J.R.D. T
THE MAGIC OF LEA

CYRUS M. GONDA

J.R.D. TATA – 'THE MAGIC OF LEADERSHIP ™'

Published in India by :

EMBASSY BOOK DISTRIBUTORS
120, Great Western Building,
Maharashtra Chamber of Commerce Lane, Fort, Mumbai - 400 023.
Tel : (+91-22) 22819546 / 32967415 Email : info@embassybooks.in
Website: www.embassybooks.in

ISBN: 978-81-933415-9-9

Printed in India by Repro India Pvt. Ltd.

'The Magic Of Leadership ™'
is a trademark owned by Cyrus M. Gonda

'The 4V Model Of Leadership ™'
is a trademark owned by Cyrus M. Gonda

'The 4V Leadership Scorecard ™'
is a trademark owned by Cyrus M. Gonda

DEDICATION

I dedicate this book to my late papa, Minoo Ratansha Gonda, who was every bit as ethical in his functioning and as caring towards his clients and as dedicated to his work and as loved by his colleagues in his own field as Mr J.R.D. Tata himself was in the Tata group. My papa was also a huge admirer and personal practitioner of the Tata ethos and way of functioning.

"Nothing worthwhile is ever achieved without deep thought and hard work "

―――――J.R.D. Tata

ACKNOWLEDGEMENTS

First and foremost, sincere and heartfelt acknowledgement is due to Mr. J.R.D. Tata himself, who through his unique blend of paternal and astute leadership, literally put Indian corporate houses on the global map, not only in terms of volume of business, productivity and efficiency, but more importantly on the parameter which will most impact corporate success in the 21st century – **ethical functioning**.

Of course, unbounded appreciation and acknowledgement is due to Mr. R.M. Lala for his detailed observations and meticulous recording and research of the incidents in the life of Mr. J.R.D. Tata. Mr. Lala's many excellent books contain a wealth of beneficial information from which I have learned so much, and I strongly feel they should be required reading wherever courses on business and management are conducted.

Indeed, every book based and authored upon the life of an individual who is no more, has to base itself upon past available information about that personality; and without the detailed information provided in Mr. R. M. Lala's many excellent books on Mr. J.R.D. Tata, this book itself could not have taken shape.

I also take this opportunity to acknowledge the excellent research done by Mr. Murad Fyzee, who in his work 'Aircraft and Engine Perfect: The story of JRD Tata who opened up the skies for his country' has intensely focused on J.R.D.'s first love – aviation.

I am also sincerely grateful to the many fine individuals who have willingly and enthusiastically shared their experiences of personal interactions with Mr. J.R.D. Tata. Their anecdotes (many of which appear for the first time ever in print) exponentially enhance the material in this book.

No words can express the thanks I owe to my publisher and good friend, Mr. Sohin Lakhani, and his entire superb team at Embassy Publishers. Sohin has wholeheartedly supported me during the last seven years that I have been working on this project.

Tons of gratitude to Mr. Nauzad D. Irani, who despite his busy schedule, has laid out this book beautifully, crafting it painstakingly as a labour of love. Thanks so much, Nauzad.

(Nauzad was humbly reluctant to place his photograph in the acknowledgements, but I insisted since he has been working along with me on this project for the last seven years.)

Many thanks to Mr. Apoorva Shah (M/s Xpressions) for assisting in the layout.

Many thanks to the Tata Central Archives, Pune, for their kind permission to use the photographs of Mr. J.R.D. Tata which appear in this book.

An extra big thank you to Mr. Zainulabedin Firoz Merchant, a genius artist, who has sketched an utterly life-like portrait of J.R.D. for the cover. I can never thank him enough. And a huge debt of gratitude to his brother and my former student, Mr. Taher Firoz Merchant, for requesting Zainul to sketch the portrait on my behalf.

Thanks to Mr. Herin Keniya, the extremely knowledgeable manager of the bookstore *Granth* (Mumbai), for suggesting the concept for the cover. And thanks to Mr. T. Jagath and Mr. Sanjeev Kamat and their very able team at the *Kitab Khana* bookstore (Mumbai) for always lending their valuable and insightful support.

And last, but definitely not the least, supreme acknowledgement and accolades are due to Mr. Jamsetji Tata, the founder/chairman, and Sir Dorabji Tata, Sir Nowroji Saklatwala, (both of whom preceded J.R.D. as chairmen of the Tata Group), and of course Mr. Ratan Tata, who, in his tenure as chairman of the Tata Group, has ensured that the levels of leadership achieved by Mr. J.R.D. Tata on the timeless parameters which matter most have been firmly maintained and unwaveringly carried forward.

Swami Vivekananda once said that if he could assemble ten like-minded individuals, each with a similar and single-minded dedication to uplift the nation, then any worthwhile achievement was well within reach. The same holds true for the Tatas – if even a handful of the corporate entities in India emulated the Tata style of functioning and supported the causes and practiced the business ideology that the Tatas are renowned for, Corporate India would stand second to none in the global business arena.

God Bless the House of Tatas. And may their example serve to inspire others to follow their noble path.

Jai Hind

TABLE OF CONTENTS

SECTION TWO – VALUES

SECTION THREE – VALOUR

SECTION FOUR – VICTORY

FOREWORD
Mr. FARROKH K. KAVARANA

I consider myself extremely fortunate and privileged to have worked closely and extensively with Mr. JRD Tata during my long tenure with the Tata group. This association of nearly 19 years till his passing away in 1993 has been one of the greatest blessings of my career.

During that period, I learnt so much not only about how a business empire is to be run, managed, led, consolidated, and expanded; but more importantly, how one individual can lead his or her people with an open heart, serve humanity with open hands, and while doing all this, also attain resounding business success. That was the magic of JRD's charismatic and humane leadership style, and therefore this fine book is aptly titled – 'JRD Tata – The Magic Of Leadership.'

I am a most unlikely writer, particularly of a Foreword to a book and one authored by a Professor at that! Nevertheless having met Prof. Cyrus M. Gonda recently and having seen his enthusiasm and the depth of research that he has done on the legendary JRD Tata, I thought I would acquiesce to his request.

But I must confess I was at a loss as to where to start. There is so much to say about JRD, so much that he managed to compress into one lifetime, that volumes would be insufficient to narrate it all.

On reflection, I feel that sometimes the 'end' is a good place to commence, especially while attempting to write a Foreword to a book which outlines an exceptionally illustrious and remarkable life. Perhaps it is only at the end of a journey that one may truly appreciate how memorable the entire journey has actually been.

1

I am taking the liberty of reproducing below a few of the incidents that I had recounted in a Tata Review on his 10th death anniversary. I believe that these are very appropriate to commence this Foreword, as they are still extremely relevant even today.

In 1974, I was on a visit to India when Nani Palkhivala invited me over to Bombay House (the headquarters of the Tata group). After a few minutes of pleasantries, he placed a call to JRD Tata and asked him if he was free, since he wanted to bring across a "young man from London". I was surprised and apprehensive; after all, I was going to meet a legend. I expected to encounter a tall and suited business tycoon, but JRD was shorter than I anticipated and he was in a safari suit. A distinguished looking person with a thinly clipped moustache, piercing eyes and a firm handshake; he seemed a decade younger than his 70 years.

He put me at ease straightaway and we had a wide-ranging discussion about the state of the world and the financial markets, about my qualifications and my career with McKinsey. JRD, and most of his colleagues later at lunch, had not heard of McKinsey the management-consulting firm. They looked rather puzzled and questioned me about when Mackinnon Mackenzie (which, though unrelated, they thought was a sister-concern of McKinsey) had diversified from shipping to consulting. Such is the course of history that, 20 years later, Ratan Tata brought McKinsey in to propose a new organisational structure for the Tata group.

JRD and Nani invited me to join the group as a Director of Tata Industries. This created a bit of a stir and some resentment, mostly because of my age (I was just 31). JRD calmed the waters, and, to be absolutely fair, he advanced by three months the appointments of two colleagues on to the Board of Tata Industries. This meant that they would have seniority and tenure which mattered quite a bit those days. That was my entry into Tatas back in 1975.

JRD was extremely keen on expanding the group globally. The growth of the Tatas was, at that point, almost totally confined to India. It was the high noon of socialist policymaking in the country and the permit, license and control raj was

2

at its zenith. But that did not deter JRD from being keenly interested in new ideas and technologies. In 1979-80, when Ratan Tata came up with the idea of investing abroad in start-up technologies such as parallel computing and plant biotechnology, with the objective of bringing them to India at a later date, JRD was one of his most passionate supporters. JRD often had to persuade his reluctant and risk-averse colleagues on the Board to support these ventures. Undoubtedly ahead of his times, he would on occasion astound us with his enthusiasm for taking big risks. In that respect, he was truly the 'youngest' director on the board.

JRD was always willing to go the extra mile to help "you youngsters," as he would call us. [This was a particularly endearing trait of his, which has been highlighted in Learning 21 of this book.] I recall the time when we had almost completed the merger discussions between our ELXSI Inc. and Gene Amdahl's (the IBM mainframe genius) Trilogy Inc., when, all of a sudden, it appeared that the deal would fall apart. JRD was in London recovering from an operation, but he insisted on hopping on to a non-stop flight to San Francisco with Ratan Tata and me. His fatherly advice to both sides saved the deal. He wasn't too impressed by our merger partners, though. With typical Silicon Valley casualness, they served us a sandwich lunch in paper plates and coffee in plastic cups, but JRD took it all in the right spirit.

On another trip to the US, this in the late 1980s, I tagged along with JRD and Ratan on a visit to Rockwell, Boeing, and other aviation-related companies. JRD started telling us about a long-forgotten South American airline of the 1930s called Aeropostale (which specialised in delivering airmail, just as JRD's initial aviation venture did), and some of the adventures of the pilots of the small propeller planes the company operated. He would repeat parts of these tales at every lunch and dinner with different guests around the table. We had begun to worry about his keenness to talk about Aeropostale and its pilots all the time; it was becoming obsessive. JRD always ended his discourse with the story of the pilot whose plane had

3

crashed in the Andes. The pilot had been given up for dead when he turned up, several weeks later, at his destination, having trudged more than a hundred miles through dense jungle with two mailbags on his shoulders. "The post has arrived; I am sorry for being a bit late," said the valiant man. [This is something similar to an incident involving JRD himself, which has been narrated in Learning 47.]

A few days later, at the Daniel Guggenheim award ceremony held in JRD's honour at the Boeing Aviation Museum in Seattle, JRD ended his speech with the Aeropostale story. The audience was gripped by his 30-minute oration, delivered without a single note in his hands. It was then that we realised that for the previous five days he had been practicing and honing at least part of his speech on his dining companions. JRD was a fantastic raconteur, an amazing storyteller, and when it came to his greatest passion, flying, he had no equal. One of his favourite books was The Little Prince by Antoine de Saint-Exupery. I later discovered that Saint-Exupery in his early days was the chief of L'Aeropostale Argentina. The Aeropostale story was JRD's way of honouring his hero while the aviation world was honouring him. [Cyrus has explained what the Daniel Guggenheim award is in Learning 50, and he has also highlighted JRD's love for reading in Learning 29.]

One can go on about the stories and episodes of JRD because there was never a dull moment with him around. His repertoire included tales of aviation and travel, doctors and hospitals, famous men and women and, in the last year or two of his life, his quest for the definitive meaning of the life one lives and the hereafter. I feel truly privileged that I could spend so much time with him.

And that is why I so like this book. It brings back memories of what a stupendous leader and what a marvellous human being JRD was. Almost every aspect of JRD's leadership style that I was familiar with (and even some elements with which I was not) have been vividly brought out. Of course, the book draws upon anecdotal references from the life of JRD which have been brought out by others previously, but that cannot be avoided when writing about a personality who has passed on.

Cyrus has not only done his homework thoroughly, he has also spoken to many individuals who have lovingly told of their own experiences with JRD, several of these stories appearing in print for the first time. I also appreciate the fact that this book has been structured into a Model of Leadership, referencing JRD as the fulcrum of this 4V Leadership Model. Here, I would like to take this opportunity to commend to the reader a full and careful reading of Lt. Gen. Iqbal Singh Singha's introduction to the '4V Model Of Leadership' at the beginning of this book. In itself it is a real-life story of an exceptional military career of devotion, discipline and service of the highest order to our nation, representing India at a global level, also leading a critical United Nations Peacekeeping Force comprising of soldiers from many nationalities. It would be hard to find an individual who is better qualified to comment on the art and science of leadership than Lt. Gen. Singha.

The quality of leadership today, especially in the business and corporate context, is an aspect which needs to be given utmost importance. It is effective and stalwart leadership by those at the helm of affairs that truly brings out the best in people, and ensures strong, honest and sustained corporate branding and profitability. I believe that if only a fraction of the often mammoth amounts which organisations spend on so-called advertising and promotional activities were to be invested in leadership development amongst its people, possibly based on concepts which have been distilled thoughtfully and excellently devised in the form of the 4V Model of Leadership, then our corporate houses would be standing on far more solid ground and attain greater longevity.

This book makes for easy and interesting, yet also thought-provoking, introspective and productive reading. I am sure that JRD would have 'encouraged' the Tata Management Training Centre (TMTC) to make this book compulsory reading for all the executives passing through their doors! My compliments and congratulations to Cyrus on this outstanding work on leadership at the highest levels.

November 2017
Mumbai

BRIEF PROFILE OF
Mr. FARROKH K. KAVARANA

Farrokh K. Kavarana retired in 2014 as a Director of Tata Sons Limited and Tata Industries Limited, the apex holding companies of the Tata Group. He was Chairman of several Tata Companies in India and abroad - notably Tata AIA Life Insurance Company, Tata AIG General Insurance Company, Tata Asset Management Ltd. (Tata Mutual Fund), Trent Ltd., Tata Tea Inc. and Tata Projects Ltd; also a Director of Tata Capital Ltd. and Tata Global Beverages Ltd. Between 2000 and 2005 he was Executive Chairman of Tata Infotech Ltd. (now merged with Tata Consultancy Services), and from 1994 to 2000 he was Executive Director of Tata Motors Limited, India's largest automobile manufacturer. Prior to that he was Vice-Chairman & Managing Director of Tata International AG, Switzerland, and Tata Ltd., U.K., responsible for the Tata Group's overseas operations and investments.

Before joining the Tata Group in 1975, he held key positions with McKinsey & Co. Inc., in London and Washington D.C. - as well as The Bowater Corporation in UK and Europe. He has advised leading international financial institutions, including the World Bank, as well as industrial companies on strategic and organisational issues.

Mr. Kavarana graduated with a B. Com. (Hons.) degree from the University of Bombay in 1963, and with an MBA from the Wharton School, University of Pennsylvania in 1970. He is a Fellow of the Institute of Chartered Accountants in England & Wales, and a Member of the Institute of Chartered Accountants of India.

He is involved with several social and charitable institutions and is a trustee of the Lady Tata Memorial Trust, the Nani A. Palkhivala Memorial Trust and the National Centre for the Performing Arts. He was a Founder Trustee of Childline India Foundation.

He is a recipient of the Dadabhai Naoroji International Millennium Award 2005, and the Wharton India Alumni Award 2009.

JOVIAL
RESOURCEFUL
DEDICATED
TRUSTWORTHY

—————— J.R.D. TATA ——————

The Tata group is an iconic Indian (as well as an internationally renowned) brand in many ways. And Mr. J.R.D. Tata was a supremely iconic leader.

Especially in this fast-paced, target-driven, ethically-challenged corporate world of the twenty-first century, the lessons and learnings from J.R.D.'s personal and professional life become even more relevant for today's leaders than ever.

Every individual having any connection with working life in some way – whether as a seasoned entrepreneur, venturing into a new business, junior executive, CEO, board member; whether a medical, finance, media or legal professional; whether employed in the manufacturing or service sector, can benefit from reading about and imbibing various aspects of the unique leadership, managerial and administrative functioning style of **Mr. Jehangir Ratanji Dadabhoy Tata**.

We often observe that when it comes to a family business, the first generation builds, the second consolidates, and the third lets go. But such was not the case with J.R.D. Although J.R.D. was handed over the reins of a solid brand, he did not relax, nor did he take it easy. He left the brand in even more solid shape than when he took over its mantle.

J.R.D. was a perfectionist with an eagle-eye for fine detail. If he was a demanding leader, it was only because for him, the Tata brand and its various stakeholders were paramount.

7

He wanted his customers to be delivered the best.

He wanted his shareholders to enjoy a safe night's sleep.

He wished his suppliers to be valued partners in the Tata enterprise.

He wished the people of the society in which he lived and within which his organisations operated and flourished, to happily share in the growth story along with him.

And, along with being a demanding leader, nothing was given more priority by him than the well-being of the employees he led. The human factor was always uppermost in J.R.D.'s vision.

Himself a great master of man management, he encouraged his generals and lieutenants to take command of the businesses in which he gave them a free hand to run. Tata Chemicals, Tata Motors, Tata Steel, Titan; all benefited from the faith and trust that J.R.D. reposed in their respective CEOs, who became virtual icons by themselves.

Air India, not only India's national carrier, but under J.R.D.'s personal stewardship renowned as one of the leading airlines of the world, on par with Lufthansa, Swissair and British Airways, was an organisation close to J.R.D.'s heart.

With all these varied corporate entities to occupy his time and vie for his attention, J.R.D. did not neglect the nation.

He financially and personally supported cultural activities:
– The National Centre for Performing Arts (NCPA), being a Tata funded venture.

His was also a leading contribution to the nation's security
– The Bhabha Atomic Research Centre (BARC).

He also gave generously of his time and money to social upliftment
– The Tata Institute of Social Sciences (TISS).

And for cancer patients, there was the finest cancer hospital that Asia could claim to have at that time – The Tata Institute of Fundamental Research (TIFR).

These are iconic institutions thoughtfully and lovingly gifted to a grateful nation by an iconic leader.

The cause of higher education through the provision of scholarships to deserving students of all communities too was not left out, and neither was any other area that the people of India could genuinely benefit from.

An intellectual and ethical giant, like any true leader, he remained simple in his lifestyle and humble in his outlook to the very end.

———

INTRODUCTION TO THE '4V MODEL OF LEADERSHIP ™'
(Developed by Prof. Cyrus M Gonda)

- By Lt. General Iqbal Singh Singha
AVSM | VSM

I t is a matter of great honour to be associated with a book on Mr. JRD Tata, India's pioneer corporate leader; who has created a special niche for himself in history and brought India into its rightful place on the world map.

Equally gratifying is the thought that Cyrus, a dear friend, has formulated a new leadership model which he has appropriately termed as the '4V Model of Leadership ™' by culling out the sterling leadership qualities of Mr. JRD Tata, and has found me suitable to write an introduction to this emerging and highly practical addition to global leadership thought.

The turn of the millennium witnessed globalisation at its peak resulting into stiff competition between corporate houses engaged in the same line of business. In India, the opening of the economy and doing away with protectionism brought in newer actors with international brands into the market. Globalisation coupled with opportunities and fat six-figure salaries brought in serious challenges to contemporary corporate leadership to keep its flock together and protect them from poaching by competing corporate houses. This

Perestroika and Glasnost ushered in a paradigm shift in the way business was to be done. And for these challenges in uncertain times, which carry with them huge opportunities as well, new and relevant models of leadership like the 4V Model become the need of the hour. The economic downturn from 2007 onwards witnessed famous names like Merrill Lynch and Lehman Brothers being acquired by Bank of America and Barclays respectively; and, so many other known firms in the USA invoking chapter 11 and filing bankruptcy and liquidation. This was the result of poor leadership and bad work ethics. Closer home, Satyam, Sahara, and Kingfisher faced similar fates, demobilising thousands of loyal workers in the bargain. In fact, in 2009, when I told a fellow student from the US at the National Defence College that my elder son Rannvijay, (a VJ with MTV and also an actor) may not get a raise that year, he said that was good news. It meant that he kept his job!

These landmark events necessitated a de novo look at the existing leadership theories and techniques, and as they were put under the scanner, the requirement of newer and more relevant models of leadership became a crying need. Disasters like Satyam and Kingfisher happened because the senior management was self-serving and broke all established norms, and the middle-order leadership did not have the moral courage to stand up to the wrong doings.

The business landscape and the boardroom battles being so intense and competitive today, I believe that what we witness on the battlefield is to some extent, metaphorically, replicated in the corporate environment. Thus, my experience and exposure to senior leadership positions on the war-front, I humbly believe, suitably qualifies me to put forth my views on what would work as far as leadership in the corporate arena is concerned.

The 4V Model has been very well conceptualised by Cyrus to meet the developing challenges to leadership in the 21st Century. Besides bringing in objectivity, the model also would come in handy for smooth succession at the highest levels. All parameters necessary to identify and evaluate leadership potential and the probability of a leader's success have been intelligently encapsulated into the 4 Vs. The Infosys succession crisis in mid-2017 further accentuated the need to have a fresh look at such leadership models.

The 4 Vs that Cyrus has identified as being pertinent to evaluate and identify leadership potential being – Vision, Values, Valour, and Victory. After going through this model, I realised that it is so all-encompassing, that it matches and fits my career graph in the armed forces perfectly well. In the armed forces, delegation of responsibility and trust are very essential to ensure your subordinates are trained and mentally prepared for succession. Whereas the execution and responsibility is delegated; accountability is retained by the higher commander. As a Divisional Commander, I desisted from visiting a newly inducted unit in the formation for the first three months of their tenure to give them adequate time to settle down after a grilling operational tenure of three years. You have to give room and space for your subordinates to evolve, bloom and perform and not keep breathing down their neck !

Vision is the quintessential quality that a leader needs to possess to chart out a roadmap for the next five to ten years in the organisation. A leader and his team without adequate vision are like a train without an engine, and such an engineless train can be shuttled up and down at the mercy of the environment. As a newly appointed Commanding Officer of Napiers Rifles, a 180 year-old infantry battalion; in 1997, I got down to serious thinking as to where I wanted to take this unit in the new millennium. Fortunately, the unit was set to go to an operational area in thick of counter-insurgency operations in Kashmir.

I decided that this illustrious unit must be conferred with the Chief of Army Staff's Citation at the end of my three-year command tenure. That was my vision for the unit. In addition, I wanted to empower all my officers and men and ensure that each one of them picked up at least one additional qualification in the three years under me. I am afraid emancipation of subordinates is not a priority for corporate sector in India. Every action of ours was thereafter directed towards attaining that goal. The commander's vision has to be broken down into several actionable and clearly definable sets of goals that the entire command understands. Sure enough, we not only achieved our goal, but based on the consistently good performance, the unit was selected for a peacekeeping tenure in the United Nations !

In order to have a clear vision, a leader must be able to detach himself and be alone for at least half an hour at the end of each day in order to be able to reflect his thought process. He should recount what all

13

has been achieved that day and what direction should be followed the next day. As a brigade commander in operational area I was part of the higher management and my efforts were towards ensuring that units were well equipped, well catered for and highly motivated to deliver results. I protected them by absorbing lots of pressure from the top for time bound performance but remained as a facilitator and motivator helping them to achieve the desired results.

When I went as Head of the United Nations Peacekeeping Mission and Force Commander to Golan Heights, my vision and desired end-state was that we have to continue keeping peace between Syria and Israel, despite the ongoing civil war, without losing any lives of peacekeepers. Under the existing mandate, we carried out capacity building and ushered in mitigating measures to ensure that this mission was accomplished.

Values are the cornerstones of a great leader's inner strength. The most important values a leader needs are integrity, impartiality, empathy, and knowledge. The belief in one's own self and in the men that one commands, sincerity of effort, and loyalty to the organisation are values of import. As a young officer, I became the lucky charm of the unit by winning most of the professional and sports competitions that I led my unit team in. However, I always stuck to the longer and difficult path of preparing hard for a competition and won it by a convincing lead by fair and square means. The journey to the objective was as important to me as its ultimate achievement. The men you command and also your children are your mirror image, and will do exactly what they see you doing. Therefore, there is no replacement for a personal example in order to instil values in your command.

My father guided me through my formative years and when I was going for my first staff appointment as a major, he told me that staff was a servant of the troops you support. If the troops were not there, staff wouldn't be required. Again when I took over command, he told me that there are 800 pairs of eyes watching each and every action of yours. Integrity and transparency had to be maintained and justice should not only be given but should appear to be given.

In the army, the value system also rubs on your family as they are an intrinsic part of a larger family. I have observed my younger son Harman as a child often asking the driver or the protection party whether they had had their food before we got down to having ours. It was no surprise that he went on to command the passing out parade on graduating from the International Maritime Institute at Greater Noida. My wife Ballie as the first lady has always known the wives of men by name and addressed their administrative and medical problems by accompanying them to the hospital or bringing it to the notice of concerned authorities. She provided moral strength to the families of officers and men when we were deployed in operational areas and the families stayed back in peace stations.

Valour is achieved after you successfully overcome your fears. As a commanding officer on the live line of control between India and Pakistan, I was expected to visit all my 24 posts at least once a month. Since we had only 200 odd bullet-proof jackets for a strength of 800 personnel, I never wore a jacket and had made it known that I will only wear one when we get bullet-proof jackets for 100 percent of our soldiers. It had a great salutary and morale-boosting effect on the men under my command, but I also realised after coming under fire several times that there is a very thin line between valour and foolhardiness! I guess fortune really favours the brave. We were able to neutralise 54 terrorists in three years without a loss of life to our own men ; as compared to an average of 03 to 05 terrorists killed by the neighbouring and previous units with equal number of fatalities to their men. We did not have a single case of an innocent dying as part of collateral damage, and that is the reason I have always enjoyed a sound sleep in life after completion of my active command in the backdrop of the Kargil War. As the Head of the Mission in Syria, I always made it a point to go and meet the men and women at the post when a crisis situation developed, against the advice of the Syrian government and my own security set up ; in order to reinsure them that we were in it together and would always back them.

Victory will always follow if you have applied vision, values and valour in the right spirit and manner. Victory by fair means should be the ultimate objective of any leader. Victory never comes cheap; it has to be earned with toil and sweat during training, and with blood during war in addition to prolonged separation from your near and dear ones. A commander's aim should always be to secure and attain victory with minimum bloodshed and losses to lives. In Syria, in my tenure of nearly three years, 180 peacekeepers were taken prisoners by Al Qaida affiliated groups like the Al Nusra Front and others, but with our persistent efforts and the application of skilled negotiations and mediation techniques, we got them all released without any loss of life. Best of my friends in the diplomatic circle were ambassadors of Saudi Arabia and Qatar, since these countries had leverage over the armed opposition groups. The saying in New York at the United Nations headquarters was that this Force Commander (myself) will go to any length to get his troops released. It feels good to live with a reputation like that and I keep on musing on it after my retirement. Addressing the Security Council at United Nations Headquarters on the situation in Syria on three occasions was a God given opportunity and a mark of success for me.

Thus, having practiced and worked hard at acquiring and achieving these '4 Vs' throughout my career, I can vouch for the fact that a concentrated focus on vision, values, valour, and victory are the primary elements essential in identifying and developing leadership potential, whether in the corporate world, in the armed forces, or in any other walk of life.

Though this book has been centred around the tremendously uplifting leadership style and achievements of Mr. JRD Tata, the '4V Model of Leadership ™' is universally applicable, and I believe that future-oriented organisations must take this model into cognizance while selecting individuals to occupy leader-ship roles and positions. This model would be very useful as an evaluation criterion as well as a development tool for lead-ers everywhere. Not only individuals, but also departments, SBUs and entire organisations would do well to evaluate their functioning on these four criteria, so that they can clearly see where they currently stand, and then identify where to focus upon to move forward in a balanced and holistic, and not in a skewed manner. In fact, so crucial and all-encompassing are they, that I believe that these 4 Vs combine to form a Balanced Scorecard for Leadership.

I am a firm believer that we Indians can hold our place with the best in the world in any sphere, including being thought-leaders in the crucial fields of leadership and management, and I am proud and delighted that it is an Indian, who through the '4V Model of Leadership ™' has made this valuable contribution to the vital discipline of leadership development.

16

A fifth generation officer, Lieutenant General Iqbal Singh Singha, AVSM, VSM (Retd), is an alumna of King George's School, Chail (now Rashtriya Military School) and National Defence Academy. He was commissioned into Rajputana Rifles in 1977 ; the oldest Rifle Regiment of the Indian Army and rose to become their Colonel of the Regiment. The General Officer is a post graduate from the Defence Services Staff College, Higher Command Course and National Defence College.

The General has had varied command and staff experience and has been the head of operational branch at brigade, division and corps levels besides having been posted to the military operations branch at army headquarters. At the Army Training Command, he was involved in writing of the sub-conventional warfare doctrine for the Indian Army. The General Officer has had tenure in Ethiopia and Eritrea in UNMEE as the Chief Logistics Officer where he devised methods to solve challenging management and logistic situations of the mission within a newly born nation state.

During his tenure as Head of Mission and Force Commander of United Nations peacekeeping mission at Golan Heights in Syria and Israel from 2012 to 2015 ; when the security situation changed drastically due to Syrian civil war, Lt Gen IS Singha infused courage and high degree of professionalism in the troops to ensure that the mission stayed on course. In his tenure of two and a half years the mission faced numerous incidents of peacekeepers being fired upon or coming under cross fire, carjacking, weapon snatching, detention/abduction and vandalisation of UN property.

The General Officer has been an active participant in various seminars on war fighting, human rights, human resources development and counter terrorism. A highly decorated officer, the General was awarded the Medal for Multinational Cooperation of I Oracle from the Ministry of Defence, Republic of Slovenia, during his tenure at Golan Heights for his dynamic leadership, ensuring high degree of intermission cooperation and excellent synergy achieved with troop contributing countries. **U.N. Secretary General**

Ban-Ki-Moon also lauded the immense contribution of the General Officer during challenging times at the end of his tenure in 2015. The General retired from the Indian Army as Director General of Operational Logistics and Strategic Movement in 2016.

In retirement at Chandigarh, besides playing golf the General writes for *lokmarg.com*, an e magazine on issues of national security and Middle East. A visiting professor to Punjab University, the officer is a guest speaker at various think tanks in India and abroad.

The General is married to Mrs Ballie Singha, a national basket baller and poet. Their elder son Rannvijay an MTV VJ, actor, producer and a youth icon is married to Prianka and they have a daughter named Kainaat. Harman their younger son is an actor, writer and producer on web entertainment and TV. Singhas share their passion for basketball, trekking, bridge, darts and golf and often partake in these events as a family.

A FAMILY PHOTO

THE 4 V MODEL OF LEADERSHIP ™

" People cannot be managed. Inventories can be managed, but people must be led "

-H. Ross Perot

As a keen student of leadership and management thoughts and practices over the years, I have made some observations which have led to the formulation of an extremely interesting aspect of leadership.

And that is, **EVERY** parameter that is considered when understanding the traits of a particular leader can be slotted into one of four categories. These being:

1. **VISION**

2. **VALUES**

3. **VALOUR**

4. **VICTORY**

With any one of these four elements missing, the study of leadership is incomplete.

With each of these four elements present, the study of leadership becomes holistic.

VISION pertains to direction. In an organisation where the leadership exhibits clarity of thought about where the organisation is headed, though all may not always be serene, the results over time are always positively favourable. Alternatively, wherever the leadership is haphazardly headed for all possible points on the corporate compass, the result over time is corporate disaster. Without vision, the speed and pace at which events happen and unfold do not matter.

VALUES are what bring meaning to the leader's vision. They are the specific drivers, the motivators, so to speak. They are what convert the leader's vision into real terms and pave the way for victory. They also include the inherent or acquired positive qualities and attributes based on the chosen values which the leader possesses or acquires. The values define the leader. They are what differentiate him in a positive way from other leaders with similar vision.

VALOUR refers to courage; bravery. Not necessarily physical courage, (though many corporate leaders, including J.R.D. Tata, displayed tremendous physical courage themselves). But also moral, ethical, emotional, intellectual, and even spiritual courage. The ability to take a decision which could put personal career or even personal safety at risk, as long as it is in the interest of the organisation and its people, or to uphold deep-rooted principles, defines valour in a leader.

VICTORY for the organisation and the people and entities associated with it (not by foul means, but fair ones) is the ultimate objective of leadership. Of course, victory or success is not necessarily calculated in financial terms alone, as the section on victory in this book will reveal, but can be viewed in many significant ways. If vision, values and valour are in place, victory for the leader and his organisation in the long-term is a foregone conclusion.

The most effective leaders would be those who have developed themselves sufficiently and holistically and proven themselves on all four points of this '**Star of Leadership.**'

The 4V Model Of Leadership ™ has been devised and designed to ensure that organisations can evaluate the effectiveness of their current and potential leaders on the four vital parameters which contribute to the success of those in leadership positions.

Thus any organisation wanting to select an individual for a key leadership role, or wanting to develop a second line of command, can make use of this Model to evaluate the fitness of that individual's potential, capabilities, and past achievements on the holistic strength of the 4 Vs.

The Model as outlined in this book is centred around the distinguished professional career of Mr. J.R.D. Tata as an example of how one individual leader, who is highly evolved on all the 4 Vs, can be evaluated on his / her leadership effectiveness.

Organisations can similarly apply this Model to meet their leadership needs, customising it to their own requirements and strategy, by identifying sub-parameters within these 4 V's which are important to them. These organisations, as per their requirements from their leaders, can formulate various sub-parameters under the four broad categories, and give them specific weightages.

According to my study and research done over the years on the subject of leadership, this Model is a comprehensive one, as almost every evaluation criterion for measuring leadership would fit under one or the other of the 4 Vs.

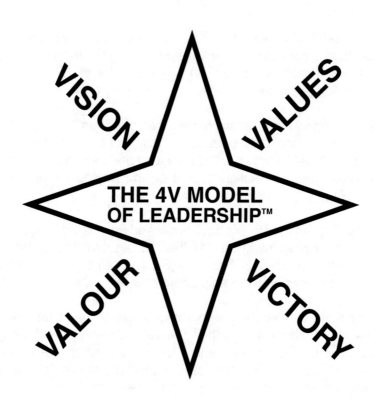

VISION · VALUES · VALOUR · VICTORY

THE 4V MODEL OF LEADERSHIP™

Think of any renowned leader in history.

From any era.

From any field of endeavour.

From any part of the globe.

A study of his/her leadership style, traits, characteristics and attributes will reveal that whatever made him or her and the organisation he or she led successful, can be categorised and slotted into one or another of the four 'V's' outlined in this model.

> *The organisation does what the leader thinks, believes, promotes and breathes. Which is why in the success story of any organisation, the key determinant is the leadership thought and philosophy*
>
> -Cyrus M. Gonda

J.R.D. TATA

VISION * VALUES * VALOUR * VICTORY

With all the focus and attention given to J.R.D.'s invaluable contribution to social causes, his humongous contribution to the business aspect of the Tata group often gets side-lined. But alongside being a true contributor to society, J.R.D. was an astute business leader. There are umpteen solid lessons for the aspiring as well as the existing leader to be learned from J.R.D.'s unique, honest, transparent and highly effective style of corporate leadership.

Many are born to illustrious families and then tend to relax and live a life of ease. But not so J.R.D. This is the first valuable lesson we learn from J.R.D.'s life. That an early advantage in life is not to be frittered away, but is rather to be consolidated and strengthened with hard, intelligent, and honest work.

Although in a way J.R.D. inherited a substantial business entity, he can be said to be a pioneering entrepreneur in the truest sense of the word. He founded an entire industry – the aviation industry, in India, and was one of the world's pioneers in this field.

Also, when J.R.D. took over as chairman of the Tata group, the Tata group consisted of fourteen companies which had a combined turnover of 17 crore rupees. When he voluntarily gave up the mantle more than fifty years later, the Tata group under his able stewardship had expanded to a stupendous ninety-five companies, and their combined turnover surpassed Rs. 10,000 crores.

Thus, when J.R.D. gracefully handed over the mantle to his able and worthy successor, Mr. Ratan Tata, the Tata group consisted of almost a hundred companies, engaged in fields and businesses as varied as salt and tea, steel and automobiles, software and information technology, chemicals and insurance, telecom and hospitality. **Many of these companies, such as Titan (for watches), Tata Chemicals, Tata Tea, Tata Consultancy Services (TCS), were not inherited by J.R.D. from his predecessors, but were ones he personally conceptualised, founded, nurtured and made profitable.**

Yet the bulk of the examples of J.R.D.'s style of functioning which form the nucleus of this work on leadership, emanate from J.R.D.'s involvement with aviation, which was his true love and passion.

And there is good reason for this being so.

Books on the leadership styles of Sam Walton, Warren Buffet, Richard Branson, Jack Welch, Lee Iacocca, Henry Ford, Akio Morita, Walt Disney, Steve Jobs, Bill Gates, Conrad Hilton, J. Willard Marriott, Sr., and many other corporate legends have been written from the perspective of the achievements of these world-famed leaders in the industry or field of their specialisation and passion: industries of their choosing, in which they achieved success of a kind never witnessed by the world before.

SAM WALTON

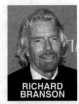
RICHARD BRANSON

While **Sam Walton** built a **retail** empire; **Richard Branson**, like J.R.D., is primarily an **aviation** enthusiast.

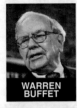
WARREN BUFFET

JACK WELSH

Warren Buffet specialises in **investments**, and the forte of **Jack Welch** was in **electrical and mechanical engineering** and **financial services**.

STEVE JOBS

BILL GATES

Steve Jobs and **Bill Gates** achieved laurels in the field of **computing**.

HENRY FORD

LEE LACOCCA

Henry Ford and **Lee Iacocca** brought quality **cars** to the common man with their own unique leadership and management styles.

CONARD HILTON

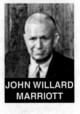
JOHN WILLARD MARRIOTT

Conrad Hilton and **John Willard Marriott, Sr.**, were pioneering **hotel and hospitality experts**.

WALT DISNEY

Walt Disney was a genius in providing world-class **family entertainment**.

Akio Morita of **Sony** made his mark in the arena of **consumer electronics**.

But the leadership lessons and learnings from these great individuals surpass the mere boundaries of their chosen industry in which they made their mark. The lessons we learn from their methods are timeless, without boundaries or limits, and are universal in nature.

What works for man management in hospitality, will be just as effective for managing men in the field of manufacturing. The discipline and drive so necessary for success in aviation will be just as essential to achieving enduring success in consumer electronics. And so on.

Thus, though a majority of the anecdotes and examples which reveal J.R.D.'s exemplary management and leadership style may be culled from his involvement with the aviation sector, as that is where he devoted a substantial volume of time and energy, the anecdotes and examples and the lessons therefrom are by no means restricted to being beneficial for an individual looking to excel in aviation alone.

The fifty-three learnings spread across the four sections in this book, pertaining to J.R.D.'s uniquely inspiring leadership philosophy and methodology are instructive to all existing and aspiring managers and leaders, irrespective of the field, industry or profession in which they have chosen or will choose to shape their career.

And since aviation has been declared by many management experts as the most difficult industry to venture into, sustain, and succeed; if a man could succeed beyond wildest imaginations in this industry, (J.R.D. commenced his airline with a team of just four, including himself as a pilot), the lessons one can learn from his success can be successfully applied to any field of human and corporate endeavour.

In the last two decades, we have seen airlines in India such as Damania Airways, East-West Airlines, Air Sahara, ModiLuft, Kingfisher Airlines and many others collapsing by the wayside.

Such was not the case with J.R.D.'s airline – Air India.

It was a highly profitable venture until it was cruelly snatched away by the government under the garb of nationalisation.

Until J.R.D. was in charge, Air India had achieved international acclaim for its punctuality and service levels, which were deemed on par with or superior to airlines such as Lufthansa, British Airways and KLM.

The moment J.R.D. was replaced with a government representative at the helm, the rapid decline of Air-India began.

This proves **BEYOND DOUBT** that it was **PRIMARILY THE LEADERSHIP AND MANAGEMENT STYLE OF ONE SINGLE INDIVIDUAL AT THE HELM OF AFFAIRS** – J.R.D. Tata – which was responsible for the levels of quality and profitability achieved by Air India over many decades.

We often speak about Indians performing at peak levels overseas, due to a favourable working environment, but this is exactly what J.R.D. demonstrated is possible right here on Indian soil – that Indian employees are equal to the best in the world, provided, of, course, like any other employees anywhere else in the world, they are **LED** with love, care and understanding.

It is these very lessons in dedication, passion, commitment to excellence, staff selection and training, and others, that a potential or existing entrepreneur in any industry, or a corporate career enthusiast in any field, can learn and derive inspiration from.

Any modern day entrepreneur or career-oriented individual cannot but help be inspired, informed, and instructed by the able manner in which J.R.D. led from the front.

He displayed qualities of corporate leadership which, if appreciated, accepted and incorporated by the Indian youth of today, would see India race well past Japan, China and Germany as an industrial and corporate superpower.

Whether it be aviation and travel, the field of pharmaceuticals, medicine and health-care, hotels and hospitality, manufacturing, services or trading, business-to-business or retail, real estate and infrastructure, information technology or education; whether small, medium, large or heavy-duty scale, the principles of superior leadership demonstrated by J.R.D. are matchless in their universal applicability and appeal.

In fact, for a period of forty years, right from 1938 up till 1978, J.R.D. simultaneously was head of the Tata group (the largest industrial house in India), as well as was running Air India (which had been nationalised by the Indian government, but which had kept J.R.D. on as Chairman, a post which he accepted without a single rupee's remuneration).

When he was asked how he divided his time between these two work areas, he responded, **"By God, sometimes upto half my time was devoted to Air India."**

J.R.D. was himself not highly qualified, and often regretted the fact that his father, rather than let him (J.R.D.) complete his education in engineering, a field he (J.R.D.) was passionate about, got him back to India and apprenticed him at a relatively early age into the Tata group. This point is important, as it is instructive in understanding that it is not essential to have a higher university education in order to successfully handle and grow a business empire. Of course, higher education does help, but if compelling circumstances have prevented an individual from attaining higher education, he or she need not worry too much on that account. Rather than fretting over what is not, they should devote their energies to what is available and at hand.

And what IS at hand, is this ready availability of leadership material from the life of J.R.D. in anecdotal and story form, which if put into practice by an individual with healthy ambition coupled with the right attitude and philosophy, will be equivalent to a master's degree in business administration.

Now that the twentieth century is over, it can be safely said that the man who had beyond doubt the single-largest, maximum positive impact on Corporate India in that turbulent, tempestuous and turning-point century, was Mr. Jehangir Ratanji Dadabhoy Tata. And by understanding, decoding, and analysing his unique leadership style (which can and must be benchmarked and adopted by leaders of today), we shall see exactly why this is so.

These lessons do not come from a leader from a foreign land, but from a true patriotic Indian, who demonstrated that such a leadership style can and does succeed even in India, by leading Indian employees, and operating in an Indian environment.

And **that** is what makes all the positive difference.

WHY ARE THERE 53 LEARNINGS FROM THE LIFE OF J.R.D. TATA IN THIS BOOK?

53 is apparently quite an odd number.

Yet there is nothing random about the selection of 53 learnings (divided logically into four sections) in this book.

The actual number of learnings from J.R.D.'s life are innumerable and infinite. J.R.D.'s life was an almost endless ongoing episode of worthy anecdotes. Everyone who came in contact even briefly with this great man had some positive story to narrate. **An entire 2-year full-time MBA course could be devised around J.R.D.'s unique brand of leadership alone.** But for purposes of a book, the pages need to be practically limited to a reasonable sum.

The number 53 is of particular significance in J.R.D.'s exceptionally illustrious career, as this number represents the number of years J.R.D. ably led the Tata group as its Chairman.

During his tenure lasting a little over half a century, the Tata group grew in:

- Revenue from approximately US$ 100 million to well over US$ 5 billion
- Number of companies from 14 to 95

And the Tata group achieved this phenomenal growth WITHOUT compromising on the core values and vision of its founders and early leaders.

NOT JUST ANOTHER 'BRICK IN THE WALL'

Taking an analogy, let us consider the 'Big Brand' as being akin to an imposing and magnificent 'Big Wall.'

Unfortunately, while this 'Big Wall' appears from a distance as a solid, magnificient, towering and imposing one-piece structure, the many small bricks which contribute towards the making of this big wall generally go unnoticed. But if you take time to ponder and look at it from up close, you will see that each brick which makes up this imposing wall has been meticulously laid, well cemented and perfectly aligned by a trained and motivated workforce under a vigilant leadership.

The 53 learnings laid out in this book in totality represent the **'Big Wall'** that J.R.D. consolidated, but more importantly, they also individually represent the **'small bricks'** without which the solid wall of J.R.D.'s inspiring brand of leadership would not have existed.

In selecting and elaborating these 53 learnings, I have attempted to present through anecdotes and stories, the multifarious organisational-building activities initiated by J.R.D. Tata, which together constitute a sample of the 'bricks' aligned to form the solid, sturdy and robust 'wall' which constitutes **BRAND TATA** today.

An important challenge that the corporate world faces is that organisational leadership often erroneously tends to view the task of Brand Building as the formation of one single large picture, magically dropped from heaven above. This is the mindset which needs to be changed, as Brand Building in reality is a complex combination of teamwork, hard work, smart work, wise work, and honest work, blended with a telescopic eye for the big picture as well as a microscopic eye for the small (yet no less important) detail, a healthy and consistent focus on internal and external customers, as well as the entire eco-system within which the brand operates, exists, lives and breathes.

Thus, J.R.D.'s most valuable leadership contribution is the strengthening of the Tata brand in the minds and hearts of the Indian people as India's MOST LOVED CORPORATE BRAND ENTITY, and more importantly, PROVING TO ONE AND ALL THAT BIG BUSINESS CAN HAVE A HUMONGOUS HEART AND YET BE HUGELY PROFITABLE.

PLEASE NOTE: Under each of the 4 sections in this book (each section representing one of the 4 Vs) multiple learnings have been identified, each focusing on diverse aspects of either Vision, Values, Valour, or Victory, as practiced by J.R.D. For you as an individual reader, and for your organisation on the whole, similarly try to identify how you (or your organisation) perform on these multiple learnings, which are nothing but sub-parameters or different aspects of the 4 Vs.

You can also create further sub-parameters which fit into these 4 Vs, other than the ones identified in these 53 learnings. The scope for further additions within these 4 Vs is literally infinite, and doing this enhances the value of 'The 4V Model Of Leadership ™.'

WHAT EXACTLY IS LEADERSHIP?
(AND JUST WHY IS THIS VITAL AND MUCH NEEDED RESOURCE IN SUCH SHORT SUPPLY?)

> " *Leadership is like gravity. You know it's there, you know it exists, but how do you define it?* "
>
> -JAMIE WILLIAMS

The resource we are most in short supply of in the corporate world (and indeed, in the world at large as well) today is that of a steady supply of strong leaders and sound leadership.

Leadership is a critical term which needs to be clearly understood so that organisations of the future are able to withstand the extremely volatile, competitive, and uncertain business space. As global markets tend to be cyclic in nature, the organisation which the leader heads should be capable of withstanding all market conditions, and the organisation should also be perceived in the wide spectrum of its customer base as vibrant and sensitive to evolving and ever-changing needs, at the same time keeping the flames of the founder's philosophy alive at all times.

Have a close look at the two pictures below.

Now answer – which of these two pictures do you think depicts the image of a glorious leader?

35

Did you select the silhouette image of the dashing man waving a sharp sword sitting astride his horse?

That man is an actor playing the role of a knight from a bygone era in a fictional film.

That same man has also played the role of a murderer and a thief in other films.

He is an **ILLUSION**.

But unfortunately a **popular** illusion, as far as the subject of leadership is concerned.

The image on the right side of the page is that of a truly successful corporate leader and a business hero. This simple but smart, cultured, decent man with the clean-shaven look, sporting scholarly spectacles, and with well-combed hair; the one who looks like everyone's idea of a favourite, kindly uncle, is **Lee Iacocca**, ranked among the best American CEOs of all time. **Through the force and power of his mercurial and inspiring leadership, he almost single-handedly brought about the turnaround of a dying gigantic brand called Chrysler.** (He is also the author of a brilliant book titled '*Where Have All The Leaders Gone?*')

What exactly is it that Iacocca **did** to establish his reputation as one of the best corporate leaders ever? He conceptualised, drove and cemented a series of apparently small changes and tweaks in the organisational setting and environment, both through personal example, as well as by initiating a culture of robust brand leadership through inculcating the right vision and values, demonstrating courage and valour, ultimately paving the path to Chrysler's victory in a highly competitive marketplace.

Unfortunately, the typical picture of a heroic leader which we carry in our mind would be that of a dashing warrior brandishing a sword and seated atop a charging horse. Or possibly, for the more contemporary-minded, the picture of leadership would be one of a man in a mask and a cape, with his underwear worn over his pants, swinging from skyscraper to skyscraper as he effortlessly wraps up entire gangs of evil-doers.

And it is **THIS** distorted picture that has done a lot of damage to the discipline of corporate leadership. In some primal, prehistoric part of our brain, this is still the image we carry of what we expect a leader to be like; an Emperor Ashoka, or Alexander the Great, or Napoleon Bonaparte, or King Arthur; or Superman, or Batman, or perhaps even Spiderman.

Somehow most of us tend to associate leadership only with dashing, heroic action, not with contemplative thought and sound decision-making.

The visions of leadership with which we are furnished and fed with today are exaggerated historical and Hollywood and Bollywood inspired versions of heroes. And it is these visions with which we are fed so often, and which we have digested so readily, which have distorted our picture of reality.

But for the world in which we live and work, the less glamorous and dashing (yet far more effective and productive) leader, the one who converts scarce resources into innovative products and services of high quality, satisfying and hopefully even delighting customers, generating reasonable, and more importantly, sustainable profits, creating meaningful jobs and careers, earning the admiration and loyalty of all stakeholders, and achieving all of this ethically without attempting to 'bend the system' is the leader towards which most of us should aspire becoming in our corporate careers.

And no better example of this brand of leader than J.R.D. can be found as an inspiration to us all.

We are today attuned through a barrage of media coverage to view the cult of 'Celebrity CEO' and the 'Big Brand' that he represents as being larger-than-life; meant to subdue and overawe, rather than to motivate and inspire.

But such need not be the case.

In fact, the most sustainable and rock-solid organisations are the ones which are led by leaders who are humble, who have a large heart and a razor-sharp mind to match it, and who view themselves not as celebrities to be glorified and idolised, but as men with an important job to do and who focus on that job and do it well.

"The most dangerous leadership myth is that leaders are BORN – that there is a genetic factor to leadership. That's nonsense; in fact the OPPOSITE is true. Leaders are MADE rather than BORN "

-WARREN BENNIS (LEADERSHIP GURU)

SO WAKE UP.

YOU, TOO, CAN BE A LEADER.

DEVELOP YOUR LEADERSHIP SKILLS AND TAKE UP A LEADERSHIP POSITION.

THE WORLD NEEDS YOU.

THE NEED OF THE HOUR – MORE LEADERS

We need people who can **MANAGE**. This is a crucial requirement for any business as well as for the nation. Which is why we have well over a 1,000 Management colleges across the length and breadth of the country. The cities of Mumbai and Pune alone having more than a hundred each.

But more importantly, we also **NEED** people who can **LEAD**. And sadly, there are not even a handful of Leadership colleges throughout the land. One may say this is because Leadership cannot be learned in colleges. It has to be learned 'on-the-job.' But this same argument could apply to the discipline of Management also. Moreover, syllabi can be designed to ensure inculcation of leadership in an intelligent combination of classroom plus practical environment, as is done in evolved universities in western countries. This is also exactly the same principle that the National Defence Academy (NDA) adopts to turn fresh recruits into world-class leaders (not managers) for our Armed Forces, which are second to none in the world.

The vital question here is – Is there a DIFFERENCE between a manager and a leader?

Certainly.

But the difference can be deceptive. Simply because the difference is not an externally visible one. For example, in an office, a robust, six-feet plus handsome hunk of a man with rippling muscles, charming smile and athletic build, occupying a position of managerial authority, could by many at first glance be mistaken by default to be a leader. It is not that he may not be one. He could well be. But it is not essential that he will necessarily be one for these reasons alone. A manager may also be a leader, but then again, he may not be. Physical appearances and occupying positions of authority are not the criteria to evaluate leadership attributes.

LEADERSHIP IS PRIMARILY A STATE OF MIND.

A QUESTION FOR YOU TO ANSWER

> If a person in a position of authority receives a suggestion from a well-meaning employee, and that suggestion would cost Rs. 10,000 to implement, but would only offer a maximum one-time benefit of Rs. 5,000, should that suggestion be implemented in the interests of the organisation?

Some would reject it outright as not being financially viable. And think no more about it. After all, the mathematics of the equation is obvious. The numbers don't lie. That is **MANAGERIAL THINKING** at work.

But at Toyota, for example, many such suggestions would be considered seriously, and some would even be implemented, though the investment is on the face of it more than the return. For at Toyota, they realise that implementing such suggestions once in a while (and even twice and thrice in a while), sends across a healthy signal to employees that their inputs and suggestions are being heard and implemented, and this encourages and motivates them to keep on giving suggestions, some of which would ultimately benefit the organisation in millions. Which is why the flow of profitable suggestions from employees at Toyota never dries up. For the record, because of this progressive thought process, Toyota receives thousands of suggestions every week from their employees. This is **LEADERSHIP THINKING** at its best. No wonder Toyota could come in from behind and beat the American automobile giants in their own game on their own turf.

Thus, the defining difference between the two is: the **MANAGER** primarily believes in **NUMBERS** and the **LEADER** primarily believes in **PEOPLE**.

Being a leader is all about a mindset – the mindset of putting your people first.

For as the leadership guru Simon Sinek puts it: '**Great leaders sacrifice the numbers to save the people, because when push comes to shove, numbers won't save you, people will.**'

J.R.D. always put his people first, and because he did so, he achieved stupendous success with the numbers as well.

40

J.R.D. TATA
THE MAGIC OF LEADERSHIP ™

Why should J.R.D.'s style of leadership be termed as **MAGICAL**?

Simple.

Because it was primarily his **LEADERSHIP** which led to the unprecedented and unparalleled success of the organisations and the business group he guided for over fifty long years. Other business leaders in other organisations, who were better qualified, and who had access to equivalent or even more resources, did not manage to replicate the stunning success on the multiple business parameters (both financial and otherwise), which J.R.D. consistently achieved.

His unique blend of visionary, value-based, courageous, and thoughtful as well as action-oriented leadership was the magic ingredient in the organisational success recipe.

Like the famed Indian magic trick, where apparently endless water flows out of a comparatively small vessel held in the hand of a master magician, J.R.D. exponentially expanded the brand he led, and what is more, did all this ethically, winning the minds and hearts of his customers, his employees and his grateful countrymen.

No wonder that J.R.D.'s special brand of leadership can only be accurately defined by one word – **MAGICAL**.

So what exactly **WAS** it that J.R.D. implicitly believed in and primarily practiced which laid the groundwork for his sterling achievements?

The answer to that question is rooted in a comment made many years ago by host Lesley Stahl in the programme *60 Minutes* on the American television channel CBS.

In that episode of the programme, Stahl had mentioned:

"The United States imports oil from Saudi Arabia, cars from Japan, TVs from Korea, and whisky from Scotland. So, what do we import from India? We import PEOPLE, really smart people."

LESLEY STAHL

It is the power of these smart, talented, and hard working people that J.R.D. managed to productively harness in the magical leadership environment which he created, proving that the best of our talent need not fly away to foreign lands; that they **CAN** be profitably retained within Indian shores if they are led with love, care, affection, and motivated and inspired with the **'Magic of Leadership.'**

J.R.D. TATA - THE COMPLETE LEADER

According to the *Management Review* magazine, in over four years of executive seminars conducted by the *Santa Clara University* and the *Tom Peters Group/Learning Systems*, over 5,200 senior managers were asked to **outline the characteristics which they most admired in a leader**.

The **TOP 10** characteristics which emerged as a result of this comprehensive exercise were:

1. **HONEST**
2. **COMPETENT**
3. **FORWARD-LOOKING**
4. **INSPIRING**
5. **INTELLIGENT**
6. **FAIR-MINDED**
7. **BROAD-MINDED**
8. **COURAGEOUS**
9. **STRAIGHTFORWARD**
10. **IMAGINATIVE**

ALL these qualities were present in and consistently displayed by J.RD. Tata in the course of his long tenure at the helm of affairs of the Tata group.

And **ALL** these qualities have been highlighted with examples and anecdotes from J.R.D.'s illustrious career in this book.

Truly, J.R.D. was a **COMPLETE LEADER** in every sense of the term.

AN ODE TO 'JEH'

In the Sunday, 2nd August, 2015 issue of the Parsi community newspaper *Jam-e-Jamshed*, reader **Armin Dutia Motashaw**, who is a great admirer of J.R.D., a former Air Indian, and a *pucca* Parsi and a patriotic citizen of our land, has contributed a beautiful poem titled '**WE MISS OUR JRD**.'

She has given me her kind permission to reproduce it in this book. This is how it goes:

Even today, live in my memories fondly you do, Jeh.
For ever with respect and adoration, here you will stay!

Besides being a tycoon, a good human being you were.
That's why this nation of ours will always love you Sir.

You taught that considerate and kind one must be.
For maintaining standards high, your employees were key.

Their overall welfare you held very close to your heart;
Of your organisation large, they were an integral part

Punctuality you strictly adhered to and not just preached.
Under your able guidance, Air India its top had reached.

Miss you and your splendid leadership we very much do.
Your loss so grave, that your absence we will always rue.

— Armin Dutia Motashaw

Armin has truly captured the essence of J.R.D.'s unique way of functioning and his nobility of character and his purity of soul in her heartfelt poem.

In fact, many of the aspects of 'Jeh's' life she touches upon –

- Being primarily a good human being
- Kindness and consideration for all around him
- Maintaining highest standards of quality in all endeavours
- Ensuring employee welfare
- Punctuality and time etiquette
- Shaping Air India into a leading international brand....

All these and many more find their place as individual learnings in this book.

———————

J.R.D. IS NOT GONE
– HIS MAGIC LIVES ON

In May 2016, a wonderful article titled **STAYING POWER - BACK TO THE FUTURE**, authored by Nikhil Prasad Ojha and Dunigan O'Keeffe graced the front page of the *Mint* newspaper.

The article analysed and ranked the performance of the leading business groups in India right from **1970** up till **2015**. (The parameter chosen for ranking the business groups as of **1970** was based on the **total net assets** of the business group, and for the ranking of **2015**, the parameter considered was that of **market capitalisation**.)

It is **STUNNING TO NOTE** that the **TATA GROUP RANKED** *FIRST* **BOTH IN THE 1970 RANKINGS, AS WELL AS IN THE RANKINGS OF 2015.**

This clearly demonstrates that not only does the Tata group **CONSISTENTLY LEAD** on **NON-FINANCIAL PARAMETERS** such as employee engagement, customer trust, and ethical functioning (which will become obvious through the course of this book), but also **CONSISTENTLY LEADS ON HARD CORE FINANCIAL, BUSINESS**, and **STOCK-MARKET PARAMETERS** such as **TOTAL NET ASSETS** and **MARKET CAPITALISATION** in a highly competitive environment for almost **HALF A CENTURY**.

The *Mint* article also affirms: 'As these groups – and new ones to come – look ahead, it is important that they imbibe the learning of the **Founder's Mentality** if they wish to thrive.

This might mean rediscovering the core insurgent mission of the company. Or we might argue that the voices of customers and the front line must be heard amid a din of competing statements – most often opinions coming from the centres of authority within a group. Or these groups might consider bringing back the idea of "**thinking and acting like an owner**," which has been ground down by complexity. Perhaps the answer is all of the above!

Continued success is a function of this mentality: a collection of specific behaviours and attitudes, best exemplified by the traits of great founders, that if properly cultivated leads more reliably to sustainable growth.

Whether a company is removed decades from the era of its founding doesn't matter. Rather, just about every company, at any stage in its existence, can benefit from the attitudes and behaviours that make up the Founder's Mentality.'

_____

It is an astounding fact that the Tata group, founded in 1868, has had **ONLY A HANDFUL OF CHAIRMEN IN ITS ALMOST 150 YEARS OF EXISTENCE**. They have been:

1. Mr. Jamsetji Nusserwanji Tata (1868 - 1904)
2. Sir Dorab Tata (1904 -1932)
3. Sir Nowroji Saklatwala (1932 - 1938)
4. Mr. Jehangir Ratanji Dadabhoy (J.R.D.) Tata (1938 - 1991)
5. Mr. Ratan Tata (1991 - 2012) and once again Interim Chairman from 2016

Each one of them has faithfully carried forward the vision and values of the founder, Jamsetji Tata, and none has done so more faithfully than J.R.D. himself.

In 1991, J.R.D. gracefully gave up the mantle of chairmanship to Ratan Tata, who proved to be a worthy and able successor in every sense of the word.

From 1970 (when J.R.D. was firmly in charge), right up till 2015 (with Ratan Tata as the father-figure, overseeing the fortunes of the business conglomerate), the Tata group maintained its Number One ranking among Indian business houses.

And what is even MORE stunning is the amazing fact that out of the OTHER LEADING NINE BUSINESS GROUPS IN 1970 (ranging from Number 2 to Number 10), NONE of them even found a place in the 2015 rankings at all.

RANK	1970	2015
1	Tata	Tata
2	Birla	HDFC
3	Mafatlal	RIL
4	KCT Group	ITC
5	ACC	Infosys
6	LNB Group	Bharti Enterprises
7	J.K. Sighania Group	Aditya Birla Group
8	Shriram Group	Sun Pharma
9	Ashok Leyland	ICICI Bank
10	Scindia	Vedanta

Thus, apart from the Tatas, who have proudly retained pole position in 1970 as well as in 2015, **THERE IS NOT A SINGLE NAME WHICH IS REPEATED AMONG THE TOP TEN BUSINESSES.**

Even if you consider the list of Fortune 500 companies, a humongous 88 per cent of companies which were there in the List in 1955 (when this List was first published) are no longer in the List at all in 2014.

It may even be a relatively easy feat to **ATTAIN** Number One position, but to **RETAIN** if for 45 years is simply phenomenal. The rules of the 'game' of business have changed dramatically in these 45 years. And when you consider the fact that in 1970, protectionism was the order of the day and the environment of liberalisation and privatisation for Indian firms was over 20 years away; and in 2015, liberalisation and privatisation had already been in force for almost 25 years, it becomes clear that **the Tata group is an all-weather, all-season, all-century, all-economy, all-situation leading brand, and thanks in no small measure is due to the fine men it has always been fortunate to have at the helm of affairs.**

J.R.D. was at the helm of the Tata group from 1938 till 1991, and then his successor Ratan Tata took over. Coincidentally, Ratan Tata took over the helm just when economic liberalisation was announced. A very difficult period to take over the reins, but Ratan Tata too still ensured that the Tata group retained its top spot, even though the business environment and policies in India had undergone a paradigm shift, literally overnight, since J.R.D.'s time.

Only when there is solid substance in the leadership is such a long and successful innings at the 'top of the charts' even remotely possible. And when you consider that when Mr. R. M. Lala pointed out to J.R.D. in 1979 that the Tatas had not expanded as much in the 1960s and 1970s as some other groups had, J.R.D. replied:

"I have often thought about that. If we had done some of the things that some other groups have done, we would have been twice as big as we are today. But we didn't, and I would not have it any other way," you can then only begin to imagine the actual significance of this achievement.

When the **VISION** is clear and **VALUES** are in place, and the leaders display **VALOUR** in right measure, **VICTORY** is never in doubt under **ANY** circumstances.

Truly – J.R.D. is not gone – his magic lives on.

If a thing is old, it is a sign that it was fit to rule. Old favourites, old customs, old styles survive because they are fit to survive. THE GUARANTEE OF CONTINUITY IS QUALITY

-Unknown

SECTION ONE -VISION

INTRODUCTION TO THE
VISION SECTION

> *We do not claim to be more unselfish, more generous or more philanthropic than other people. But we think we started on sound and straightforward business principles, considering the interests of the shareholders our own, and the health and welfare of the employees, the sure foundation of our success*

-JAMSHETJI TATA

No organisation or leadership career can ever truly succeed without vision.

Vision is the beginning (though not the end), of any worthwhile endeavour.

> *Without vision there is no direction, though there may be blind speed. And blind speed without vision is infinitely more dangerous than no speed at all*

-CYRUS M. GONDA

Yet, there are today many organisations and 'leaders' who are in a tearing hurry to get 'somewhere' – 'anywhere' – **AS LONG AS THEY GET THERE FAST.**

Such organisations and their leaders remind one of the absent-minded professor who jumped into a standing taxi and shouted out to the driver – **"Fast. Hurry. There's no time to lose."** Then the professor got absorbed in reading some papers. The taxi driver, galvanised into action, sped off straight down the road. A few minutes and many miles later, the driver gathered courage and timidly asked the fierce-looking professor who was still absorbed in his papers, **"Pardon me, Sir, but where are we supposed to be going?"**

Speed truly counts for nothing, if you don't know where you're headed for.

Of course, some little children have greater and clearer vision than many absent-minded professors, and even higher and loftier vision than some CEOs. There was this small girl of five, seated at her desk in school, busily sketching with some crayons on a sheet of paper. The teacher came up to her and asked, **"What are you drawing?"** The child earnestly said, **"I'm drawing a picture of God."** The teacher smiled and responded, **"But nobody knows what God looks like."** The girl looked at the teacher and solemnly replied, **"But they WILL know how God looks like when I've finished drawing the picture."**

Just like that little girl, **leaders too need to have a vision deep within them, and be convinced of the goodness and the righteousness of their vision**. Only then will leaders be able to inspire others and develop more leaders.

Queen Elizabeth I

Many years ago (in the sixteenth century, to be precise), during the reign of Queen Elizabeth I, she noted the absence of one of her favourite courtiers, named Sir Walter Midway, from her court for a few days. When he was back, she asked him where he had been. Sir Walter had been engaged in a noble task – he had been busy establishing Emmanuel College at Cambridge. He did not see this task as merely the laying of the foundation stone, but rather envisioned the future college as a place where young minds would receive a valuable education. Which is why he replied courteously, "Madame, I have been planting an acorn seed. And when it becomes an oak tree, God only knows what fruits it will give."

Emmanuel College - Cambridge

Visionary leaders are often **first movers** – they see further over the horizon than their counterparts, not because they have better eye-sight, but because they have developed their **'third eye,'** which lies deep within all of us.

Volumes have been written upon the subject of vision, and most of us vaguely understand what the word means. What is more important, (and less commonly understood), is what exactly the element of vision comprises of, and **how vision is to be conceived and practically implemented by a leader within an organisational context**.

To understand that, we do not need to look to foreign shores. The learnings that follow, which display a sample of J.R.D.'s visionary brand of leadership, adequately show the way forward.

STRATEGIC VISION IS KEY

" *If you are working on something exciting that you really care about, you don't have to be pushed. The vision pulls you* "

-STEVE JOBS

WHAT **J.R.D.** BELIEVED IN AND **PRACTICED**

" *Give to us clear vision that we may know where to stand and what to stand for – because unless we stand for something, we shall fall for everything* "

-PETER MARSHALL

J.R.D. had a far-sighted vision for his beloved airline – Air India – as well as for the Tata group which he ably stewarded for over half a century.

Bobby Kooka, a key figure in the brand-building saga of Air India, analysed that although J.R.D. was himself a hands-on pilot, he did not simply view aviation as an enthusiast and as a flyer. He also looked upon aviation as an industrialist and a businessman responsible for the continued functioning, growth and profitability of an airline. **Back in the early days of commercial aviation in the 1930s, when flying was a luxury meant only for the super-rich, J.R.D. demonstrated the vision to understand that air travel would become economically viable only if it could be made a large-scale industry which would trickle**

down and have mass-market appeal. A few years later, his vision made him realise that Air India could become a key service provider of choice for passengers among existing aviation giants, only if it could manage to present a unique offering to its passengers.

This vision translated into practical reality, as J.R.D. became keenly interested in ensuring that Air India offered something special to its passengers if it was to become a global force to reckon with. **The profit motive was secondary in the short-term, and it is this VISIONARY focus on a special offering (in the case of Air India, its service levels), that elevated the airline to join the highest ranks of the leading international players.**

The way I explain this in the Customer Experience Excellence workshops I conduct is: "There are only two primary manufacturers of commercial aircraft in the world today, and these are **Airbus** and **Boeing**. Most airlines in the world have a fleet consisting either of Airbus or Boeing aeroplanes. The fleet of even most low-cost airlines would in all probability consist of machines of either of these two manufacturers. Yet, while airlines such as Emirates and Singapore, Lufthansa and Swiss, consistently win the international awards for best airlines, and are able to charge a premium from their passengers, **the difference does not lie in their aircraft, but in the entire chain of customer service experience**, crafted with thought and loving care by razor-sharp analytical minds at the helm of affairs, who have the **VISION** to realise that today, more than ever before, the differentiation between one organisation and its competitors will be based on soft-skills and the element of service."

This requires exceptional clarity of vision on behalf of the key decision-makers in the organisation, as we are yet living in a world which traditionally revolves around a product-based mindset rather than a service-oriented one.

As T.E. Lawrence (also known as 'Lawrence of Arabia'), wrote: '**All men dream, but not equally. Those who dream by night in the dusty recesses of their minds wake in the day to find that it was vanity. But the dreamers of the day are dangerous men, for they may act their dream with open eyes to make it possible.**'

J.R.D. was one such visionary, and he had learned the art of **dreaming in the daytime**, and this is always a profitable form of dreaming.

John Scully said: "**The future belongs to those who see possibilities before they become obvious.**" How aptly this applies to visionaries like J.R.D. Tata.

LEARNINGS

FOR LEADERS

" The companies that survive longest are the ones that work out what they uniquely can give to the world – not just growth or money, but their excellence, their respect for others, or their ability to make people happy. Some call those things a soul "

-CHARLES HANDY

No buzz-word is more heard in corporate circles today than 'vision.' It seems to be on every CEO's lips. Yet few have apparently been able to understand its true meaning, and fewer still have managed to convert vision successfully into execution.

The hitch appears to be that while for vision to bear fruit, the element of time is of utmost essence, CEOs today seem to be driven by the merciless whip-hand of the stock market, which with its focus on short-term speculation rather than long-term investment, does not appear to have much real use for philosophies such as 'Vision' and 'Strategy.' Yet ironically, even in today's times, sustained profits and organisational success can only be achieved through a visionary long-term approach.

The key lies in leaders developing the self-discipline to realise that while short-term inconveniences may 'hinder' them now, it is better to sacrifice a little in the short-term so that long-term benefits assuredly accrue. There is always a trade-off between the two approaches, and the leaders who can '**see**' further, the leaders with '**vision**,' always ensure they take actions to secure the long-term future of their organisations.

Another element which seems to 'restrict vision,' even among stalwarts of management, is the lack of ability to foresee the **avenues of utility** to which their own product or service could possibly be put to use by potential customers in myriad ways. There are umpteen examples of such apparent 'short-sightedness' throughout corporate history. As illustrations of the same, the following are particularly instructive:

- **"I think there is a world market for maybe five computers"** –Thomas Watson; chairman of IBM, said this in 1943

THOMAS WATSON

- **"There is no reason anyone would want a computer in their home"** –Ken Olsen; president, founder and chairman of Digital Equipment Corp., and renowned as one of the ten most memorable CEOs of the digital era, said this as recently as 1977

KEN OLSEN

- **"Television won't be able to hold on to any market it captures after the first six months. People will soon get tired of staring at a plywood box every night"** –Darryl Zanuck, executive at 20th Century Fox (winner of three Academy Awards as producer for Best Picture), said this in 1946, when television was in its infancy

DARRYL ZANUCK

What you will read on this page is a goose-bump raising anecdote of what **VISION** in the corporate context truly means. The following is highly inspiring material extracted from *Think Out of the Box* by Mike Vance and Diane Deacon:

'Vision is a crucial component in the formula for success. It holds the keys to the future. The inspirational lives we look to for guidance remind us of this time and again.

The following incident will illustrate our point.

WALT DISNEY

At Disney Studios in Burbank, California, Mike (former Disney executive Mike Vance) could gaze out of his office window, across Buena Vista Street, to St. Joseph's Hospital where **WALT DISNEY** died.

His death was preceded by an amazing incident that reportedly took place the night before in Walt's hospital room.

A journalist, knowing Walt was seriously ill, persisted in getting an interview with Walt and was frustrated on numerous occasions by the hospital staff. When he finally managed to get into the room, Walt couldn't sit up in bed or talk above a whisper.

Walt instructed the reporter to lie down on the bed, next to him, so he could whisper in the reporter's ear. For the next 30 minutes, Walt and the journalist lay side by side as Walt referred to an imaginary map of Walt Disney World on the ceiling above the bed.

Walt pointed out where he planned to place various attractions and buildings. He talked about transportation, hotels, restaurants, and many other parts of his vision for a property that wouldn't open to the public for another six years.

...A man who lay dying in the hospital whispered in a reporter's ear for 30 minutes, describing his vision for the future and the role he (himself) would play in it for generations to come. This is the way to live – believing so much in your vision that even when you're dying, you whisper it into another person's ear.'

J.R.D. had developed the similar visionary foresight and passion to visualise and recognise, that without a positive organisational differentiator, neither survival nor success would be possible. His sharp leader's mind immediately latched on to the one differentiator that could be the key to success, and thus raised a fledgling organisation (Air India), into one of the most successful aviation brands the world had ever experienced.

Truly, the future belongs to those who can visualise it coming well in advance.

" The empires of the future are the empires of the mind "

-SIR WINSTON CHURCHILL

POINTS TO PONDER AND PRACTICE

- Remember one constant: Evolved leadership thinking is always visionary and long-term

- **Look around you and identify the strongest brands you can find. Brands in which you would personally invest without much debate, deliberation or thought. In almost all cases, these would be brands which commenced with a clear and focused vision, brands with a sterling legacy; brands which have stood the test of time. This should get you thinking faster than anything else ever can, that when it comes to a trade-off between the short-term and the long-term, which road you need to choose**

- Then there are other smart-alecs who joke, "Why bother about the long-term? In the long-term, we are all dead." We as individuals may be dead, but organisations are not individuals. If crafted with vision and nurtured with care, organisations live on and carry the legacy of the founder and subsequent leaders with them far beyond the natural life of individuals. As just one example, there are many organisations in Japan which are well over a thousand years old, existing and thriving even today under the same brand-name, owned and managed by the same family, and offering the same (although modified), products and services envisioned by their founders over a thousand years ago

- You will hear and read a lot of hogwash from certain management 'experts' about how if you don't think of the short-term, you will not even be around in the long-term. These are nothing but weak excuses for not wanting to stay the mile, for not wanting to walk on the straight and narrow path. **Men like J.R.D. and his predecessors and successors never cut corners or took short-term measures, which is why the business group they headed still runs strong and remains India's leading business house even today**

A VISIONARY LEADER SETS STANDARDS NOT ONLY FOR HIS ORGANISATION, BUT ALSO FOR THE INDUSTRY WITHIN WHICH HE OPERATES

"Don't be content with just being a leader. Strive to become a leader's leader"

-CYRUS M. GONDA

WHAT **J.R.D.** BELIEVED IN AND **PRACTICED**

"You can become an even more excellent person by constantly setting higher standards for yourself and then by doing everything possible to live up to those standards"
-BRIAN TRACY

J.R.D. was a pioneer in more ways than one. Not only did he establish an entire industry (aviation) in India, he also 'raised the bar' and set industry standards in the aviation industry for the rest of the world to follow.

65

The Boeing 707 aircraft was a plane that J.R.D. was rightly proud of. It formed the nucleus of the Air India fleet for many years. **But J.R.D. was not merely satisfied with having these planes on board his fleet. He identified an area of improvement in these excellent aircraft, that even the highly qualified and experienced Boeing designers and engineers had not thought about.**

Since Boeing is an American company, initially, the 707s came fitted from the Boeing factory with American-made Pratt and Whitney engines. While these engines were definitely good, for J.R.D., they were not good enough. With deep study, he found that not the Pratt and Whitney engines which the 707s came originally fitted with, but British-made Rolls-Royce Conway engines, were a superior option. Thus Air India became one of the first airlines in the world to place an order with Boeing for 707 aircraft customised and fitted with Rolls-Royce Conway engines.

Other international airlines observed the performance of this combination, and finding that J.R.D. had made a winning decision, these airlines also commenced ordering Boeing 707s with Rolls-Royce Conway engines for their own fleets. Even many airlines based in America saw the wisdom of this, and changed over from American-made Pratt and Whitney engines to the British-made Rolls-Royce ones for the Boeing 707s they purchased.

BOEING 707

NOTE: The following news was received in February 2018, a few days before this book first went into print.

India's largest carrier IndiGo grounded three of its A320 neo aircraft due to engine-related issues. The grounded aircraft were fitted with Pratt and Whitney engines. This safety measure follows a directive from European aviation safety regulator EASA (European Aviation Safety Agency). EASA had issued an emergency airworthiness directive for A320 airplanes fitted with PW1100 engines having a particular serial number. The directive was issued due to cases involving several incidents of engine in-flight shut-downs (IFSD) and rejected take-offs (RTO) in airplanes fitted with these particular Pratt and Whitney engines.

This is the second occasion on which IndiGo has had to ground aircraft on account of Pratt and Whitney engine problems. Just a year prior (in 2017) IndiGo had to ground a few aircraft which then began flying again after the problems were resolved. The current issue with the engines is a different one from the problem which had led to the grounding of IndiGo aircraft the previous year.

Some flights also had to be cancelled as a result of grounding the aircraft, leading to disrupted schedules and passenger inconvenience. A statement issued by IndiGo said: 'Our precautionary measure of grounding the three aircraft resulted in cancellations of some of our flights. But we feel it was the best decision in the interest of our safe and reliable operations.' IndiGo ensured that the affected passengers were offered refunds of their fares.

Of course, although there is no immediate and apparent co-relation between J.R.D.'s decision taken many decades ago to have the aircraft he ordered from Boeing to be fitted with Rolls Royce engines rather than the standard Pratt and Whitney ones which Boeing traditionally came fitted with, it is almost uncanny how J.R.D.'s visionary insight in this regard (as a result of his deep study on the subject) rings true even today.

LEARNINGS
FOR LEADERS

" *Uncommon thinkers REUSE what common thinkers REFUSE* "

-J.R.D. TATA

This learning, of course, is about an attribute linked with vision, and pertains to a thorough and complete, rather than a superficial understanding of the industry the leader operates in. This is another reason why **a leader should not have his hand in too many pies**. (Later in this book, under the section of 'Valour,' the concept of 'Span of Control' will be discussed, which will validate this lesson further.)

Henry Ford focused his attention on a single industry and thus was able to come out with the **path-breaking concept of assembly-line production**, which drastically reduced production time, and also reduced costs. Not only did assembly-line become an industry standard for the automobile manufacturing industry, but also for many other industries, which saw the wisdom and benefit of Henry Ford's pioneering concept.

Similarly, once **Toyota** developed, fine-tuned, and popularised the concept of **Total Quality Management** (TQM), it was rapidly adopted by every other industry, not only in manufacturing, but also in the service sector.

Standards of **service excellence** and **customer-delight** designed and developed at the highly-focused **Walt Disney World** are now practiced by leading service organisations across industries as diverse as hospitals and management consultancies.

Leaders are not given their positions so that they can merely go with the existing flow. They are there to envision and study and chart out new and better paths, and also be the first to tread on them. Others then see the wisdom of the leader's approach, and then follow; and what the leader has pioneered then becomes the *de facto* new and improved standard for other organisations in that industry, and even for organisations in other industries, to adopt and practice.

It requires courage, wisdom and insight to not only identify a better way, but to move away from the existing and entrenched. Primarily, it requires a different kind of **vision** compared to what contemporaries are adopting.

The word 'Leadership' itself is derived from the Old English word '**Lethin**' which means '**to make go**' or '**to make happen**.'

So don't stagnate. Don't be still.

Go ahead. Make things happen.

That is when you can honestly wear the mantle of leadership with pride.

AN EFFECTIVE EXERCISE

Ask Yourself: How often do you follow and adopt current industry standards and practices, without attempting to wonder whether you can change the existing paradigm for the better, by taking efforts to identify and develop superior alternatives?

POINTS TO PONDER AND PRACTICE

- The difference between a follower and a leader is that while a follower is content to tread the beaten path, the leader knows that there are many newer, better, interesting and more profitable paths just waiting to be discovered

- Leaders do not wait for others to take the first step to find out whether the water is too cold for swimming. Neither do they recklessly plunge into the water themselves in their bid to be the first one in, without any thought or study. That, too, is not a trait of mature leadership

- Rather, you as a leader need to be cautious and not needlessly risk organisational resources, but first work-out and understand the pros and the cons of your proposed decision of sailing on uncharted waters, by conducting a detailed SWOT analysis. This is a management tool wherein one identifies the strengths, the weaknesses, the opportunities, and the threats, and through this identify all possible implications associated with any decision, situation, or course of action. This is exactly what J.R.D. did before he took the decision to change the engines on the Boeing 707 aircraft he ordered for his fleet

- Once the SWOT analysis is rigorously and scientifically conducted, and if after this analysis it appears that the 'pros' exceed the 'cons,' that the odds appear to be in your favour, go ahead with the decision, **even if it means going against what the rest of the industry is currently doing**. However, while conducting your SWOT analysis, it would be wise to include parameters which would tell you why the industry is currently adopting what it is adopting. As it is said: '**never pull down a fence until you understand why it was erected in the first place**.' That is sensible leadership thinking at work

RECOGNISE
THE SUPREME IMPORTANCE
OF TRAINING

We must remember that one man is much the same as another, and that he is best who is trained in the severest school

-THUCYDIDES
(Greek General and Historian)

WHAT **J.R.D.** BELIEVED IN AND **PRACTICED**

It's all to do with training. You can do a lot if you're properly trained

-ELIZABETH II, *Queen of Great Britain*

J.R.D., like all great leaders, envisioned the importance of comprehensive and thorough training to ensure that high standards which management had set for the organisation were converted into reality at the front-level by operational staff.

Addressing the final Annual General Meeting of Air India International in 1953 (before the airline got nationalised and was renamed as Air India), he concluded his address by saying, "**I must utter a word of warning that unless the greatest attention continues to be paid to the maintenance of high standards of training and discipline amongst flying and ground crews, the resulting deterioration might destroy the good name of Indian civil aviation.**"

71

K.G. Appuswamy, who joined Air India as an engineer in 1946, and who later rose to become the Managing Director of Air India, recalls the importance that J.R.D. gave to the function of training. When Air India first bought the Boeing 707 aircraft, J.R.D. and his team decided to develop 100 percent of the maintenance facilities domestically. Air India developed its own engine overhaul system, instrument overhaul system, and so on. It was also arranged with Boeing to directly train all technical personnel of Air India. Pilot instructors and operating pilots were sent to Boeing, America, one-and-a-half years ahead of time, to receive thorough and comprehensive training on all aspects of that aircraft. Other personnel apart from instructors and pilots were also given robust aircraft-related training in India.

Jawaharlal Nehru

The Tata passion for providing thorough training was appreciated even by **Prime Minister Jawaharlal Nehru**. After India attained independence in 1947, communal violence was rampant in the states of Punjab and Bengal. Many volunteers from all over the country rushed to these troubled spots to undertake relief work. Among these was also a team from the **Tata Institute of Social Sciences (TISS)**, Bombay.

Nehru later singled out this particular team for special praise. He said, "We found the difference in their (TISS team) work and the work of many others who were earnest and who had done their best but who did not have the training to do it well. There is a difference between the trained workers and the merely enthusiastic workers."

J.R.D. always evinced an interest in observing the functioning of educational institutions and their diverse methodologies, wherever he travelled. In the 1960s, while visiting France, he was interested to note that more than three-fourths of the top positions in the French Civil Service and in leading scientific institutions of France were held by individuals who had trained in the four leading polytechnics of France. (It is an interesting fact that the first of these four polytechnics was originally conceived and established by Napoleon Bonaparte to train his civil engineers.) After noting all this, J.R.D. invited the Director-General of Education, Paris, to visit India and identify whether a similar institution could be successfully set-up in India to train our people in similar style.

72

J.R.D. also had in mind the inception of a Staff College for his senior executives where Tata Directors and senior faculty from management institutes would lecture to and interact with Tata officers, sharing their rich and varied experience in various aspects of business management and leadership.

With this in mind, a suitable premises surrounded by serene greenery was acquired by the Tatas in Pune, where the **Tata Management Training Centre (TMTC), was established.**

This centre today is considered one of the finest of its kind in India, where regular training programmes are conducted in a conducive environment by the best of trainers for Tata personnel, as well as staff of other corporate houses and public sector organisations.

THE BEST INVESTMENT YOU COULD EVER MAKE

A wealthy businessman came to seek his mentor's advice on a matter which had been at the back of his mind for some time.

"I have earned great wealth in a short time, which I want to leave to my children. I know they are still very young, but I feel it is better to plan for the future as early as possible. What I would like to know is, should I invest it in real estate, but that could be dicey. Gold also fluctuates. And fixed deposits do not really give a high rate of interest. Where should I invest for them so that it will give them the most benefit?"

The wise mentor advised, **"Provide for your children the kind of wealth that will always appreciate and which no one can take away from them, ever, in any way. Invest in the best education for them, and couple it with a sense of values. You can do nothing better for them. Not only will they then be able to make their way ahead in life with the education you have given them, they will also move forward in the right direction based on the values you have instilled in them."**

The businessman, having received the answer he was seeking, went away a happy man.

LEARNINGS ▮
▮ FOR LEADERS

> *Excellence is an art won by training and habituation. We do not act rightly because we have virtue or excellence, but we rather have those because we have acted rightly. We are what we repeatedly do. Excellence, then, is not an act but a habit*
>
> -ARISTOTLE

Since the benefits which accrue from investment in training and development activities are naturally not immediately visible, but happen and enhance exponentially over time, it requires a **visionary** leader with foresight to invest substantially in the same.

Evolved leaders understand that training and development activities are an **investment**, and not a **cost**. The returns that can be achieved from investing in training activities (of course, provided they are done in the right manner), are truly phenomenal.

The benefits of initiating and undertaking training activities include:

- Reduced rate of attrition

- Feeling of loyalty towards the organisation

- Reduced wastage and accidents

- Increased productivity

- Enhanced quality of product or service

- Higher customer satisfaction and resulting positive word-of-mouth publicity

In fact, if one delves into the Japanese Quality Movement, which is primarily based on Dr. Deming's *Fourteen Points of Excellence Model*, the importance of training becomes clear. These fourteen points, the application of which have made Japan the quality super-power it is acknowledged as today, were developed by Dr. Deming, who is considered as the father of Japan's quality revolution.

In his list of fourteen points, training is the only point which Dr. Deming considers so important, he has mentioned it twice, in different contexts.

The first time he mentions training, Dr. Deming mentions that thorough and complete training should be provided to every new recruit who joins the organisation. Not only should he be thorough with his own job, but also be trained to be thorough with related jobs, as well as completely and holistically inducted into the philosophy of the organisation.

Next, he mentions that providing on-going training even for existing employees is an absolute imperative. For example, if an employee has been with an organisation for, say, thirty years, he still needs re-training every year to ensure that 'the axe remains sharpened.'

No wonder then, that with this literally obsessive attention towards the training function, the Japanese have beaten almost all nations world-wide when it comes to quality considerations and a healthy attitude and positive and quality-oriented approach towards work.

It is an established fact that the armed forces adopt the most structured and severe approach towards training, and if it is their men who are the most dependable in crises situations, credit goes to the thorough training they receive right since the time they are inducted, as well as the regular training which they receive on an on-going basis, throughout their career with the forces.

Many brands today attempt to save and scrimp on the training function, thinking it is not a priority. But it is a trained employee who is the most valuable asset for an organisation, especially in today's era where customers access the Internet and are themselves knowledgeable, and expect employees to be still more knowledgeable than them.

It is not enough for your front-end people to know the basics of your product or service. They need to have knowledge which goes 'above and beyond,' so that their interactions with customers can truly be memorable and a value-add, and be the cutting edge which makes your brand the preferred choice for customers in your industry.

A global example as to the level to which some brands go in today's times to ensure their front-end people are fully informed, is the New York-based supermarket brand *Wegmans Food Markets Inc*. Wegmans is a family-owned business, having more than eighty outlets, and blessed with an extremely loyal customer base. **The customer loyalty of Wegmans stems primarily from the fact that their front-end employees are a joy to interact with.** The employees are selected based on their passion for food and their willingness to learn more about food. Then they are made to undergo rigorous and thorough training, which makes them masters of the food products they are in charge of. David Burkus, in his book *Under New Management*, elaborates on the thrust that Wegmans delivers to training its employees:

'Once Wegmans finds passionate people, it invests significant time and money in training them. New employees in customer-facing positions go through up to fifty-five hours of initial training before hitting the floor. Cashiers, for example, are not allowed to talk to customers until they have completed forty hours of primary training. **For on-going training, the company even sends individuals overseas on training trips. Cheese department employees may be sent to Italy to learn about how Parmesan (cheese) is made, and bakery employees may be sent to France to learn the French style of baking.** Wegmans invests all this training in employees so that they will bring their expertise to customer interactions, advising customers on everything from foods to pair together to how to best cook and serve a meal.'

Because its employees are so passionate about food to begin with, and because they have been so well trained, Wegmans becomes a great place to shop. And as a result of this emphasis on training and other employee-oriented initiatives, Wegmans ranked Number One in 2005 in the *Fortune's* 'Best Companies to Work For' list.

Investment in training requires the leader to display a medium to long-term outlook towards business, as the results which accrue from the right training do not fructify overnight.

The positive results obtained from investing in training and development activities may not always be visible in the short-term. Therefore, it requires the inculcation of a **long-term leadership vision**, if the leader is to commit and invest sufficient organisational resources to this vital function.

Some short-sighted 'leaders' who lack sufficient vision take the approach: **'Why invest so much in training and developing staff? Let our employees learn 'feet-on-street.'**

There is a humorous but revealing anecdote where the CEO of an organisation tells the Finance Head, **"The new batch of trainees are joining us next week. We need to organise an intensive and detailed induction and training programme for them."**

The short-sighted Finance Head who is obsessed with reducing the training budget, responds, **"We are always spending so much on training these new recruits. WHAT IF THEY GET TRAINED AT OUR EXPENSE AND THEN LEAVE?"**

The CEO smiles and wisely counters, **"What if we DON'T train them and they STAY BACK?"**

Training (or lack of it) strongly impacts the experience your customers receive.

The most important purpose for which training activities should be invested in is that it **shows regard and respect for your customer, who will be the ultimate recipient of improved and enhanced product and service as a result of your employees being thoroughly and intensively trained in all aspects of their job.**

'THE KNOWLEDGE'

We in India have always taken pride in the fact that the IIT and the IIM entrance examinations are the toughest entrance examinations in the world to clear and get through.

But there is another test, not so well known in our part of the world, which may be even more of a challenge than the entrance examinations for the IITs and the IIMs.

That test is appropriately called '**The Knowledge**,' and it is the test that a person has to pass before he or she can qualify to become a taxi driver for the famous **London Black Cabs**.

The test has been described as the equivalent of having a detailed atlas of the mega-city of London implanted in the brain.

Before we see how detailed the 'syllabus' for this test is, and how much time an average person takes to train himself or herself to pass it, and how exactly it results into ultimate customer delight, let us have a look at the interesting story behind **HOW** this test came about to be.

Although taxi cabs in London were first licensed early in the 17th century (at that time they were obviously horse-drawn carriages and not motorised vehicles), 'The Knowledge' test was put in place as a pre-requisite for a person to be authorised to ride/drive a taxi cab in London, way back in the 1850s.

It was in 1851 that the *Great Exhibition* of Great Britain was held in Hyde Park, London. At that time, Great Britain was the most powerful empire in the world, and the Great Exhibition had been organised to showcase the best that the British Empire had to offer in terms of engineering, technology, and innovation. It was a grand event, the first ever of the major international exhibitions (which were later held in New York and also in Paris, for which the famed Eiffel Tower was constructed), and people flocked from all over the world to devour what it had to offer.

........*continued*

The exhibition itself was a grand success, but one complaint the visitors who came from other parts of the world had was that the drivers of the horse-drawn cabs were ill-informed about the geography of their own city (London), and often had little idea where they were going.

This feedback was taken very seriously, and Prince Albert, (the husband of Queen Victoria, who was the ruling monarch at that time), devised the idea of **testing a London taxi driver's knowledge about the city before he would be given a license to ply his trade**.

This idea developed into *The Knowledge* (as this test is now known), and it is still the entrance examination that an aspiring cabbie needs to get through today, if he wishes to ply his taxi in the city of London.

A FAMOUS BLACK LONDON TAXI

........*continued*

■ SHIFT FOCUS TO TODAY ■

It takes on an average for a person with decent intelligence and retentive memory over **four years of preparation** to pass this test, so detailed and in-depth is it in nature and scope.

The information that an aspirant has to store in memory covers a **complete and thorough knowledge of a twenty-kilometre area in diameter**, at the centre of which lies the 'heart' of the city of London.

There are over 25,000 roads and streets to be memorised.

Also to be memorised are **several thousand 'points of interest' which a passenger could request a taxi-driver to ply him to**. These 'points of interest' include, but are not restricted to, **restaurants, hotels, pubs, bars, cinemas, theatres, courts, parks, places of worship, stadiums, shops (large and small), statues, museums, art galleries, and almost every other thing one can expect to find in the city.**

Of course, they are also expected to familiarise themselves with one-way streets and all traffic regulations and keep updated of any changes therein. And not only is it their knowledge which is evaluated, they need to have their shirt collars buttoned up, their hair neatly trimmed, their shoes gleaming. In short, they need to make a presentable picture, as well as be seen as a walking-talking encyclopaedia of the city they represent.

'The Knowledge' has been described as the ultimate mind-teaser. It is said to be a real-time, grass-root level test of memorisation skills so intense, that it literally physically alters the brains of those who pass it.

For the prospect to pass the test, the examiner may ask any permutation or combination of possible routes within the area under consideration, and the prospective cabbie has to rattle off the precise sequence of streets, junctions, bypasses, round-abouts, over-bridges, no-entry barriers, and left and right turns to reach from Point A to Point B, anywhere within that 293 square kilometre area which comprises the area that any London cabbie is supposed to know even if woken up from sleep.

........*continued*

........continued

And this is not just a one-off examination where you may get lucky as you may be asked just that part of the syllabus in the examination which you have coincidentally prepared for. It is an on-going series of tests which will keep on being conducted until the examiners are truly satisfied with the person's thoroughness, and believe he is deserving of being awarded that Green Badge which signifies him as an authorised London cabbie who truly has 'The Knowledge.'

In this era of satellite technology and GPS, why is so much stress laid on memorising the intricacies of the locality?

Because when it comes to quick reactions, emergency situations, and sheer 'street-smarts,' a person who has 'The Knowledge' can beat technology hollow.

THIS – IS THE SUPERIOR LEVEL OF TRAINING TO WHICH THE BEST OF ORGANISATIONS EXPECT THEIR PEOPLE TO ASPIRE, AS IT IS ONE OF THE BEST WAYS OF ENSURING CUSTOMER DELIGHT.

(I am extremely thankful to my former student and an MBA Mumbai University topper, and now my good friend - Prof. Danish Memon, for having brought *The Knoweldge* to my attention. A more well-read person than Danish it would be hard to find.)

An article titled 'Taking A Crack At Rails: Why Railway Track Fractures Have Gone Up' which appeared in the *Mumbai Mirror* dated 15th November, 2016, highlights the many perils that can accrue due to lack of adequate training. An extract from the article follows:

'A lack of expert welders in the Central Railway's workforce threatens to push commuters' safety off the rails and further worsen the network's punctuality record. In the past three days alone, there have been at least six track fractures in the strained network and four of them occurred at points where rails had been welded together during line laying or repairs. While temperature fluctuations are blamed for an unusually high number of track problems during winter, the national railway workers' union claims that Central Railway's Mumbai Division doesn't have a **SINGLE TRACK WELDER WITH TRAINING OR CERTIFICATION** from the Regional Design and Standards Organisation (RDSO). This body advises zonal railways on a range of issues, including construction, operation, and maintenance.'

POINTS TO PONDER AND PRACTICE

- Never under-estimate the value of training. **The best organisations world-wide, invest 1 to 2 percent of their annual turnover into the training function**, which can work out to millions of dollars a year

- For organisations which carry out the entire process and cycle of training and track the results, (organisations such as Motorola and Xerox are renowned for this), the **returns on the training investment** are calculated at around 50 to 60 percent, a fantastic rate of return by any standards. (**According to the American Society for Training and Development, an increase of $680 in a company's training investment per employee, generates, on average, a 6 percent improvement in total shareholder return. These organisations also enjoy higher profit margins and higher income per employee**)

- Even if you are currently not in a position to decide the training budgets for your organisation or your department, you can at least set aside some of your time on a regular basis to share your experiences with your people. Guide them where they need to improve and explain or demonstrate how they could do a task better or faster or with reduced wastage. Train them thoroughly on all aspects you feel may help them perform their job in a superior manner. **With a trained team to support you, your own performance and productivity will see marked improvement**

POINTS TO PONDER AND PRACTICE

- Training is provided so that the individual can enhance his performance in three broad areas – **Attitude, Knowledge**, and **Skills**. Ensure you focus on all these three areas while providing training. Often, managers focus only on providing training to enhance skills, as job-related skills are visibly and immediately linked with enhanced job performance, and thus, short-term profitability. **But it is a healthy ATTITUDE and broad-based KNOWLEDGE that enable specific SKILLS to be put to practice; hence training for attitude and knowledge improvement also need to form an important part of the training package**

- As a leader, give the training function sufficient importance. **Resist the temptation to slash training budgets for your organisation or for your department when revenues are down**. Or at least continue conducting training in a cost-effective manner by using in-house faculty, as it is the training function which is the proven life-blood of organisational success

" *It is easier to build stronger children than to repair broken men* "

-FREDERICK DOUGLASS

83

THE ROLE OF
STATISTICS

" *You can't manage what you don't measure* **"**

-W. EDWARDS DEMING

WHAT **J.R.D.**
BELIEVED IN
AND **PRACTICED**

" *Statistics may be defined as "a body of methods for making wise decisions in the face of uncertainty* **"**

-W.A. WALLIS

J.R.D. was the **first individual** in Corporate India with the foresight to not only **envision**, but also take concrete steps to ensure that the collation of statistical data and its subsequent analysis was taken seriously.

He identified the need for corporate-level decision-making to be done in a scientific manner, with the use of numbers as well as the complement of judgment and experience. Decisions made with the head as well as the heart would obviously be superior decisions, as compared to those based on intuition and gut-feel alone.

85

With this end in mind, and finding that there was a severe lacunae of statistical information based on which economic initiatives and decisions and resource allocation could be based, **J.R.D. initiated a Statistics Department within the Tata Group**.

To spearhead this department, J.R.D. brought in Mr. Y.S. Pandit, who was then the Statistical Superintendant in the Bombay Government Labour Office. Mr. Pandit left his job with the labour office and joined the Tatas in their new statistics department.

Mr. Pandit said of J.R.D., "**J.R.D. had a hunger for statistics**. In those days – the 1930s – they were not readily available. The only source that showed an interest in compiling them was the Government. In Bombay House (the Tata group headquarters building), we used to compile statistics on different subjects and stencil them on a rather unpresentable page or two. We soon found they were much appreciated not only in India but also abroad."

This statistics department initiated by J.R.D. was soon expanded to include the study of economics as well, and was renamed as the 'Department of Economics and Statistics.'

Dr. F.E. Mehta, a senior Tata group functionary, reminisced that it was **J.R.D. who was the first in India to realise that staff-functions needed to have a knowledge-base**, which is a prime reason why the Department of Economics and Statistics was initially established by the Tatas.

Then, in the early 1940s, Dr. John Mathai, another of J.R.D.'s hand-picked men, took over as head of the expanded Department of Economics and Statistics of the Tata group. The department gathered and collated valuable information, which in the early days was made available only to Directors of the Tata Group to facilitate decision-making. **Over time, the department initiated the regular publication of *The Statistical Outline of India*, published by the Tatas, for public consumption**. This publication became almost the sole and definitely the most reliable source of vital, practical, statistical information for use by all Indian business entities, and also for Indian Government officials, including economic planners at a senior level.

Thus, J.R.D. with his astute vision can also be credited with the formal introduction of statistics as a tool and as a discipline into the Indian corporate world.

LEARNINGS FOR LEADERS

" In God we trust: all others must bring data "

-W. EDWARDS DEMING

It is unfortunate that the moment many of us hear the terms 'statistics' or 'analytics,' our minds 'turn off.' This aversion has probably arisen due to the fashion in which mathematics was taught to us at school level. **Forward-thinking schools are now looking 'backwards' and incorporating ancient but time-tested methods such as 'Vedic Mathematics' and 'Mathematics through Abacus' into their syllabi.** This, say students who have undergone mathematics training using these methodologies, makes them feel comfortable with numbers, and better equipped to tackle complex formulae with which they are faced later on in life, as the years progress.

Decision-making is a key function of leadership. And the best decisions are taken when quantitative as well as qualitative data have been correctly and carefully collated and intelligently analysed. If this is not done, decision-making becomes more of an intuitive activity, where the probability of the decision taken going wrong is almost as much as the probability of it being the right one. As Dr. Deming said: **'The ultimate purpose of collecting the data is to provide a basis for action or a recommendation.'**

87

Today, every business entity, whether in the field of **mutual funds, insurance, health-care, construction, manufacturing, retail, aviation**, or any other, relies (or should rely) considerably on statistical analysis to take key decisions in almost every aspect of its functioning. Leaders at all levels need to incorporate some element of statistical understanding into their decision-making, to ensure solid substance is added to intangible intuitive judgment and the element of experience.

According to my good friend and statistical genius **Dr. Kalim Khan**, the Director of Rizvi Institute of Management Studies and Research, Mumbai, and a PhD in Statistics: **'Every aspect of corporate functioning across hierarchies and domains involves dealing with numbers and making decisions based on them. It is thus imperative that number literacy and ability to fathom data, making sense out of them and using them as a guiding light for decision-making, be a strong weapon in the armoury of any executive who intends to scale corporate glory.'**

As seen, statistics in some form or the other can be used to make superior decisions in all functions across the corporate spectrum, including in the domain of Human Resources. Decisions regarding aspects such as manpower planning, staff selection, promotions, and even location postings of employees can be made more effective by the intelligent and thoughtful application of different statistical techniques, coupled with various behavioural models. In this context, the following makes interesting reading.

In February 2018, Punjab Technical Education Minister, Mr. Charanjit Singh Channi, invited 37 lecturers for offering them posting orders to the location of their choice after having an open discussion with them. The 37 lecturers had been recently appointed and were to be posted in various institutes across the state of Punjab. While 35 of the lecturers reached consensus over the location of their choice, two of the candidates both insisted on getting a posting at the same location in Patiala, which resulted in a deadlock. To resolve the deadlock, the minister decided to toss a coin, which he said he chose to use as the decision-making method, after both the candidates had agreed to it. This arbitrary method of taking an official decision at such a high level was widely criticised in political and professional circles, as it was felt that a more structured method, taking some sort of numerical and behavioural parameters into account would have been appropriate and suited to the occasion.

POINTS TO PONDER AND PRACTICE

- You may not be a mathematical and statistical genius. But you do not need to be one in order to understand basic numbers and analytics which would assist you in your decision-making as a leader

- **Resources (both material and human) in any organisation are scarce, and if you need to put them to best use and re-direct and allocate them to areas where they would be most beneficial and productive, you need to incorporate an element of numericals into your decision-making**

- Take the help of qualified individuals on your team to understand and apply numbers to maximum effect. There should be at least one or two people on your core team who thoroughly understand and love numbers; not just superficially, but in-depth. **Take the inputs of these people to help simplify the information and reports you receive, so they can be presented in a way that even non-mathematically inclined persons within your organisation can appreciate and understand and put to productive use**

- A word of caution – do not become over-dependant on numbers alone, but also incorporate a judicious blend of the human element and personal judgment into your decision-making. **A healthy combination of the numerical as well as the intuitive (based on experience) would result in vastly superior decision-making**

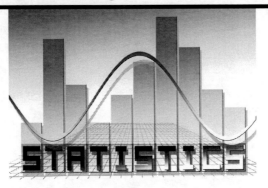

AN INSISTENCE ON ACCURACY BY THE LEADER MAKES ALL EMPLOYEES RAISE THEIR STANDARDS

" *Fast is fine, but accuracy is everything* "

-XENOPHON
(Greek philosopher, soldier, historian)

WHAT **J.R.D.** BELIEVED IN AND **PRACTICED**

" *The pursuit of perfection, then, is the pursuit of sweetness and light* "

-MATTHEW ARNOLD

J.R.D. implicitly believed in accuracy in all endeavours, large or small, as being essential for building a strong brand and a culture of excellence, and to ensure efficient, error-free functioning.

Captain Visvanath, an early employee of Tata Airlines, recalls that after J.R.D. became Chairman of Tata Sons in 1938, he would still fly aircraft for 15 days a month as a pilot, and another pilot would accompany him in the air as an assistant responsible for preparations with maps, navigation, and so on. Every pilot tried to find some excuse for not

91

accompanying J.R.D. on a flight, as nobody seemed to be able to satisfy J.R.D.'s need for efficiency and accuracy in flying operations. Some pilots even pretended they were sick in order to opt out from flying with him.

Captain Visvanath however says that he has learnt more from flying with J.R.D. than from anyone else. He recalls how once while on a flight, J.R.D. asked him (Captain Visvanath), to calculate the ground speed, which is different from the air speed. In those days, instruments which automatically provide these readings were not fitted onto the dashboard of a plane. **Captain Visvanath says he made some quick manual calculations and informed J.R.D. that the ground speed at that moment was 145 miles per hour. J.R.D. then took out his slide rule (an instrument used for making calculations), worked out the ground speed for himself, and politely told Captain Visvanath that IT WAS NOT 145, BUT RATHER 145.5 MILES PER HOUR. Captain Visvanath says that from that day on, he personally practiced and insisted on the same levels and standards of accuracy from the pilots whom he trained and worked with.**

Nathaniel Hawthorne, the famed American novelist once said:

"Accuracy is the twin brother of honesty; inaccuracy the twin brother of dishonesty."

J.R.D. Tata would have heartily agreed.

And on a lighter note, there are also occasions on which an insistence on accuracy is really not that important.

A little old lady was attending a lecture being delivered by a scientist. The scientist declared, "It is estimated that the earth will come to an end in 4 - 5 billion years." At this, the little old lady looked shocked and timidly raised her hand, asking, "Please, what exactly did you say?" When the scientist repeated his statement, the little old lady heaved a sigh of relief and said, "Thank God. I thought you had said **MILLION**, not **BILLION**."

LEARNINGS
FOR LEADERS

> *Accuracy of observation is the equivalent of accuracy of thinking*
>
> -WALLACE STEVENS

It is rightly said that **the fish rots from the head**.

Whenever standards of accuracy and efficiency of any parameter of functioning of an organisation see a marked drop or decline, the failure can be always directly attributed to top management lethargy and lack of interest and involvement to that parameter.

For example, in the aviation industry, the parameter of flight safety (a relatively difficult task to accomplish), is always observed as being achieved at a far superior level than the parameter of accuracy in baggage-handling of passengers' luggage (a relatively easier task to accomplish). From this observation, it is crystal clear that if airline managements focused on the process of baggage-handling with the same stringent attention and criteria that they applied to flight safety, far fewer passenger bags would be lost, tampered with, damaged, or misplaced.

There is a very interesting observation which mentions that with only a 0.01 percentage level of inaccuracy in operations, what a huge number of entries in a dictionary would be incorrect, how many planes would crash each day, what volume of the water we drink would be dangerously polluted, and so on. It really makes a person think, and think hard, on the importance of accuracy in all endeavours, not merely in life-threatening ones.

It is the duty of a leader to personally set high standards in accuracy of thinking and of functioning, and inculcate and insist on the same from all concerned through the length and breadth of the organisation.

Leaders need to **VISUALISE** the impact that lack of accuracy in any aspect of functioning in their organisation can have on outcomes. Only then will they adopt high standards of accuracy themselves and insist upon the same from those they lead. **Thus, the insistence on accuracy begins with the visualisation of what may happen if inaccuracy is tolerated.**

Only when the employees see their CEO or their department head or supervisor personally practicing high standards of accuracy, do they realise its importance and practice the same themselves.

Some 'leaders' in the corporate world today scorn the focus on extreme accuracy, laughing and mocking at those who do insist upon it. These 'leaders' would do well to remember what the great Irishman, George Bernard Shaw had said, many years ago: **"The power of accurate observation is commonly called cynicism by those who have not got it."**

AN INTERESTING ANECDOTE – The front page headlines of the *mid-day* newspaper (4th May, 2016, Mumbai edition), made interesting reading. '**BURGLARS BURROWING INTO JEWELLERY SHOP DONE IN BY WEAK MATH**' was the story.

It elaborated how two construction workers employed at a site in Mumbai found an opening of a drainage line at their site, and realised that if they entered the line and walked a kilometer, they would be very near to where four jewellery shops were located and they could then dig their way inside the shops. They convinced their supervisor to let them work a night shift (giving the excuse of the summer heat). Then they spent twenty-three back-breaking days digging through the sewer, only to find they had miscalculated the length of the tunnel they needed to dig. Instead of emerging **inside** the shop they planned to burgle first, they dug just one foot short and emerged **outside** the shop. A local resident spotted them huddled on the road near the pit they had emerged from, informed the concerned authorities, and their dreams of a golden future evaporated.

ALL BECAUSE OF A SLIGHT MISCALCULATION.

CAPTAIN EDDIE RICKENBACKER was an American ace fighter pilot in the First World War. He was also, at other times in his life, a racing-car driver, an automotive designer, and held many senior designations in the corporate sector as well as in the government. But probably his most notable contribution to aviation was his long-term leadership of Eastern Air Lines.

As chairperson of Eastern Air Lines in the 1940s, Eddie was faced with a customer-related dilemma which was getting out of hand. Passenger complaints were increasing exponentially by the day as the airline was mishandling baggage far too often. When things got absolutely out of hand, Eddie decided to take action.

He called for a special meeting of his management team in Miami, Florida. Members of the management team flew in to Miami, and were told that their baggage would be delivered to the hotel where rooms had been reserved. **But Eddie ensured that their luggage never left the airport, where he got it safely stored away.**

CAPT. EDDIE RICKENBACKER

The management team reached the hotel; waited and waited for their luggage, which did not arrive. Next morning, the managers showed up for their scheduled meeting unshaven, teeth not brushed, and wearing the same travel-stained, unironed clothes they had worn the previous day. Throughout that day, there was no sign of their luggage, but at three the next night, when the exhausted managers were in bed, Eddie had their luggage delivered to their respective hotel rooms, accompanied by thunderous pounding on the doors.

The next morning, he commenced the session with the managers by saying, **"Now you know how our customers feel when we mishandle their bags. Don't you think we should be working towards achieving greater accuracy in this important function?"**

Complaints in baggage handling reduced drastically in a short while after the conference ended. Eddie had got the message across.

BEAUTY AND ACCURACY *CAN* GO HAND-IN-HAND

An amazing clock is housed in the Strasbourg Cathedral in France. The complex masterpiece functions on an intricate network of hundreds of hidden gears. The numerous dials and beautifully-crafted figurines on the visible surface of the clock literally comprise a mechanical circus, with 'performances' taking place every fifteen minutes, as regularly as clockwork.

Near the top of the clock are depicted the four ages of man; represented by figures of an infant, an adolescent, a warrior, and an elderly man. Every fifteen minutes, each of these four figures takes a couple of steps forward, rings a bell, and then disappears. Then the figures of the 12 apostles appear through a small doorway. A mechanical rooster greets the arrival of the apostles by raising its head, bristling its plumage, opening its beak, and crowing three times. Then two figures of angels swing hammers against bells, resulting in a glorious swirl of figures and pleasing sound. Below the angels, another seven figures, representing the seven days of the week as well as the seven planets closest to the sun – revolve in a ring, with one figure visible each day. The other attractions present in this wonderful clock are a figure of Christ, a revolving celestial globe, an angel with a functional hourglass, and many other sculptures, including the figure of the maker of this clock – Jean-Baptiste Schwilgue.

Another unique aspect of this clock is that the clock faces illustrate multiple distinct methods of keeping time – standard time in hours and minutes, apparent time indicated by the sunrise and the sunset, phases of the moon, the coming of eclipses, as well as sidereal time which is governed by the stars through the movement of the zodiac.

Altogether, the various fascinating figures and movements which comprise this clock make it not only one of the most intricate, complex, attractive as well as entertaining clocks in the world, but also one of the most accurate.

The message? – Even without the help of modern technology, it IS possible for BEAUTY to go hand-in-hand with ACCURACY.

Once Mahadevbhai Desai, Mahatma Gandhi's trusted personal secretary, was seated opposite Gandhiji, when Gandhiji asked him what the time was.

Mahadevbhai glanced at his watch and casually responded that it was 5 o'clock.

Gandhiji noticed Mahadevbhai's watch while Mahadevbhai had been glancing at it, and noticed that the time showed one minute before 5 o'clock.

And then Gandhiji explained to Mahadevbhai the importance of accuracy, and ended by asking Mahadevbhai, **"Would it have cost you more energy to say it is one minute to five, rather than say it is 5 o'clock?"**

Mahadev Desai and Mahatma Gandhi

If you want excellence, you must aim for perfection. It has its drawbacks, but being finicky is essential

-J.R.D. TATA

POINTS TO PONDER AND PRACTICE

- Of course, a philosophy of perfection does not develop overnight, but until you consciously and deliberately commence the journey, neither you nor your organisation can move on to the 'highway of perfection'

- The first step on this path is an awareness of the importance of accuracy in all aspects of functioning. If something has to be done, it needs to be done well

- Accuracy in observing, recording, and reporting leads to improvement in standards of quality and efficiency, and the level of accuracy achieved depends upon the importance you give it. There are times when it may be outside your sphere of control to be absolutely accurate, but in most cases, as J.R.D. demonstrated to Captain Visvanath, it is merely a function of attitude. **Be a role model for accuracy to the members of your organisation by visibly practicing it yourself on every possible occasion.** Your organisation and all those associated will benefit as a result

- Only if you practice ensuring accuracy at all times and on all occasions, even when you feel it **'really does not matter,'** will an insistence on accuracy become a habit which will serve you and your organisation well when it **'really DOES matter'**

A TRUE LEADER IS ALWAYS WELL ORGANISED

> *A place for everything, and everything in its place*
>
> -MRS. BEETON
> *(The book of household management)*

WHAT **J.R.D.** BELIEVED IN AND **PRACTICED**

> *Information is a source of learning. But unless it is organised, processed, and available to the right people in a format for decision-making, it is a burden, not a benefit*
>
> -WILLIAM POLLARD

J.R.D. had always been mechanically inclined, and he enjoyed creating objects out of metal and wood. In his modest home, he had a tiny workshop, with rows of shelves along the walls, meticulously stacked with various instruments – screwdrivers, spanners, hammers, and the like.

Once, it is narrated, J.R.D. was confined to a wheelchair with a hairline fracture, and a friend who was present with him in his workshop asked J.R.D. if he needed any assistance. J.R.D. did require a specific spanner from one of the shelves for some work he was engaged in, and from his wheelchair he directed his friend, guiding him exactly to the shelf and right to the spot where the spanner was: **"Second shelf, third item from the right,"** said J.R.D. to his friend, without even glancing at the shelf. And that is exactly where his amazed friend found it. **J.R.D. had organised his workshop so meticulously, that seated on his wheelchair, out of sight of the tools on the shelves, he could clearly, in his mind's eye, VISUALISE exactly where each instrument was located and what the layout of every shelf looked like.**

 **Mr. Robert Henry George Mendonsa** (the father of my good friend Mr. Vivek Mendonsa), was the Chairman and Managing Director of Lawrence & Mayo, when the following incident took place.

Mr. Mendonsa was aboard a domestic flight from Mumbai, when he casually happened to turn around and noticed that the person seated diagonally in the row behind him was none other than Mr. J.R.D. Tata. What Mr. Mendonsa then saw and observed not only gave him a valuable lesson for a lifetime, but he also ensured that he passed on the same learning to his son Vivek.

He noticed that Mr. J.R.D. Tata had unfolded the small 'table' (meant to hold the meal tray) in front of him, and on it, had neatly laid out a stationery kit and a whole lot of papers in single file, which he then proceeded to diligently work on until the flight landed. Most other passengers in the flight either dozed, or chatted with those seated beside them, but J.R.D. did not squander his precious time. Rather, he meticulously and systematically got through a whole lot of paperwork which he neatly put away along with his stationery kit just before the flight landed.

Mr. Mendonsa was so impressed and inspired by this, that from his next flight on, he too carried a complete stationery kit with him as well as papers to work on, and thus being well organised, spent his time on flights in a productive manner.

LEARNINGS ▮▮▮▮
FOR LEADERS

" *Organisation isn't about perfection; it's about efficiency, reducing stress and clutter, saving time and money and improving your overall quality of life* "

-CHRISTINA SCALISE

The five functions of effective management have been identified by experts as: planning, staffing, directing, **organising**, and controlling.

Organising is an extremely vital function, becoming even more important the larger the organisation grows and the more it expands. Paperwork, schedules, meetings, timetables, deadlines – all these and many more similar things occupy a substantial portion of the professional energies and time of the leader.

A leader, apart from being dynamic, needs to be productive, to achieve the maximum that he can within the limited time he has at his disposal. This can only be possible if the leader keeps himself well organised, and is not scattered and haphazard in his approach towards his work. There are leaders who are dynamic and able to handle all their other responsibilities well, are good decision makers, good people managers, but fail when it comes to being well organised. This results in wastage of time and duplication of effort, something which a busy leader can ill-afford.

Also, many business opportunities are squandered and lost as the leader may not be sufficiently equipped with necessary paperwork, documents, facts and figures at his finger-tips, to take immediate advantage of these opportunities as and when they arise.

To be well organised requires a special type of **VISION...**

To 'see' in the mind's-eye, how things should be structured and laid-out for efficient retrieval and enhanced productivity.

The Japanese technique of '**5 S**' is a marvellously simple and effective technique, which if adopted and practiced as a philosophy, ensures that things are neatly arranged and organised. It ensures that what is most regularly needed is most conveniently accessible, and the least amount of time and effort is needed to be efficient and productive. **The key lies in investing time and thinking in the act of organising.** The philosophy of '5 S' can be truly summed up as – '**A place for everything, and everything in its place**.'

Leaders need to ensure that not only are they and their immediate team well-organised for maximum impact, but this philosophy is shared with and percolates right down to the bottom-rung of the organisation.

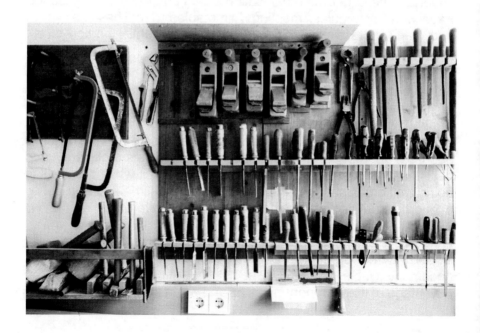

POINTS TO PONDER AND PRACTICE

- It is not difficult to be well organised. What it requires is discipline. Self discipline. In fact, the Japanese technique of '5 S' mentioned previously, is based on five words in the Japanese language, each word beginning with the letter 'S'. The English equivalents to these five words are: **Sort, Set in Order, Shine, Standardise, Sustain.** This technique is not only restricted to nor only applicable to manufacturing activity. It is also applicable to the organising of icons on your computer screen and the logical creation of folders, files, word-documents and Excel sheets on your computer. A little foresight and thought before creating these entities can result in huge savings of time later on. This learning also applies to the proper filing and organising of paperwork. Recently, a very large Indian bank was plagued with an increasing number of complaints from its customers that paperwork was getting misplaced, requests for things like change of address were not being carried out as bank employees stated the requests could not be found, and so on. This bank trained its staff on '5 S,' and then had a '5 S' audit conducted by the consultants for identifying improvement in terms of organised paperwork post-training. Within a few weeks of conducting this training, customer complaints had drastically reduced

- Practice being organised – keep your paperwork and other necessary tools and equipment in order. Maintain a diary for your daily schedule, note down whatever needs to be remembered as you could otherwise tend to forget. If you had previously been a victim of disorganisation, you need no longer suffer the ill-effects of the same. Encourage those in your department and in your organisation to practice an organised way of working as well. Increased efficiency and enhanced internal and external customer satisfaction will be the happy result

- As someone once said: **"My biggest motivator for being organised: I have more time to have fun, to pursue my hobbies, spend with my family, and take on new, interesting and profitable projects"**

IDENTIFY
BUSINESS POTENTIAL
AND INDIVIDUAL TALENT

" *Identify Potential And Talent* "

-J.R.D. TATA

WHAT **J.R.D.**
BELIEVED IN
AND **PRACTICED**

" *The potential of the average person is like a huge ocean unsailed, a new continent unexplored, a world of possibilities waiting to be released and channelled towards some great good* "

-BRIAN TRACY

Not all people are aware that the **Taj Mahal group of hotels** (India's finest and most renowned hotel chain) is also a Tata concern, operating under the name of Indian Hotels Company. (I personally learned whatever little I know about service quality standards there, as the first job of my career was with the Taj Mahal Hotel, Mumbai.)

Although the Taj Mahal Hotel, Mumbai, is today over a century old, having been constructed by Jamsetji Tata in the true Tata spirit of patriotism of building a world-class hotel for Indians to reside in during the British era, **the planned and systematic expansion of this one flagship hotel into an entire world-class hotel chain was the result of J.R.D.'s visionary foresight into the potential for tourism in India.**

J.R.D., in his capacity as an expert in commercial aviation, identified early on that quality accommodation facilities for tourists would be needed once the age of mass travel and tourism truly got underway.

With this in mind, he planned for the expansion of the Taj chain of hotels, which grew in number from just one hotel in Mumbai, to over forty world-class hotels in prime locations in India and overseas within a span of twenty-five years. The Taj chain of hotels is instantly recognised by many as the apex brand of hotels that India has developed; their warmth and service quality being legendary and second to none.

This planned expansion of one hotel into over forty properties; all of them being situated at prime tourist destinations; all offering world-class standards of ambience and service, **demonstrates the ability of J.R.D. to identify potential in a business area well before others who possessed an equal amount of resources, but who, lacking foresight, failed to secure first-mover advantage for their organisations.**

At the same time, it is vital that a leader not get carried away by hype that is taking place all around him. J.R.D. displayed this attribute of leadership as well. In the 1970s, when most other leading international airlines were purchasing the newly developed *Concorde* aircraft, J.R.D. with a calm, collected, and cool mind realised that these supersonic aircraft, although indeed glamorous and eye-catching, were more suitable for flying over the ocean and were not meant to fly long distances over land, because of the sonic boom they caused when they broke the sound barrier. **In this he was proved to be correct, and displayed the vital visionary leadership ability to RESIST adopting an attractive new technology merely because others were doing so. The Concorde has now been discontinued from service by every airline in the world.**

CONCORDE

J.R.D. not only had the vision to identify potential (or lack of it), in BUSINESS SITUATIONS, he was also quick to identify talent in PEOPLE.

He spotted latent potential in young **Sumant Moolgaonkar**, a shy but brilliant individual, who at J.R.D.'s insistence, joined TELCO as Director-in-charge. Once he had placed Sumant in a position of responsibility, J.R.D. never interfered with his style or method of functioning, but let him deliver results in his own quietly efficient manner. It was one of the best decisions that J.R.D. ever made.

Dr. Homi Bhabha

Even in the case of **Dr. Homi Bhabha**, the father of India's nuclear programme, it was J.R.D. who first envisioned the talent in the young doctor. Dr. Bhabha was a brilliant scientist from Cambridge, England, who had come down to India in 1939 for a visit to his homeland, and got stranded in India, unable to return to England, as World War II broke out during his visit. It was J.R.D. who identified potential in Dr. Bhabha, and it is J.R.D. who had the Tatas establish a Chair in the field of cosmic ray research for Dr. Bhabha at the Indian Institute of Science. This visionary decision taken by J.R.D. ensured that Dr. Bhabha's talent would one day lead India to secure her rightful place among the nuclear powers of the world.

Such was the eagle eye that J.R.D. developed for envisioning and identifying potential in business opportunities, as well as talent in people at an early stage, before others could identify and take advantage of the same.

This quality in a leader is essential, as it leads to the vital first-mover advantage, so coveted in the rapidly evolving corporate world of today.

In this respect J.R.D. was similar to the famed master craftsman **Michelangelo**. A lovely story about this great sculptor is relevant here.

Once, Michelangelo picked up an oddly shaped chunk of marble which other sculptors had rejected as being unworthy of chiselling into a statue of any kind. Michelangelo took up this piece of marble which had been discarded by his fellow sculptors, and chiselled a marvellous statue of David from it. Seeing this statue, people wondered and asked Michelangelo how he had been able to craft such a lovely statue from a piece of stone which his fellows in the same profession had felt was not suitably shaped to work with.

Michelangelo replied – **"I saw David in that stone, when it was just a stone."**

STATUE OF DAVID
-sculpted by Michelangelo

LEARNINGS ███████

FOR LEADERS

> " *No institute of science and technology can guarantee discoveries or inventions, and we cannot plan or command a work of genius at all. But do we give sufficient thought to the nurture of the young investigator, to providing the right atmosphere and conditions of work and full opportunity for development? It is these things that foster invention and discovery* "
>
> -J.R.D. TATA

Identification of genuine potential in new business areas is by no means an easy task.

Many entrepreneurs have got carried away with surrounding hype and expanded into areas which are the 'flavour-of-the-month,' without fully understanding whether sufficient potential indeed exists to justify the investment of their organisations' money, time and energy.

One classic example is the hollow dot.com boom in India in the 1990s, which turned into the **dot.com bust**. Many otherwise sensible businesspersons, without application of mind or understanding, got carried away by the opinions of 'experts' and by frenzied media publicity.

But if you **do** feel that the business area in which or the person in whom you have identified talent is worth investing time, money, and effort, do so wholeheartedly. But do so because **you** believe it, **not merely because others feel or say so**. The following story about having faith in the talent you have positively identified is instructive:

Enrico Caruso

Many years ago, a young boy of about ten, coming from a poor family, used to work in a factory in Naples, Italy. This was much before the present laws prohibiting child labour were put in place. His mother was instinctively convinced that this young boy would make a fine singer as he had a good voice for a ten-year-old, and that by having him work in the factory, he could earn money to pay for music lessons. Unfortunately, the music teacher he went to was blunt and said the boy clearly lacked singing talent, and that it would be a waste of time and money to pursue this idea any further.

The mother of the boy, a poor peasant woman, kept faith, and encouraged her son, telling him that she believed he had singing talent, and she even went without shoes and walked barefoot to save money for her son's singing lessons with some other teacher. Her faith in her boy's potential was justified. The boy went on to become **Enrico Caruso – The Great Caruso – acknowledged as the finest opera tenor singer the world has ever had the pleasure of hearing.**

Unfortunately, many managers also make purchase decisions not on the basis of how good and useful the machinery or equipment would be, but rather on the basis of whether other managers in other organisations have decided in a similar manner.

Such managers believe in safety in numbers, rather than focusing on taking the correct decision based on their experience, expertise, judgment and intuition for the benefit of their organisation.

The favourite motto of such managers is – 'You can't go wrong with IBM.' By which they mean, if the manager opts for the best and the most expensive brand-name in the market, then even if something **DOES** go wrong with it, or it does not live up to expectations, the manager has already covered his tracks, as he can say, "It's not my fault if something went wrong. I bought the best."

A similar scenario unfolds in the recruitment function. Recruitment managers often only visit 'top-ranked' institutes to recruit talent. (These 'rankings' have no official standing, and in most cases have either just carried on across the years through inertia, or, worse, are often obtained through dubious means by the academic institution placing costly advertisements in magazines which provide these 'rankings'.) Again, if the new recruit from this 'top-ranked' institute turns out unsuitable, or leaves the organisation within a month of joining, or just plain and simply 'messes-up,' the recruitment manager can safely say – "It's not my fault. I went and recruited from the best college."

(A wonderful book which explains how talent can be found in the most unlikely of places is *The Rare Find* by George Anders. It explains in beautiful detail how the best talent is often not found where most tend to look for it, but is hidden where recruiters least expect.)

Managers with such a play-safe attitude can never aspire to succeed as leaders, until their mindset undergoes that vital paradigm shift of becoming true leaders and not remaining mere followers.

This is where the concept of '**Out-of-the-Box**' thinking comes into play.

If J.R.D. had thought the same way as a 'safety-first' manager would have done, he would have opted to purchase the Concorde for Air India, as all other leading airlines were adding it to their fleet.

But J.R.D. did not 'PLAY SAFE.' He 'PLAYED INTELLIGENTLY.'

And by doing so, he saved Air India crores of rupees in the bargain.

Often, what works for someone else may not work for you.

Often what has been praised by someone else may have been praised for the wrong reasons.

Often what has been purchased by someone else may suit their organisation, not yours.

But such bold and visionary thinking requires that you put the interests of your organisation above your personal career safety. And if you have thought well and intelligently and then made your decision, chances are high in your favour that your decision, though unconventional and non-traditional, would be appreciated as being the right one.

The key essential needed to function in this manner is to **THINK**:

- Think
- Think hard
- Think smart
- Think with the organisation's interests in mind
- And only then make your decision

THAT is the reason why you are in the leadership chair.

A word of advice for leaders. If your subordinates take decisions with the interests of the organisation in mind, and for some reason, in case such a decision does go wrong, support your subordinates. Consider the intent of the subordinate, and if he took the decision for the right reasons, assure him that this is the way he needs to work and take decisions in future as well.

For example, if you feel the subordinate was not up to the mark in his data collection or analysis, which is why his decision went haywire, help him improve on analytical skills. But take all efforts to make him feel that as long as he is working with the interests of the organisation at heart, and not relying merely on others or on outside agencies to take his decisions for him, he has a valued place on your team.

The following are some practical tips which can help you identify and select high-potential individuals to occupy leadership positions from among your existing employees. You would do well to focus on individuals who:

- Voluntarily accept accountability and shoulder responsibility
- Proactively go beyond their assigned role for the benefit of the organisation
- Display empathy in their dealings with others
- Remain calm under pressure
- Demonstrate exceptional communication and listening skills

When British prime minister Benjamin Disraeli was shown the first dynamo by its inventor, Michael Faraday, Disraeli looked disinterestedly at what was the first version of all future generators, and asked, **"What good is this?"**

Faraday responded with an incisive and thought-provoking question of his own – **"What good is a baby, Mr. Disraeli?"**

Anyone and everyone can spot talent and potential once they have blossomed and reached their peak. The leadership genius lies in spotting them when they are at the 'baby stage.'

Michael Faraday

Benjamin Disraeli

PEOPLE WHOSE IMMENSE TALENT WAS NOT SPOTTED BY THE 'EXPERTS'

There have been too many instances in recent history of 'experts' who were trained to spot talent in their field, missing out completely on the opportunity, when a highly talented individual or group of people were in front of them. To name just a few of these talented individuals who were not identified at first glance:

- **J.K. ROWLING** of 'Harry Potter' fame, who was initially rejected by 12 publishers before she got her first break. She was also advised, "Do not quit your day job."

- **ELVIS PRESLEY** was fired by the manager at the auditorium after he gave his first performance, and was told, "You ought to go back to driving a truck."

- **OPRAH WINFREY** was fired from her initial job as a television reporter, being told she was "Unfit for TV."

- **The BEATLES** were turned down by a record company executive, and were told, "You have no future in show business."

- **MARILYN MONROE** was told she should become a secretary rather than aspire to become a model.

- **WALT DISNEY** was fired as a cartoonist from a local newspaper, being told he "lacked imagination and had no good ideas."

- **VINCENT VAN GOGH's** paintings were rejected throughout his lifetime, with only one painting sold.

- **STEVEN SPIELBERG** was thrice rejected by the University of South California - School of Theater, Film and Television.

Nathaniel Hawthorne

In later life, **Nathaniel Hawthorne** became a renowned American novelist. But this was not the profession he commenced his working life with, although he had always wanted to become an author. He was initially employed with a customs house, and one day he lost his job. With a sad heart, he gave his wife the news, but she was happy when he told her he had lost his job. She smiled and told him that now he could do what he had always wanted to – write. But the practical Nathaniel asked her what they would live on till he started making money as an author. His wife led him to a drawer, in which she had stored a large sum of money she had saved over the years. She told him, "Over the years, I kept aside some money every week, because I knew I was married to a man of genius and one day you would write an immortal piece of work. There is enough money saved here to comfortably get us by for another year." His mind at peace, the very next day Nathaniel sat down to write a book – *The Scarlet Letter* – which today is regarded as a classic work.

POINTS TO PONDER AND PRACTICE

- A leader, however hard-working, charismatic, and intelligent he or she may be in all respects, cannot operate alone. He needs a core team of individuals which he can depend upon to advise him, to carry out his instructions faithfully and thoughtfully

- Your leadership team need not be large. In fact the smaller and more compact the team is, the better. But since this team will shoulder vast responsibilities, it is vital that they be people of **impeccable integrity**, **substantial talent**, and enjoined by a **common philosophy**. Select the right people for your core team, and share your burden of leadership with them and also the joys. **Take special care that you do not have a single person on your core team whom you do not implicitly trust, and who is not adding considerable value**

POINTS TO PONDER AND PRACTICE

- **Instil in your key people the philosophy that they NEED not, SHOULD not, and MUST not play safe, when it comes to making corporate decisions.** Not playing safe does not mean taking rash and risky decisions which can negatively impact the organisation. But it **does** mean taking decisions which are out-of-the-way, not normally taken by managers in other organisations, but taken because the individual feels it would be a more beneficial decision for the unique requirements and circumstances of the organisation he or she represents

- Also, another area where you as a leader need to have the **vision** to be able to identify potential is business opportunity. In most cases, it requires a thorough understanding of your industry at a local, national and global level, keeping updated with the latest technology and innovations, the recent changes in customer preferences, tastes and trends. In short, it requires hard and smart work, but after all, that is what you as a leader are there to do

- Just as you need to develop the ability to identify potential and act upon it, you also need to develop the ability to **resist** pursuing a business opportunity or hiring the services of an individual, merely because others have said that is the right thing to do. Think for yourself, and as far as possible, make decisions based on primary data which you have obtained through keen observation. Your personal judgment and intuition, developed and sharpened through experience, can be your own best guides, if only you allow them to be so

- In short, as a leader, develop and constantly fine-tune your own personal vision on multiple parameters, as well as the vision of the organisation you have the good fortune to lead

DEVELOP AN EYE FOR DETAIL

> *It is said that one should not miss seeing the forest for the trees. But it is also important that one should not miss seeing the trees for the forest*
>
> -CYRUS M. GONDA

WHAT **J.R.D.** BELIEVED IN AND **PRACTICED**

> *The difference between something GOOD and something GREAT is attention to detail*
>
> -CHARLES R. SWINDOLL

J.R.D. was always keenly observant about aspects of the organisations he led which he felt needed nurturing and improvement. However small, low-down on the hierarchy, or negligible these aspects would possibly have appeared to chairpersons of other organisations, (who often tend to look at the bigger picture alone, leaving minute detail to their subordinates), J.R.D. felt they were his responsibility.

For example, J.R.D. was renowned for the quantum of detailed feedback he provided to his management team at Air India about various aspects of operational functioning. **One day, he received a note from Air India which informed him that he had written a total of a million words as detailed feedback to them.** He was pleasantly surprised to hear this.

His reaction to this feedback towards his focus on such intricate detail was: **"The only thing that can be said is that I as an airline Chairman took much more trouble and I attended to smaller things, more personal things than did those of the bigger airlines who were on the administrative side and couldn't possibly attend to details."** This statement also demonstrates J.R.D.'s nobility of character, as he attempts to find a genuine reason for other CEOs who were unable to match the eye-for-detail J.R.D. himself displayed.

As Alvin Toffler incisively expressed: '**You've got to think about big things while you're doing small things, so that all the small things go in the right direction.**'

A few tips which will help you develop an eye-for-detail in your area of work:

- Avoid multi-tasking and focus on one activity at a time

- Take a short break when you feel your attention to a task draining away

- As far as possible, create an environment free from distractions

- Make a 'to-do' list (short-term as well as long-term) so you do not miss out on even the smallest of tasks you were meant to do

---

A student of Zen was once asked by the Zen Master as to how the work that had been allocated to that student was progressing.

The student smiled and replied that the work was going fine and in fact was almost done. **"There are just a few details to wind up,"** added the student.

The Zen Master looked puzzled as he responded, **"Just a few details left? But everything from beginning to end is detail, isn't it?"**

LEARNINGS
FOR LEADERS

❝ With honest and straightforward business principles, close and careful attention to details, and the ability to take advantage of favourable opportunities and circumstances, there is a scope for success ❞

-JAMSETJI TATA

As an instrument of sight and vision, the **microscope** is just as important as the **telescope**.

Maybe far more important.

While a telescope uplifts us by letting us gaze on the stars, planets, comets and other heavenly bodies, the microscope serves a far more humbler, yet a more practical purpose and function.

It is through the microscope that we learn about molecules and atoms, germs and viruses and microbes, about DNA and genetics, and other things which help in the development of medical science, genetic engineering, the understanding of the entire human structure; and it is knowledge of all these disciplines which has resulted in the development of the X-Ray machine, the CT-Scan equipment, antibiotic medicines, and many more life-saving technologies and vaccines.

A telescope serves to make distant objects appear close, while a microscope enlarges small objects and makes them clearly visible.

While the Telescope can be equated with ORGANISATIONAL VISION, it is the Microscope which allows for an EYE-FOR-DETAIL.

But it is 'Vision,' that lofty, glamorous, and 'upward-looking' (and obviously useful) word, which tends to get far more importance from most leaders, than the term 'Eye-for-Detail,' which sounds more mundane, trivial, and narrow and restrictive in focus.

Unfortunately, many senior leaders feel that focusing on minute detail is not part of their job. They feel they can safely leave such tasks without supervision from their end to those at a junior level.

This single tragic factor, I believe, is responsible for a majority of customer grievances at the operational level across industries.

I have heard many managers and even some CEOs say to their subordinates: "**I don't need the details. Just give me the bottom line.**" Such persons will never be well-informed, simply because they don't **wish** to be. It is also possible that they may have taken on far more responsibility than they can efficiently handle, which is why they lack time or inclination to get into important detail. They need to master the fine art of delegation and develop the discipline to maintain a span-of-control which is within physical limits. (More on J.R.D. and his approach towards span-of-control in a later learning in this book.)

If the leader does not bother to display an active interest in detail, it is difficult to get staff at a lower level to do so. Indeed, why should they bother, if there is no one to check them, or reward them for doing so? As a very true management maxim goes: '**WHAT GETS REWARDED GETS DONE.**'

Remember, customers may not be able to relate to your 'Corporate Vision' (though they do benefit from it), but they can and will see, observe, notice, and be immediately impacted by the attention you as a leader have given to minute detail.

Vision should be focused on by a leader in both directions – from the far to the near (telescopic), as well as from the small to the large (microscopic).

Leaders need to judiciously 'utilise' both these 'instruments' (the telescope as well as the microscope), in their 'vision armoury.'

J.R.D. displayed bifocal vision, by focusing on lofty heights as well as on minute detail. And this is exactly what every leader needs to do to succeed in a holistic manner in a competitive environment.

ALFRED CHARLES WILLIAM HARMSWORTH, (1st Viscount Northcliffe) was a British newspaper and publishing magnate and editor.

As owner of the *Daily Mail* and the *Daily Mirror*, and a pioneer of tabloid journalism, he exercised vast influence over British popular opinion.

At one time in his illustrious career, he was troubled with his eyesight. Many specialists examined him, but found no physical defect which could explain his faulting vision. Ultimately they concluded that he had been overusing his eyes to look at the newspaper fineprint each day in the course of his duty, and had not been lifting his eyes often enough to look at distant objects.

His doctors advised him to take a vacation in the countryside for a while where he could gaze at the distant horizon. Gradually, as he used his eyes to look at distant rural scenery, he began to repair his failing eyesight.

———

Similarly, when it comes to the subject of leadership, a true leader does not look only at the larger picture nor the fine detail alone, but judiciously uses his leadership 'vision' to good effect in both these vital areas.

POINTS TO PONDER AND PRACTICE

- Imbibe a sense of importance towards the aspect of 'Eye-for-Detail' early on in your career. The sooner you incorporate it into your system as a habit, the stronger it entrenches into your personal leadership DNA

- **Identify the areas of detail which matter most to the customers in your industry, and then ensure that you, as well your team, give importance to these details**

- Attention to detail is an aspect which leaders simply cannot ignore. It is a known principle in management that **if a leader can take care of the small things, the big things will by default be taken care of**. If customers are aware and observe that the management has paid attention to fine detail, they will be assured that such management could never have ignored the larger issues. But unfortunately, the reverse does not hold true. Which is why wise leaders pay at least as much attention and give at least as much importance to the 'small' issues as well as to the large

- Use J.R.D.'s examples provided in this learning and elsewhere throughout the book as your guideline. Understand how he gave the greatest priority to probably the smallest, (and what would appear to many other leaders, 'trivial' things), and how it is this very attention to detail that made Air India **the** leading international airline during the era of J.R.D.'s able stewardship

VISIONARY LEADERS NEVER IGNORE THE LESSONS OF HISTORY

" The farther back you are willing to look, the farther forward you are likely to see "

-SIR WINSTON CHURCHILL

WHAT J.R.D. BELIEVED IN AND PRACTICED

" Learn from the past, set vivid, detailed goals for the future, and live in the only moment of time over which you have any control: now "

-DENIS WAITLEY

During World War II (while India was still under British rule), J.R.D. was instrumental in organising a core group of leading Indian industrialists to put their collective heads together and come up with a sound and practical plan to identify how the economic structure of India would evolve and be put in place after the War ended. This plan was later named the Bombay Plan, and it was published in two instalments; in 1943 and 1944. (World War II lasted from 1939 - 1945.)

It was for the first time ever in recorded history that a team of industrialists planned for the economic, industrial and also the societal future of a nation. J.R.D. himself later mentioned that the whole concept started with the patriotic feeling that Indian businessmen must prepare for their role in developing a free India. He said he knew that independence was bound to come soon after the War ended, and that India's economy would have to be handled in the appropriate manner to ensure that the subsequently ensuing economic prosperity would reach not only a chosen few, but also the deserving many.

The plan he initiated commenced by considering factors such as estimating what kind of standard of living the average Indian would expect after independence. The plan was not merely theoretical but highly practical and identified and included specific parameters such as what would be needed in terms of volume and quantum of grain, cloth, housing, educational institutes and so on to meet these expectations, and how these objectives could be achieved in reality.

J.R.D. explained that he felt the urgent need for such a plan as he was sure the British would be economically destroyed after the War, even if they were to win it, and that India would soon achieve independence, and needed to be prepared to move on the long road ahead.

He said **he was sure of this outcome as he had always taken a keen interest in history**; whether contemporary history, or that of ancient Greece and Rome, and also the Napoleonic wars. **As a result of his understanding and solid grasp of the lessons of history**, he analysed and was convinced that the British could never afford to hold on to their empire (including India), after the War, irrespective of its result. **A study of history had taught him so**. And he was proved correct in his analysis as events unfolded.

> *History is for human self-knowledge.....the only clue to what man can do is what man has done. The value of history, thus, is that it teaches us what man has done and thus what man is*
>
> -R. G. COLLINGWOOD

LEARNINGS FOR LEADERS

" A people without the knowledge of their past history, origin and culture is like a tree without roots "

-MARCUS GARVEY

Today, a lot of stress and emphasis in academics is being given to mathematics and the sciences. This holds especially true in India, where engineering and medicine are considered the epitome of higher education (and no doubt they are important disciplines), while other subjects are given almost step-motherly treatment.

In fact, after completing high-school, the three obvious options available to a student in India considering enrolment to junior college are: Science, Commerce and the Arts. While Science and Commerce are considered 'manly' and 'practical' options, Arts is still widely considered as a field of study opted for by those not really interested in further studies, or for those who simply did not score well enough to secure admission in either the Science or the Commerce disciplines. However, the current global reality is quite different.

A recent article in an issue of the *Harvard Business Review* magazine reveals that in evolved and developed western countries, many leading corporate houses now prefer to recruit graduates from the Arts and Humanities courses, rather than from Business Schools or MBA institutes, for their Management Trainee positions.

The reason for this is simple. At the apex level of corporate leadership, the skills considered essential for success need a strong foundation and thorough grounding in areas such as:

- Languages
- Philosophy
- History
- Culture
- Sociology
- Psychology
- Anthropology
- Economics
- Literature

– In short, subjects which form the nucleus of the Arts and Humanities syllabus. Knowledge of the core components of these subjects leads to holistic development and produces a well-rounded, suitably-informed personality. The inputs derived from a study of the above-mentioned subjects are exactly what a CEO needs most in order to lead his organisation forward in a competitive, globalised economy.

History as a discipline is so important that in some form or the other, it literally forms the core and nucleus of most research, as it is a proven fact that trends and cycles are repeated over periods of time. Those leaders who focus on, study, analyse, introspect upon and learn from the lessons of history: whether it be military history, business history, history of fashion, history of tastes of people, history of a particular industry, and also study the key points and milestones in that industry's growth and development, are the leaders who perform far better at ENVISIONING the future trends and needs. They are also often SUPERIOR AT STRUCTURED DECISION-MAKING.

And it is structured decision-making that forms the fulcrum of effective management and sound leadership.

- Modern-day doctors, pharmacists and medical and nursing professionals can learn a great deal by studying the lives and methods and thinking processes of pioneers in their field such as **Louis Pasteur** and **Florence Nightingale**.

- Advertising professionals would learn a lot by reading the works and understanding the philosophies of advertising legends of the likes of **David Ogilvy**.

- Accountants and financial professionals could avoid career-destroying mistakes by studying the case histories of organisations such as **Enron** and **Arthur Andersen**.

Thus, in every field of human endeavour, sufficient historical material of great value is available if only managers and leaders take time out from their busy schedules to peruse and imbibe it. A certain amount of time **MUST** be set aside by aspiring leaders on a weekly basis to read, register, remember, reflect, and ruminate upon past happenings and important milestones along the pathway on which their industry in particular, as well as management practices in general, have evolved.

I have even seen the advertisement of a private Business School, inviting prospective students to enrol for their undergraduate course, in which the advertisement proudly announced that in order to save time and fast-track the education process, the institute has eliminated 'useless subjects and portions of syllabi related to history and geography.' J.R.D. would have pitied the unfortunate students of such a narrow-minded and 'visionless' institute.

In fact, a fantastic book, *The Timeless Leader*, authored by John K. Clemens and Steve Albrecht, examines in brilliant fashion the lessons that the modern leader can learn from real-life as well as fictional leaders throughout history. The book is definitely worth a read.

Truly, those who ignore or forget the lessons of history can never be leaders in the true sense of the word.

POINTS TO PONDER AND PRACTICE

- **However intelligent one may be, there is always something to learn from those who have gone before**. You may not enjoy learning about kings and queens and battles long ago, but the least you can do to enhance your leadership quotient is to study from business history – biographies and auto-biographies of thought-changers in the field of business, books about leading corporate houses and the path they took to growth and the challenges they faced along the way

- Remember what Otto Frank said:

  "To build up a future, you have to know the past"

- Read *Made In Japan* by Akio Morita of Sony or books authored by Lee Iacocca of Chrysler or books written about pioneers such as Henry Ford and Walt Disney. These are just a few of the many great business biographies available. If your organisation has a well-stocked library, well and good. Else initiate one and recommend these books for its shelves and encourage others in your team to read such books as well. Ideas that strike any of your team members after reading something and which are shared with others could be of great benefit to your organisation

- Keep aside a minimum fixed healthy portion of time in your own weekly schedule for researching such historical material. This investment of your time and effort will be well worth it

Wilt Chamberlain

In closing, recall the words of the basketball legend, **Wilt 'The Stilt' Chamberlain,** who remarked:

"I believe in history and I'm a part of history. I believe that only by knowing yesterday are you really able to enjoy your day and be prepared for tomorrow"

BENCHMARK WITH THE BEST

> *I am always ready to learn, although I do not always like being taught*
>
> -SIR WINSTON CHURCHILL

WHAT **J.R.D.** BELIEVED IN AND **PRACTICED**

> *If you know the enemy and know yourself, you need not fear the results of a hundred battles*
>
> - SUN TZU

J.R.D. was always looking to improve processes and systems in his organisations and enhance even further the already high existing levels of product and service which his airline, his hotels, his automobile companies and other units were at any moment-in-time providing to customers.

With this end in mind, he often deliberately travelled on other international airlines, and kept his eyes and ears open on these flights as well. Any positive points he observed either in terms of decor or processes or service levels or food and beverage offerings made by these airlines, he carefully noted down and tried to implement similar or even higher standards on these parameters in Air India. **He was ever alert and on-the-job for his beloved airline, always striving to ensure that he could learn from wherever and whomsoever possible to make Air India the best airline in the world.**

When a leader has such an overwhelming desire to constantly think of ways and means of bettering his organisation and its product and service offerings and value propositions, the organisation and all the concerned stakeholders are fortunate indeed.

WHAT EXACTLY *IS* BENCHMARKING?

Benchmarking is often misunderstood to mean the setting of standards. It is not so. Actually, the process of benchmarking involves the observing of best practices already implemented in other organisations within your industry as well as organisations in industries other than your own, and also best practices and evolutions found in Nature and in the Animal Kingdom; and adapting whichever of these are relevant to fit into your organisation wherever applicable.

Today, the art of movie cartooning and animation is well established, but in the early days of cartoon films, the animators had very little past work in their field to study, learn and improve themselves from. So these early animators observed and benchmarked against Vaudeville stage artists and performers, and then translated the exagerrated hand movements and gestures of these Vaudeville artists to sketch life-like animated cartoons.

NOTE: Vaudevillle was a type of entertainment popular chiefly in the US in the early 20th century, featuring a mixture of speciality acts such as comedy and song and dance.

LEARNINGS
FOR LEADERS

"Leadership and learning are indispensable to each other"

-John F. Kennedy

A true leader is always ready to learn. A leader has no false ego about learning from and appreciating what his competitors (whether large or small) are doing, if it leads to delight for the employees and customers of his organisation.

Even if your organisation/brand is currently the industry leader on multiple parameters, and is acknowledged to be the best on most aspects which are of importance to the target customer base, there is always something worthwhile that you can learn from someone, somewhere.

Benchmarking is a very effective managerial tool for achieving such learning and improvement in a scientific, structured manner.

Benchmarking can be defined as the process of observing and identifying best practices and processes, within and outside your industry, and adapting them to suit your organisation.

While a lot of learning takes place from observing your competitors' processes within your industry, learning can also happen from the most unusual of places, provided you have **an attitude to learn, no false ego about learning from those junior to you, and the imagination to see how these practices could be adapted to the unique circumstances of your organisation, the abilities of your employees, and the tastes and preferences of your customers.**

As an example of learning from literally everywhere, **when the Wright brothers were developing the prototype for the first ever aeroplane, they had no previous aeroplanes available based on which they could observe and develop and perfect their model. So they spent months on hilltops with binoculars, watching birds take-off, glide, and land, noting their observations, and then incorporating them into the design of the first aeroplane ever**. And of course, since what they observed could not be directly copied, (as the structure of birds is inherently similar to but differs in many aspects from what an aeroplane would be), the observations and learnings were adapted and modified to suit the requirements of their initial aeroplane. The following instance will illustrate this better:

The Wright brothers had worked out that successful flying was all about maintaining balance in the air. If a plane tilted to one side due to the force of wind, it usually resulted in a crash because the machine could not recover its balance again. By watching how birds flew and balanced their bodies in the air, the brothers hoped to find a solution to this dilemma.

Through their observation of birds in the air, they identified that birds adjust the tips of their wings while in flight and thus create an upturned angle on one side and a downturned angle on the other. The wings function like a windmill and enable the bird to turn to the desired direction while in the air. And when the bird completes the turn, it reverses the angles of both wing tips to regain its balance, By applying this observation to their prototype aeroplane, Orville and Wilbur Wright solved this problem they had faced and had not known how to overcome.

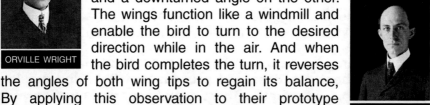

ORVILLE WRIGHT

WILBUR WRIGHT

Another excellent piece of benchmarking which the Wrights can be credited with was with regard to developing the mechanical skills essential to construct their first prototype. Since there was no existing aircraft manufacturing facility where they could master aircraft construction skills, they gained the mechanical skills necessary to construct their first aircraft by working for years in their bicycle shop cum printing press and translated these related skills to aviation design and construction. In fact, in 1901, they fitted a third bicycle wheel horizontally above the front wheel of one of their bicycles and used this apparatus to successfully study airfoil design.

Obviously, it may not be possible to directly copy what you learn from observing your competitors and the processes in other industries, but such learning can and should be done and then modified and adapted to fit your unique requirements. As an example, your distant competitor (or maybe not a competitor at all, in the true sense of the term), may be a two-star hotel, and you may be the CEO of a five-star deluxe property. You could possibly have observed a cost-cutting measure practiced by the two-star hotel which saves that hotel a lot of money, but slightly impacts customer satisfaction. For a two-star hotel, this may not really matter, as customers don't expect too much in the way of posh service and great experiences from a two-star hotel anyway. You too, would like to control costs in your five-star deluxe property, but without negatively impacting your customers' experiences in the slightest. So you could take the crux of the cost-cutting idea you have observed, and modify it to suit your circumstances so that a little cost is saved, but not any element of cost which would reduce customer satisfaction in the slightest. **This is what is meant by adapting the observations to fit your situational context.**

As a corporate example, a leading automobile brand desired to provide its prospective customers the best possible experience while they waited in the showroom for a sales executive to attend to them. They did not merely benchmark by looking at what other premium automobile brands were offering, but observed the business-class waiting rooms at airports and also the layout of five-star hotel lobbies. Thus they came up with the idea of adding a mini golf-course, a bar counter, and other facilities to engage and entertain the prospects while they waited their turn for an attendant to demonstrate the vehicle to them.

As a leader, you cannot afford to and should not be spending your valuable time reinventing the wheel which has already been invented by sombody else. Benchmarking, if intelligently used:

- Helps save time
- Gives you the spark for ideas which you can then modify
- Ensures reduction of unnecessary costs and wastage
- Makes processes more efficient, your organisation more productive
- Enables you to achieve enhanced levels of customer satisfaction

POINTS TO PONDER AND PRACTICE

- The first step is to develop healthy curiosity in all that goes on around you and to actively seek to learn something new each day

- **Next, it is the art of observation which needs to be strengthened. Not just merely seeing, but actually observing.** The difference between these two activities is similar to the difference between passive hearing and active listening

- And of course, benchmarking is not just about observation, but also the application of a scientific process with the use of numbers and statistics to study the extent of differences and improvement possible, which professionals within your organisation or outside can assist you with

- But step one and two in profitable benchmarking will always remain the developing of a healthy curiosity and the power of keen observation. Any leader in any industry can benefit by sharpening these essential qualities

If 'giving it your all' isn't working, stop and follow someone else's lead. It'll give you a completely new perspective

LEANDER PAES

CORPORATE SOCIAL RESPONSIBILITY IS EVERY LEADER'S RESPONSIBILITY

> *Every company has a special continuing responsibility towards the people of the area in which it is located. The company should spare its engineers, doctors, managers, to advise the people of the villages and supervise new developments undertaken by cooperative effort between them and the company*
>
> -J.R.D. TATA

WHAT **J.R.D.** BELIEVED IN AND **PRACTICED**

> *Goodness is the only investment that never fails*
>
> -HENRY DAVID THOREAU

Apart from the many initiatives which J.R.D. undertook to uplift society in umpteen ways, such as the National Centre for Performing Arts (**NCPA**), the Tata Institute of Social Sciences (**TISS**), the Tata Memorial Cancer Hospital and the Tata Institute of Fundamental Research (**TIFR**), the Bhabha Atomic Research Centre (**BARC**), and others of a diverse nature, **J.R.D. was the first Indian industrialist of stature to consider the responsibilities of the corporate towards rural upliftment.**

In 1969, while addressing a meeting in Madras (now Chennai), he said, "Let industry established in the countryside 'adopt' the villages in its neighbourhood; let some of the time of its managers, its engineers, its doctors and skilled specialists be spared to help and advise the people of the villages and to supervise new developments undertaken by co-operative efforts between them and the company. Assistance in family planning in the villages would be a particularly valuable form of service. **None or little of this need be considered as charity** .....The benefits of such a joint venture will no doubt initially flow to the village, but **it is also clearly in the interests of industry that surrounding areas should be healthy, prosperous and peaceful**."

J.R.D. did not make this speech to simply sound noble and look good and win popularity. That was never his style. He put his thoughts into immediate practice. Once back in office after that Madras visit, he initiated action on his speech. **The Articles of Association of leading Tata Companies were amended to include social obligations which now reached above and beyond the welfare of only Tata employees.** These amendments were accepted as part of the renewed objectives of these Tata companies, and thus **J.R.D. initiated the concept of Corporate Social Responsibility as it is understood today into the DNA of the Tata group in a formal manner.**

In Jamshedpur, where Tata Steel was established, as well as at Mithapur, where Tata Chemicals had its plant, J.R.D. ensured that his organisations launched welfare programmes of various types to assist and even 'adopt' many of the neighbouring villages.

JAMSHEDPUR

Even when it came to the establishment of TELCO's second plant near Pune, Maharashtra, on barren and rocky land, the first thought the Tatas had was the planting of thousands of trees in the vicinity. But even if saplings were to be planted, there was no water available to nurture them, so an artificial lake was created for the storage of water.

Now these trees have grown and blossomed, and the attached nursery has supplied umpteen fruit trees to the villages around the factory, making the entire area lush and green from what was just some years ago barren land. J.R.D. said with pride: "We did not **have** to create a lake and plant trees to produce a truck. (Which is what TELCO as a business is primarily established to do.) **But we did. What I am most proud about is not the making of steel or trucks but our social concern.**"

It is clear to see where J.R.D.'s passion for social responsibility came from. It emanated from the **Tata Corporate Vision**. Years ago, Jamshetji Tata had written to his son Dorab about his vision for a township that would ultimately become Jamshedpur: **'Be sure to lay wide streets planted with shady trees, every other (alternate tree) of a quick-growing variety. Be sure that there is plenty of space for lawns and gardens. Reserve large areas for football, hockey and parks. Earmark areas for Hindu temples, Mohammedan mosques and Christian churches.'**

Then there have been times in post-independence history when the government policies provided tax relief to those organisations which would invest in projects for social upliftment. At such times, one witnessed many corporate entities literally jumping onto the Corporate Social Responsibility bandwagon. The moment the government policies were reversed, these organisations stopped their CSR projects.

But for the Tatas, CSR has never been an activity to be pursued for tax relief or to attain other material benefits. The Tatas practice Corporate Social Responsibility year in and year out, irrespective of government and taxation policies, because they implicitly believe in the power of CSR to build a better India for all of us. This has been the **vision** of each of the Tata leaders, including that of J.R.D.

In my personal view, the crucial thrust of CSR lies not merely in the fact that the organisation envisioned and did something worthwhile for someone in need, but rather, that by doing what it did, the organisation took a leading role in demonstrating the road for others to follow. This becomes the responsibility of a leader, and the Tatas, through J.R.D. and their other leaders, have fulfilled this responsibility admirably.

As Neale Donald Walsch put it: 'If the whole world followed you, would you be pleased with where you took it?'

J.R.D. could have rested easy and said an honest and heart-felt "Yes" to that piercing question, for he had truly done his part even early on in life. But he kept on contributing more and more to the society he was part of, and that is one of the hallmarks of a true leader.

J.R.D. was (and even Ratan Tata is) an ardent animal lover, and it is my humble appeal to corporate houses to allocate at least a portion of their CSR budgets to causes which support animal welfare. After all, as the Father of our Nation, **Mahatma Gandhi**, rightly observed: **"The greatness of a nation can be judged by the way its animals are treated."**

LEARNINGS ▍
FOR LEADERS

> *I never had any interest in making money. None of my decisions were influenced by whether it would bring me money or wealth*
>
> -J.R.D. TATA

Corporate Social Responsibility, as J.R.D. envisaged in 1969, is not a form of charity. It does not have to make the receiver feel as though he were receiving a hand-out. It is not meant to be a one-way street. It involves much more than mere money being handed over to those who are in need of it.

Today, legislation in India has made Corporate Social Responsibility mandatory. Organisations are scrambling to understand the implications of this new legislation and are busy consulting their financial and tax advisors as to how they can best 'invest' the mandatory minimum two percent of their profits as required by the legislation to gain maximum corporate advantage and leverage in terms of publicity, tax saving, and so on. **Unfortunately, many business entities view CSR as a purely business proposition.**

It is sad that corporate leaders have to be forced by legislation to contribute even two percent of their profits towards CSR-related activities, when the Tatas have been contributing over fifty percent of their profits towards social causes since the last many decades, and have done so willingly and voluntarily.

It is always better for all concerned when good deeds are done from the heart and not due to compulsion. J.R.D. (and also the other fine gentlemen who led the Tata group before and after him), was a **visionary** who was far ahead of his time. He initiated and put firmly in place a formal system for CSR within the Tata group long before other organisations took an opportunistic interest in it and far before it became a mandatory requirement. CSR was not initiated because the Tatas wanted the associated publicity and goodwill, but because they genuinely believed that if a corporate entity operates in a society and consumes its limited resources, it has a duty and responsibility to give back to that society.

Today, the Tata group reaps the enormous goodwill resulting as a by-product from its focus on investing a huge component (over fifty percent of their profits), into societal causes of all types.

In modern accounting techniques, new ways are being identified to calculate the goodwill component of an organisation's assets, as goodwill today accounts for a substantial portion of assets on the balance sheet of many firms which focus on CSR. In fact, a whole industry has recently developed around how to monetarily evaluate intangible assets, including goodwill.

Customers in the 21st century are an evolved lot, and more and more customers are becoming socially aware and environmentally conscious, preferring wherever possible to purchase the products of firms which are positively contributing to society. These customers are even willing to pay a higher price for the products and services offered by firms practicing CSR.

As just one global example, we can study the organisation 'The Body Shop' founded by **Dame Anita Roddick** in 1976. The organisation is in the business of the production and sale of shampoos, body lotions and the like, which are manufactured in a totally environmental-friendly manner and not tested on animals. The Body Shop also invests tremendously in various CSR activities, and although its products are priced relatively on the higher side, that has not deterred the brand from becoming a global powerhouse in its domain within just forty short years. **(Please glance through the multifarious CSR activities of this brand on the Internet; it is an eye-opener as to how a brand can surpass all stakeholder and societal expectations and yet remain highly profitable.)**

So investing time and money in CSR ultimately becomes a fortunate win-win for all concerned – the society, the organisation itself, the customers (who are also part of the society), and the employees, who feel proud to be associated with an organisation which truly cares for the environment, the people, as well as the eco-system within which it functions and operates.

Steve Hilton and Giles Gibbons write in *Good Business - Your World Needs You* (Texere Publications):

'In the 1980s, Arie de Geus carried out research into the lifespan of various companies in the US, Europe, and Japan, and examined their characteristics. He reported that on average companies stayed in existence for twelve years, that the really major companies that could be described as pillars of their economies lived for around forty years, and that **those which survived longer were the ones that saw their role not merely as profit generators but as members of the community**.

Similarly, James Collins and Jerry Porras, in their book *Built To Last*, present evidence that the world's most successful companies are those that have some kind of **social vision** beyond making money, and **are prepared to stick to their core values even if that sometimes means sacrificing profits in the short-term**.'

William Allen White (1868 - 1944) was a renowned American newspaper editor, author, politician, and philanthropist. Among other things, he once donated a 50-acre plot filled with lush greenery and beautiful trees to his city as a site for a park which all the residents could relax in and enjoy.

While making this gift, he asserted: "**This is the last kick (moment of fun) in a fist-full of dollars I'm getting rid off. I have tried to teach people there are three kicks in every dollar: one when you make it; one when you have it; and the biggest kick of all is when you give it away.**"

WILLIAM ALLEN WHITE

Once, the pioneer of automobiles – **Henry Ford**, asked a young engineer working in his organisation as to what his main ambition in life was.

The young engineer, proud at being singled out for attention by the great Henry Ford, gave what he thought was an impressive reply, "**I'd like to become very wealthy, and I'd like to do it as fast as possible. Nothing else matters,**" was the reply.

Ford did not say a word.

A few days later, Ford again sought out and called for the young engineer, and then removed a pair of spectacles from his pocket. **The spectacles were unique and obviously specially designed – they had silver dollars in the place where the glass lenses should have been.**

Ford handed the pair of glasses over to the bewildered young engineer and asked him to put them on. The engineer did so.

Then Ford asked the engineer what he could see.

The engineer replied: "**Nothing. The money blocks out the view.**"

"Precisely," smiled Ford. "**Now don't you think you should reconsider that ambition of yours which you stated so strongly a few days ago?**"

Many businesses with great potential have collapsed by the way-side, simply because the chief decision-makers in these companies have been men who were concerned more with immediate and short-term profits rather than long-term brand repute and sustainability.

But the Tatas, and also the Ford motor company under the leadership of Henry Ford, demonstrate through their actions that there is **LIFE BEYOND THE BALANCE SHEET**.

POINTS TO PONDER AND PRACTICE

- As a leader, your vision needs to be a broad one. Your focus cannot be so narrow as to keep your eyes and attention on organisational profitability alone

- Of course, profits are the life-blood of any 'for-profit' business entity, but focusing solely on profit is actually self-defeating in the long run. **By making profits the sole focus of a business, quality will be compromised, customers will be treated and dealt with aggressively, accounts and financial statements may be manipulated in order to achieve unrealistic short-term targets.** Also, the society which is observing the corporate entity's contribution may feel alienated from the organisation if it sees the organisation distancing itself from societal concerns and focusing on profits alone to the exclusion of all else

- Be a holistic leader. It does not mean that you need to contribute over fifty percent of your profits to societal causes as the Tatas do. This may not be feasible for every organisation. If not your money, you can at least give of your people's time, knowledge, and expertise to societal and environmental causes which could benefit from them. This too, will be highly appreciated

- **In many organisations in western countries, employees are actually given a half-day off from work each week by their organisation if the employees offer to spend that half-day in voluntarily working for the charitable organisation of their choice, such as an animal welfare organisation, an orphanage, or an old-age home**

- Incorporate or suggest such visionary policies and practices in your organisation. They do not really cost you anything, and they generate enormous goodwill from all concerned. The half-day (or a few hours) off which you give your employees for a cause close to their hearts will be more than recovered by the extra effort they put in at work the rest of the week, as they proudly realise that they are associated with a leader who is truly an evolved soul

REALISE THE VALUE OF THE SLOW BUT STEADY PATH

Samay se pehle aur bhagya se adhik kisee ko kuch nahi milne wala hai

-GEETA SAAR, SHIRMADBHAGWAT GEETA

(Translation of the above quote: *None will get anything before the time is ripe and right, nor will they get more than is their destiny in this life)*

WHAT J.R.D. BELIEVED IN AND PRACTICED

Everything on Planet Earth is controlled by the Laws of Nature. Nothing can supersede them. Wise leaders realise this, and do not attempt to DEFY, but sensibly operate WITHIN the boundaries of Mother Nature's eternal and omnipresent law

-CYRUS M. GONDA

145

J.R.D. himself spearheaded the Tata Group for over fifty long years. A remarkable achievement by any standards. This was partially possible because J.R.D., right from the beginning, realised the importance of achieving and maintaining growth in the only historically proven manner possible – **By following the slow and steady path.**

In 1977, J.R.D. wrote: 'Air-India is indeed doing well. In fact, remarkably so as compared to many other airlines in the world. Apart from using the best available equipment and giving what is now recognised as first-class ground and in-flight service, **our progress is largely due, I think, to our consistent policy of slow but steady growth.'**

Even the shares and the stocks of the various Tata companies have never seen rapid escalations, and thus have never seen rapid declines either. They are Blue Chip shares, the elite among the stocks, and are as safe an investment (maybe more so), than the fixed deposits of public sector banks. This fact, too, is due to the Tata policy and vision of focusing primarily on the long-term. The Tata stocks are most sought-after by genuine investors and not by fly-by-night speculators.

The Tata group is today well over a hundred years old and yet steadily growing. In fact, at the time this book went to print in 2018, the Tata group is by far India's most valued, and most well-loved brand. Many other businesses started later, with more fanfare, 'progressed' much faster, and then inevitably stumbled and collapsed by the wayside.

MR. RATAN TATA

But the Tata group, with fine men of the sterling calibre of J.R.D., succeeded by Ratan Tata, continues to grow slowly yet steadily, moving irresistibly onward like a juggernaut, because the men at the helm of the Tata group have always set their true course by latching their vision to the distant but brilliant North Star.

LEARNINGS ▉▉▉▉▉▉▉▉▉▉
FOR LEADERS

"Of course, in business, the short-term matters, but the short-term is not what a LEADER is primarily there for. Looking after the short-term is a MANAGER'S job. The leader is there to illuminate and light up the path, to show the way, to focus the torch onto the far horizon, all the while inspiring and motivating the individuals in his organisation, demonstrating faith in them, helping them up when they stumble, sharing their joys and sorrows, and giving them hope that after the sun sets on today and tomorrow, there will be a new dawn the day-after"

-CYRUS M. GONDA

A very interesting experiment in human behaviour, termed the **Marshmallow Test**, was conducted many years ago, with young schoolchildren in a western country being the subjects of the experiment. The children were each given a marshmallow (a kind of sweet), by their teacher, who told them not to eat the sweet till she returned from an errand. When the teacher returned after fifteen minutes (the errand was just an excuse to conduct the experiment), she identified and praised those children who had followed her instruction and not eaten the marshmallow, and gave them two extra marshmallows as a reward. Those who had disobeyed the instruction and eaten their marshmallow despite having been instructed not to do so obviously got no reward.

The very interesting finding from this experiment came many years later – the future lives and careers of these young children in this classroom who had undergone the Marshmallow Test were tracked through college and early work-life. **It was observed and found that the children who had delayed their gratification in school by obeying orders and instructions and displaying self-restraint with the marshmallows, later on in life also did much better on their GMAT tests and in college examinations. Still later into adulthood, at work, these same individuals were found to be, in general – better decision makers, more self-confident, more assertive (not aggressive), and were more likely to assume leadership roles.**

147

It is not that these individuals who early on in life displayed admirable self-restraint were **NOT** tempted to eat the marshmallow. They too were tempted, as were their classmates, who succumbed to the temptation. **But early on in life they realised the importance of operating in a disciplined manner and sacrificing immediate benefits so that larger rewards could follow later.**

True leaders have developed the capability to delay their gratification and get larger rewards at a later date. This benefits both the organisation, the people who form part of it, and also the leader himself.

We would know the story of *The Goose That Laid the Golden Eggs*. A man was gifted a magic goose, which would daily lay him a golden egg. One golden egg a day was more than sufficient to keep the man in the lap of luxury. But greed got the better of him. He wondered since if the goose was able to lay a golden egg each day, would it not be much better to cut open the goose and get all the golden eggs at once? He carried out his plan, found the insides of the goose empty of eggs, and never received a golden egg ever again. This is a fable from the master story-teller, Aesop. His fables contain practical morals, for children and adults alike, and are of great use for leaders as well.

THE PURPOSE OF BRAKES

Once a learned professor asked the students of his MBA class - "Can anyone tell me why we have brakes in a car?"

Different students expressed their different views.

"To stop the car when needed," said one.
"To prevent accidents," added another.
"To help slow down and reduce speed," opined a third.

The professor listened to all of these answers, smiled, and shook his head to indicate a "no" to each of them. "The **REAL** purpose of brakes in a car," he explained to his students, "is that the brakes actually help you drive **FASTER.** Think of it this way. Assume for a moment there are no brakes in your car. Won't you then drive very slowly and cautiously? Ironically, it is **BECAUSE** you have powerful brakes in your car which you can apply when needed, that you dare to drive the car at a decent speed, and yet rest secure in the knowledge that you are on the safe path."

POINTS TO PONDER AND PRACTICE

- One of the primary Laws of Nature relates to the quantum and period of return. A tree takes a certain amount of time to bear fruit. If the period is artificially hastened, poor quality of fruit results. The same holds true for baking a cake or baking bread. **With all the technological advancements and the latest cooking and baking equipment, the time taken to bake bread still hovers around twenty minutes. Any attempt to speed up the process by correspondingly increasing the temperature of the oven would not result in edible bread, but a lump of charcoal**

- A good leader realises that anything worth achieving requires **a certain process to be followed,** and a certain minimum gestation period to pass, before which desired results are not possible in the natural way. **This Law of Nature relates to the business sector as well, as it does to every activity upon God's good earth**

As the traditional (and very true) proverb says:

'SLOW AND STEADY WINS THE RACE'

ALWAYS VISUALISE THINGS FROM YOUR CUSTOMERS' PERSPECTIVE -NOT FROM YOUR OWN

> ❝ *The customer's perception is your reality* ❞
>
> -KATE ZABRISKIE

WHAT **J.R.D.** BELIEVED IN AND **PRACTICED**

> ❝ *Whether you operate in the aviation sector, and you call him the PASSENGER; or in the health-care industry, and you refer to him as the PATIENT; or in hospitality, and you welcome him as the GUEST; or in professional services and consultancy and you term him the CLIENT, or whether you call him just a plain, vanilla-flavoured CUSTOMER, he is quite simply – the KING – and EVERYONE in the organisation, INCLUDING THE LEADER AT THE TOP, SHOULD BE AT HIS SERVICE* ❞
>
> -CYRUS M. GONDA

One of the many reasons why J.R.D. was such a successful leader was that he was not at all self-obsessed. **He was truly magnanimous and large-hearted, never considering himself as the centre of the Tata universe.** He always ensured that he looked at things from his customers' and from his employees' (internal customers) perspective. It is largely due to this that any brand which he was associated with, grew, prospered, and flourished.

A memo that J.R.D. wrote to the General Manager of Air India on 30th April, 1951, with regards to his observations on an Air India flight he had flown by on 8/9th April, 1951, shows that the observations he made during the flight and the suggestions for improvement he made thereon through his memo could only have been done by a customer-service genius; an individual who was truly concerned and had a **CLEAR VISION** about offering the maximum convenience to his customers on matters which leaders from most other airlines and organisations would have considered too trivial and negligible to even think about.

For example, in the above-mentioned memo, he made an observation that the beer which was served on-board was a brand of dark, heavy, British beer. He rightly opined that not many people prefer drinking heavy beer while flying, and that a lighter brand of beer should be stocked.

He also noted that on that aircraft, some of the seats tended to recline more than others. As a result, he observed that such seats were more comfortable, and suggested that all seats on the aircraft be adjusted to recline at the maximum angle possible to ensure passenger convenience.

Another observation he made was that the colour of the tea served on the flight was indistinguishable from the colour of the coffee. He suggested that the concerned manager look into the matter.

In a memo written in 1970 by J.R.D. to a senior Air India official, J.R.D. raised a point about on-board breakfast service. He wrote: 'I am told that while the scrambled eggs and omelettes we serve for breakfast in the first-class are excellent, the bacon and tomatoes that go with them are often served stone cold.....I suggest that appropriate action be taken to ensure that bacon and tomatoes are served hot along with the eggs.'

In a memo addressed to a member of the Board of Air India (in 1960), J.R.D. wrote: 'You may not be aware that I have throughout the history of Air India made it my special responsibility to keep in touch with, and have the final say in all matters directly concerned with passenger service.'

If such a memo had originated from another person, someone who merely wished to exercise his authority without actually having gone into depth of matters related to customer service, this might have seemed high-handed. But J.R.D. truly considered his passengers to be the most important stakeholders of Air India, and was justified in his decision to have the final say, as this say was not based on his designation alone, but on pure merit of his having the patience and the ability to observe, understand, and appreciate things from his customers' perspective.

Once, in a personal addressal to the cabin-crew of Air India, he advised them to serve on-board meals with the overhead lights switched on, even during the day-time. He had noted when he travelled by Air India recently that this had not been done. The reason for having the lights on, he said, was that it made the silverware and crockery sparkle and gleam and created a positive impression in the minds of the passengers. He also added that if a particular passenger wanted the lights switched off, that was fine and the passenger's request should be heeded, but he instructed the cabin-crew that the lights must be switched on initially.

Truly, J.R.D. ensured that Air India made use of every opportunity it had to create a rock-solid brand image and identity in the minds of its valuable passangers.

No wonder then, that Bakul Khote, who was selected to initiate the customer service department of Air India, recalls, "J.R.D. was meticulous where the passengers interfaced with the airline, and displayed a real concern for the travelling public."

In the 21st century, where customers have access to social media and are prompt to highlight any lacunae in service, it has become the norm for almost every organisation to claim it is customer oriented. But J.R.D. (and indeed every senior Tata group leader before and after his time), had the foresight and vision to put this into practice when it was 'not in style.'

LEARNINGS ██████
██ FOR LEADERS

> *We see our customers as invited guests to a party, and we are the hosts. It's our job every day to make every important aspect of the customer experience a little bit better*
>
> -JEFF BEZOS, FOUNDER & CEO - AMAZON

The importance of the customer in the life of a corporate leader cannot be over-emphasised. Even for a political party, or in the context of a non-profit set-up, customers in one way or the other are (or, should be) paramount, and indeed are the prime purpose that organisations exist. **For a leader to train and focus his vision on the organisation from the customers' perspective; to view the organisation as an outsider sees it, is imperative, and requires a paradigm shift in current management practices.**

With many other similar organisations competing for the attention of the same set of customers, does it not make sense to understand the unique needs and requirements of your customers and then service those needs in the best way possible? To be constantly upgrading your product and service offerings, maybe marginally if not exponentially, but always moving in the forward and upward direction?

Unfortunately, this is a point where many business leaders of today differ from J.R.D. Oh, yes, they will **talk** about how important the customer is, and even term the customer as a '**King**' or an '**Emperor**' or even '**God**' in their annual reports and in workshops and in seminars.

But the sad fact remains that most leaders in senior positions leave the nitty-gritties and day-to-day 'minor' issues with regard to customer service in the hands of their subordinates. They feel that with a customer-service team in place, it is that team's duty to look after these issues. Which is fine as far as it goes.

But the personal involvement of the leader in these 'minor' issues would send a strong and healthy signal throughout the customer-service team, and indeed throughout the organisation, that customer-service issues are not 'minor,' but sufficiently paramount to be taken seriously by the top man himself.

Carolyn McCall

The truth is, the customer notices things about the organisation and forms strong opinions on the quality of leadership present (or absent) in an organisation. On the episode of the BBC programme *Hard Talk* aired on 16th June, 2014, **Carolyn McCall** was the corporate leader being interviewed. Carolyn had spent decades in the media industry before taking over as CEO of **easyJet**, a popular low-cost airline with a huge customer base, rivalling the customer bases of Lufthansa and Emirates airlines. **The first question put to her was about how difficult had the transition been for her** – after decades of working in media, with no aviation industry experience – to overnight taking over directly as CEO of a large airline. Her response was apt. **She replied that she may not have been previously employed in the aviation industry, but she was a regular airline passenger, and thus had good experience about how airlines functioned from a customer perspective.** And she said she liked what she had seen as a passenger of easyJet, which is what prompted her to take on the role of CEO of easyJet when it was offered to her.

WHOSE PERSPECTIVE DO *YOU* VIEW THINGS FROM?
– AN INTERESTING EXPERIMENT YOU CAN CONDUCT UPON YOURSELF TO FIND OUT

In the fine book *Friend & Foe*, authored by Adam Galinsky and Maurice Schweitzer, the authors conduct an interesting experiment to identify whether a leader is sufficiently large-hearted and broad-minded to view things from the others' perspective, or selfishly views them from his/her own. The following experiment is adapted from their book:

Are people in power really that oblivious to the plight of others, or is that just something the less powerful say to feel better about themselves? We designed an experiment to find out. Here is what we asked our participants to do. Hold up the index finger of your dominant hand (depending on whether you are right-handed or left-handed) and using that finger, draw the outline of a capital "**E**" on your forehead. Do this as quickly as possible, without stopping to think.

What does your E look like? Does it look like a normal E to those facing you, or is it backward? **To draw an E on your forehead normally (so that it can be read the right way by others facing you) requires that you think about what the E looks like from the others' point of view. In contrast, a self-facing E (reverse for those facing you) indicates you think and view things less from others' perspective than you do from your own.**

And the higher up you go in the hierarchy and the more power you wield, it becomes more difficult for the leader to view things from the others' perspective. This means the higher up you go, the more effort you need to take to focus your perspective on the points of view of those around you.

POINTS TO PONDER AND PRACTICE

- The higher you move up the hierarchy, it is bound to happen that more and more areas of responsibility will fall under your purview. Handling finances and budgets, satisfying needs of investors and shareholders, handling government officials and other authorities, complying to statutory requirements, all these and more will keep you up late at night

- And this is as it should be. You have chosen the path of leadership. And it is a good choice. There are many personal and professional benefits which accrue along the way. You will also handle and wield considerable power as a leader. And this power increases in scope and intensity, the higher up you go. But never forget – **with great power comes great responsibility. And the first and primary responsibility you will always have as a leader is towards your customer**

- It is the development of '**vision**' to see beyond your specific job-profile (even though you may be in a senior position, you still have a job profile), and also focus your eyesight at the operational level of your organisation – where the 'rubber hits the road' – which ensures that you have truly understood what visionary leadership is all about

- Remember the **words of J.R.D.**, who was fond of saying: **'COMMON PEOPLE HAVE AN APPETITE FOR FOOD. UNCOMMON PEOPLE HAVE AN APPETITE FOR SERVICE'**

SYSTEMATIC SUCCESSION PLANNING
PAYS DIVIDENDS

" As I lay down office as chairman of the firm, I do so in the conviction that the future of the Tata group, the continuing growth and prosperity, are in safe hands "

-J.R.D. TATA

WHAT J.R.D. BELIEVED IN AND PRACTICED

" The final test of a leader is that he leaves behind him in other men the conviction and the will to carry on "

-WALTER LIPPMANN

It was J.R.D. who evinced an interest in initiating a system which would ensure a steady stream of trained managers and leaders, over time, who would be imbibed into the Tata group philosophy, ready to move wherever required within any Tata group company, prepared and trained to hit the ground running.

J.R.D., even in the early days when the Tata group was a relatively smaller entity than it is today, envisioned that in the not-too-distant future, the Tatas would grow steadily and exponentially, and would

159

require some type of management school of their own from which they could source the senior executives they would then need.

This vision was the genesis of what came to be known as the **Tata Administrative Services** (TAS).

J.R.D. conceptualised TAS as a highly mobile unit of experts, who could and would gravitate from one assignment to another within the Tata group companies, whenever and wherever their individual skill and expertise was needed most. This would ensure that these senior executives, who would be instrumental in devising strategy and policy and implementing the same for the Tata company which they were currently part of, would think holistically on behalf of the Tata group when devising such strategy and policies, and not only from the point of view of the individual Tata company they represented at that point of time. The individuals selected through the TAS programme, once they completed fifteen months of training across Tata companies, could also opt to be placed with the Tata company of their choice and in their area of interest to work with.

TAS was one way in which J.R.D. ensured that all the multiple Tata group companies would bond close together under common leadership, and not adopt differing ideologies and drift away from one another over the years.

It is obvious that by devoting energies to setting up a concrete and practical project such as TAS, J.R.D. Tata implicitly practiced what **Ralph Nader**, the renowned American civic activist, described as the true function of leadership:

'The function of leadership is to produce more leaders, not more followers.'

RALPH NADER

160

LEARNINGS ∎
FOR LEADERS

If you cannot make it greater, at least preserve it. Do not let things slide. Go on doing my work and increasing it, but if you cannot, do not lose what we have already done

-JAMSETJI TATA

(to his son Dorab, while on his death-bed)

The 2015 *State of Succession Planning Report* describes succession planning as, **"Any effort designed to ensure the continued effective performance of an organisation, division, department, or work group by making provisions for the development, replacement and strategic application of key people over time."**

Many otherwise great leaders have suffered from a common failing. While they were at the helm, their organisation appeared invincible. But the moment they moved away or passed on, as all men (and women) do, the glory they brought to their organisation faded away (relatively) with their departure.

Narayana Murthy (to a certain extent), Steve Jobs, and many others are cases in point.

Leaders need to have the vision to realise, as J.R.D. did, that the organisation outlives (or ought to outlive) the individual.

A great leader is a visionary who takes concrete steps to ensure that a steady stream of qualified, trained and experienced individuals, immersed in the corporate philosophy, are readily available to fill an immediate requirement or vacancy, to take control of positions when an incumbent suddenly leaves, and in general to provide the organisation with their capable leadership expertise over periods of time.

161

Another organisation which adopts a similar planned and well-structured approach towards this vital parameter is **FedEx**, which has initiated a programme called **LEAP** – the Leadership Evaluation and Awareness Process.

Of course, all organisations may not be as large and as diverse as the Tata group, and may not need as many individuals in senior positions with the variety of skill-sets as the Tatas do. **But that is no excuse for a leader, whether he or she be the department head, the divisional chief, or even the CEO of an organisation, to not put in place a structured, systematic methodology such as the Tata Administrative Services model, in however small a way, to anticipate and supply the future knowledge needs of the organisation.**

Only a leader who focuses on this as a primary responsibility can be said to truly have his organisation's best interests at heart.

According to the *Talent Space* blog, 'All businesses lose good people. Whether it's for personal or professional reasons, planned or unplanned, losing talented employees can leave a large gap in any organisation. Filling critical vacancies can prove to be challenging, expensive and time consuming. That's why succession planning is vital. It ensures businesses are well-positioned to continue growing and performing, minimising the impact of losing key talent and leaders.'

A Sufi mystic once asked his students to identify what they felt was **the most satisfying thing in life**.

All answered intelligently. One said that it was '**loyal friends**,' another suggested it was a '**happy marriage**,' and yet a third opined that it was a '**clear conscience**.'

The mystic smiled and said that all these were indeed good things, but they had failed to give the right answer. Then he revealed, "**The most satisfying thing in life is to observe a child confidently walk down the road on his own after you have guided him the way to go.**"

POINTS TO PONDER AND PRACTICE

- Of course, TAS is a very large-scale project, requiring considerable resources, and also the support of the very senior organisational leadership. If your organisation is of a substantial size, and you are at the apex level of decision-making, it is certainly worth considering a similar model within your organisation to ensure that a common leadership and decision-making culture binds the organisation together over a period of time

- But even if your organisation is mid-sized, and you yourself are currently designated at a middle-management level, you can informally adopt such a philosophy for the work area which is under your responsibility and purview. **Ensure that you allow and encourage job-rotation for high-achievers, so that they are ready and prepared to take up challenges which may materialise in emergency situations.** Groom and train new entrants into the corporate and organisational philosophy, so that they understand not just **WHAT** is to be done, but also **HOW** it is to be done, and most important of all, **WHY** it is to be done. Such investments of your time will seem worthwhile when situations arise which require people to take over responsibilities in diverse areas within relatively short time spans

- **Remember, that only when you develop others below you to take your place will you be released to take up higher levels of responsibility. So focusing on developing the next line of leadership actually helps you further your own career path**

163

SECTION TWO - VALUES

INTRODUCTION TO THE
VALUES SECTION

> " *Try not to become a man of success. Become a man of value* "
>
> -ALBERT EINSTEIN

The right set of values drive the vision forward and onward in the correct direction, and ultimately convert vision into victory.

Different individuals are driven by different values, and often it is the value systems and beliefs of the top man in the organisation which decide the direction the entire organisation will take. If the leader is driven by values which have stood the test of time, and conveys them consistently through word and through deed, then the people in the organisation, however many there may be (and when J.R.D. led the Tata group, there were well over hundreds of thousands of people employed there), act as a united whole.

The impact of the leader's value systems on the entire organisation are very similar to a story which appeared in a November 1965 edition of *Time* magazine.

The story was about an electrical fuse (weighing less than a couple of kilograms at the most, and the size of a bread-box), which failed, plunging over 80,000 square miles of territory along the U.S.A.–Canada border into darkness.

The entire electrical power for that vast region had passed through that small, single, but critical fuse. Once that fuse failed, no power could be provided to any point across that vast region until the fuse was replaced.

The presence of J.R.D. and the impact of his values and beliefs on the functioning of Air India and the other Tata group companies was akin to that single vital fuse. It were his personal beliefs and value-systems which carried and instilled the right set of values throughout the vast organisational structure of Air India and its employees. Once he stepped down as Chairman of Air India in 1978, the immediate and visible decline of Air India began. This did not happen because employees forgot the values he had instilled. Rather, the new Chairman of Air India, a short-term political appointee, had apparently no interest nor inclination in allowing Air India to remain as a value-driven organisation, treating it more like a political plaything. **Thus clearly proving that it is the set of values that the leader at the helm practices, propagates, and holds dear, which decide the fate of a vast organisation.**

The other Tata Group companies, apart from Air India, of course had the benefit of retaining J.R.D.'s values as he later handed over the baton to another individual of the similar high calibre, namely, Mr. Ratan Tata.

> *Values hold the team together, provide stability for the team to grow upon, measure the team's performance, give direction and guidance and attract like-minded people*
>
> -JOHN C. MAXWELL

Ben and Dale Midgley write in their excellent book *Golden Circle Secrets*: 'In business these days, values are '**popular**.' So they are given a great deal of lip service, relegated to corporate vision statements, customer service slogans, image advertising, and other superficial means. They are used to help make a quick sell, a fast buck, and rarely anything else. Too many corporations act under the pretense of having these values, when in truth they are used as just another means to an end. The result of this selfishness is the erosion of trust in business.'

So true.

When values are not only talked about, but visible in practice, the brand gains immense credibility. In the absence of values, or when values are paid only lip service, trust is lost.

Most businesses and leaders start off with the right values, but somehow tend to lose their way over time.

Often, these leaders and brands don't lose their values overnight. The shift happens slowly and silently, gradually and even unnoticeably, till the leader or the brand realises they have drifted so far they cannot get back to the strong spot at which they had **anchored themselves safely with the strength of their values**.

Remember the wise words of John G. Blumberg, who said, "**We don't go running away from our values. We go drifting away, and one day wake up in a place we never meant to be, drifting in a direction we would never have chosen.**"

First develop the right set of values, then instil them into your people through the power of example, and lastly, never sway from the values which made you great. This will ensure perpetual organisational as well as individual success. **The learnings which follow in this section will show you the value-driven way – J.R.D.'s way.**

> " *Back of every noble life, there are principles that have fashioned it* "
>
> -GEORGE H. LORINER

> " *Open your arms to change, but don't let go of your values* "
>
> -DALAI LAMA

(I believe that what the Dalai Lama has observed above is the single most important reason the Tata group has not only survived, but thrived over the decades.)

PUNCTUALITY IS KEY TO CREATING AND MAINTAINING A POSITIVELY PROFESSIONAL IMAGE

" *Time and tide wait for no man* "

-GEOFFREY CHAUCER

WHAT **J.R.D.** BELIEVED IN AND **PRACTICED**

" *Punctuality is the politeness of kings* "

-LOUIS XVIII

J.R.D. personally accomplished a most remarkable feat of punctuality when he physically re-enacted, in October 1982, at the age of seventy-eight, the fiftieth anniversary of his first operational flight as a Tata Air Lines pilot from Karachi to Mumbai. (More on this path-breaking flight later in this book.) He flew in solo, and was due to land at 4 p.m. at Juhu aerodrome, Mumbai. Waiting to receive and felicitate him, along with a huge crowd of his fans, were the Chief Minister and Governor of the state of Maharashtra.

As the gathered crowd watched and waited, a speck indicating J.R.D.'s plane approaching became visible in the clear blue sky. Excitement on the ground mounted. **The plane approached the gathered crowd, came in low, but did not land, and flew over the covered stage where the dignitaries had gathered. The plane then took a graceful circle in the air, and then landed with perfect control, ON THE DOT of 4 p.m. as scheduled.**

If J.R.D. had landed on his first approach, before he made the circle in the air, he would have landed five minutes early. This is why he made that extra circle. **Even at the age of seventy-eight, flying solo in an old-fashioned plane, on such a momentous and possibly perilous occasion, J.R.D. ensured he was on the dot, NOT A MINUTE EARLY, NOR A MINUTE LATE.**

That – is punctuality.

Another incident demonstrating J.R.D.'s obsession with punctuality and the way it translated into punctual functioning for Air India was narrated by Nari Dastur, who after a long stint with Air India in various countries in Europe, was appointed Regional Director for that continent. He recalls that in the 1950s, Air India flights used to arrive in Geneva at 11 a.m. (as was their scheduled time). Once, at the airport, he overheard one Swiss gentleman asking another as to what the exact time was. His companion looked out of an airport window and said "11 o'clock." The first man asked how he knew the exact time as he hadn't even glanced at his watch. The second replied, **"Air India has just landed."**

Even the epitome of punctuality – the Swiss – saluted the punctuality of Air India in the halcyon days when J.R.D. led this once-grand airline like a piece of precision clock-work.

J.R.D. was a firm believer in the value of time – his own time as well as the time of others. This reflected in the importance which the organisations headed by him gave to punctuality in all their actions. In fact, having spoken with many old-time Tata employees who were around during J.R.D.'s tenure, they all reminisced that when J.R.D. was in Mumbai, his car could always be seen at exactly 9.30 a.m. dropping him off at the Tata headquarters building, Bombay House.

As an example from his early days, the following is instructive.

Tata Air Mail and Tata Aviation Service (the forerunners of Air India), commenced operations in 1932 with the aim of carrying airmail across the country.

After their first year of operations, the Directorate of Civil Aviation (then controlled by the British), had the following to say about the Tatas and their air services in its annual report of 1933-34: '**As an example of how an airmail service should be run, we commend the efficiency of Tata Services who on October 10, 1933, arriving at Karachi as usual on time, completed a year's working with 100% punctuality.....even during the most difficult monsoon months when rainstorms increased the perils of the Western Ghats portion of the route, no mail from Madras or Bombay missed a connection at Karachi, nor was the mail delivered late on a single occasion at Madras.'**

The report also had some advice for their own British-run airlines back home, mentioning – '**...our esteemed trans-Continental Airways, alias Imperial Airways, might send their staff on deputation to Tatas to see how it is done.'**

Imagine, the British-run Directorate of Civil Aviation in British-controlled India, recommending to British airlines operating back home in Great Britain, that they should send their staff on deputation to a fledgling airline run by the Tatas in India to learn lessons about punctuality.

It is not surprising that with his keenness for punctuality and his devotion to keeping to time; J.R.D. was the founder (in the 1980s) of a Tata company – **Titan** – which rapidly grew to become India's leading watch-manufacturing company. A sizeable chunk of Titan's revenue now comes from exports, since Titan watches are being accepted as quality time-pieces the world over.

A final word – the section on **VALUES** commences with this learning on punctuality, as evolved leaders are those who **VALUE** their own time as well as the time of others around them.

LEARNINGS ▮
▮ FOR LEADERS

> ❝ *If I have made an appointment with you, I owe you punctuality. I have no right to throw away your time, if I do my own* ❞
>
> -RICHARD CECIL

A management book titled *Free – Perfect – Now* provides telling insights into what ought to be the priority areas for organisations and their leaders in their dealings with their employees and their customers.

The title of that book itself says it all. What matters the most for customers today are these three parameters which make up its title: **free**, **perfect** and **now.**

The first of these parameters is **low** or **reasonable price (FREE)**. This does not obviously literally mean 'free' but refers to the fact that the customer desires value-for-money, and not an over-priced, needlessly expensive product. This parameter can be achieved by eliminating waste throughout the organisation in all processes, and passing on this benefit to the customer in terms of reduced price without impacting organisational profitability. One organisation which has truly mastered this art and science is **Toyota**. A factory-head of Toyota recently mentioned that in their efforts to bring down wastage of water in their factory, they had managed to bring down the volume of wastage in an entire Toyota plant to **just one single mug of water a day**. But not being satisfied with even this miniscule wastage in such a gigantic plant, they were aiming to improve their processes to bring down the wastage still further. This is the approach that organisations need to adopt when it comes to eliminating waste, thus reducing cost and offering the product or service at a lower price to their customers without compromising on quality. The organisational leadership owes this to their employees and to their customers.

The second parameter is **quality (PERFECT)**. This relates to error-free and defect-free performance, and if possible the customisation of the product or service according to the customer's requirements. After all, quality has been defined by a quality guru, Joseph Juran, as – **'Fitness for use, as defined by the customer.'**

And the third vital parameter of concern to today's time-deprived customer is **punctuality**, **urgency** or **immediacy (NOW)**. In a world where people are increasingly busy, have lesser and lesser free time on their hands, and where their needs and requirements are no longer leisurely but immediate, **'NOW' is no longer a luxury but a necessity.**

Delivery times, service schedules, promptly attending to customers, all these are aspects of corporate punctuality which customers yearn for. Yet, in spite of increased and enhanced technology at their command and superior equipment and facilities available to organisations today, even the representatives of large organisations find it a constant struggle to:

- Keep to scheduled appointments as committed

- Commence work punctually as committed

- Complete work on time as committed

- Deliver on time as committed

- Install on time as committed

- Service or repair on time as committed

It is a telling commentary that the one organisation of substantial size operating in India which is able to consistently meet customer requirements on the parameter of punctuality is the *Dabbawalas* – Mumbai's famous tiffin carriers, who deliver meals from customers' homes to their offices, on time, every time. They are not able to achieve this because they are highly qualified – the average *dabbawala* has not even completed a high-school education; nor because they are equipped with superior technology – they operate on a simple, manual marking system with colour codes to tell them where a specific tiffin-box has to be delivered within the vast metropolis of Mumbai.

173

Rather, they are able to achieve the vital parameter of punctuality, simply because their leader believes in the importance of every minute. Their leader's (and therefore by default every *dabbawala's*), priority, is ensuring that every single one of the approximately 1,60,000 tiffins they carry each day, must not reach the customer even a minute later than the scheduled time.

The leader of the *dabbawalas* does not believe in providing excuses for delayed delivery on the line of – "Oh, we have so many customers, some are bound to suffer." **He believes that every single paying customer deserves to receive the benefit of the *dabbawala's* accuracy and punctuality, which is what the customers are paying for.**

It is this ingrained philosophy of their leader, who is almost paranoid and obsessive about punctuality, that has earned them the well deserved reputation of being the most punctual organisation in India today.

Prince Charles

In fact, a few years ago, when Prince Charles of England was scheduled to visit India, he had written through his secretary to the head of the *dabbawalas*, mentioning that Prince Charles would like to meet him during his visit. (The *dabbawalas* have achieved world-renown by being featured on the BBC in a documentary, which is how Prince Charles had heard of them.)

The leader of the *dabbawalas*, who conducts and oversees operations from an office at Andheri railway station in Mumbai, politely replied that he would be pleased to receive Prince Charles, **but only if the visit could be scheduled for after two o'clock in the afternoon.**

Dabbawalas

Till that time, every working day, the priority of the leader of the *dabbawalas* was controlling operations with supreme efficiency from his centralised command post at Andheri railway station, ensuring that not a single one of his customers received their tiffin even a minute late.

It is such dedication to the customer from the organisational leader in terms of punctuality which ensures that the importance of time is inculcated in and practiced throughout every level of the organisation.

It is said that in Bombay House (the Tata Group headquarters), outside the boardrooms, there was a 'charity box' into which the directors and other Tata personnel who reached late for any meeting, or for their lunch (which they used to have together), had to donate a certain amount as a penalty. This amount would then be donated to ceratin charities.

But it is also said, that J.R.D. Tata, who donated untold wealth to other charities, never once in his entire career had to deposit even a single rupee into this box. Such was his legendary punctuality.

Arnold Bennett, a man who made time work for him, wrote in his classic work, *How to Live on Twenty-Four Hours a Day*:

'You have to live on this twenty-four hours of daily time. Out of it you have to spin health, pleasure, money, content, respect, and the evolution of your immortal soul. Its right use, its most effective use, is a matter of the highest urgency and of the most thrilling actuality. All depends on that. Your happiness – the elusive prize you are clutching for, my friends – all depends on that.'

POINTS TO PONDER AND PRACTICE

- The time available for every individual on this earth is the same. Twenty-four hours gifted to us every day, to use as we please

- Not only should a leader use his own time productively by planning his day well in advance and leaving sufficient time slots in between for unscheduled emergencies, but more importantly, he should ensure that he inculcates a spirit in his employees to ensure that they do not waste a single minute of customer time

- If the leader does not display punctuality as a vital quality to be practiced always, under all circumstances, his followers too will take time lightly. And that is a recipe for personal as well as organisational disaster

GREAT LEADERS PERFORM SILENT ACTS OF NOBILITY WITH HUMILITY

> *Great leaders act silently but surely. Maybe not noticeably, but definitely nobly*
>
> -CYRUS M. GONDA

WHAT **J.R.D.** BELIEVED IN AND **PRACTICED**

> *Your thoughtful actions, however small, set in chain a series of positive karmic events which will spread goodness to the four corners of the earth. As is scientifically proven, the beginning of an avalanche can be traced back to the fall of an individual snowflake; a butterfly flapping its wings can initiate a hardly noticeable breeze which can ultimately culminate into a hurricane*
>
> -CYRUS M. GONDA

177

The following is an anecdote which is absolutely true, but not widely known.

An acquaintance of mine once narrated the following about the time when he was a young lad. Back in the early 1990s, he had qualified as an MBA and secured his first job, and had invited his parents to the *Jewel of India* restaurant at Worli, Mumbai, for dinner to celebrate his achievement.

Once seated at the restaurant, he noticed Mr. J.R.D. Tata dining alone at an adjacent table. He hesitantly approached J.R.D., apologised for disturbing him during his meal, but explained that J.R.D. had always been his role-model during his MBA days, and that he simply couldn't resist the opportunity of just shaking his hand.

J.R.D. invited him to sit down, graciously conversed with him for a few minutes, and casually asked him whether he had just come over for dinner or was he celebrating some occasion. He told J.R.D. that he was treating his parents to dinner, since he had just finished his MBA and had secured employment with a reputed firm.

J.R.D. said he was pleased that the young man gave due respect to his parents' contribution in his academic success and wished him all the best. The young man returned to his table, leaving J.R.D. to resume his meal in solitude.

Later, with the meal complete, the young man asked to be presented with the bill.

He was told by the restaurant staff that his bill had already been settled by Mr. J.R.D. Tata, who had by then completed his meal and left the restaurant.

Astounding.

Another incident which demonstrates J.R.D.'s nobility was narrated to me by Mr. Mahesh Shah, the owner of a manufacturing unit named *Aaditya Polymers*. Mr. Shah was a participant at a keynote address I had been invited to deliver to the members of the *Gowalis Industrial Association* of Vasai and Thane, Mumbai, on the subject of the leadership style of Mr. J.R.D. Tata. After my talk, Mahesh approached me and said he would like to share a personal experience. The following is the gist of what he said.

11th August, 1992, was a day pouring with rain in Mumbai. Mahesh was standing outside the Churchgate railway station in Mumbai, waiting for a taxi to drive him to his destination, the Bombay Stock Exchange. Not a single taxi heeded his request for a ride. Mahesh was getting wetter by the minute, standing almost in the middle of the road, frantically trying to hail a cab.

That is when a Mercedes pulled up beside him and the gentleman seated in the back asked him to get in. **It was Mr. J.R.D. Tata, on his way to the Tata headquarters – Bombay House**. Mahesh mentioned that he (Mahesh) was so wet and soggy that even a taxi-driver avoided giving him a ride, feeling he would dampen the taxi seat, but Mr. J.R.D. Tata had no such worries about his own vehicle.

On the way, J.R.D. chatted with Mahesh and put him at ease. Once they reached Bombay House, Mahesh started to alight, but J.R.D. insisted that his chauffeur would drive Mahesh to his destination, the Bombay Stock Exchange, and would not even dream of leaving Mahesh to make his way to his destination on his own in the rain. J.R.D. even courteously asked Mahesh if he (J.R.D.) could lend Mahesh an umbrella

Mahesh said he simply had to share this incident of J.R.D.'s nobility with me as my talk had brought that incident afresh to his mind.

Mr. Mahesh Shah had been so impressed by this humbling interaction with J.R.D., that he had immediately written a thank-you note to Mr. J.R.D. Tata. He also wrote a letter outlining this incident to the mid-day newspaper, with a request to print it in their letters column. Since at that time, Mr. Mahesh Shah was representing the firm of Aditya Investment, all the correspondence penned by him is on the letterhead of Aditya Investment. The mid-day newspaper printed his letter, and J.R.D. also courteously replied to the same. A couple of newspaper readers, on reading Mr. Mahesh Shah's letter, also responded with their own remarks in the mid-day. All this correspondence and newspaper clippings was faithfully kept by Mr. Mahesh Shah, and he most obligingly forwarded me the same to insert in this book. (mid-day reader Mrs. Perin Jeejeebhoy has erroneously written Mr. Mahesh Shah's name as Mr. Mahesh Sharma in the letters column.)

The following 5 pages contain scanned images of all the correspondence which Mr. Mahesh Shah has faithfully kept as a reminder of this memorable incident.

ADITYA INVESTMENT

Date 17 August, 1992

Bharat Ratna J.R.D. Tata,
Bombay House,
Bombay.

Respected Sir,

While it may be difficult for you to recall a small incident that occurred on 11th instant, when you sportingly offered me a lift in your car from Churchgate to Fountain.

It was a great day for me and shall cherish the memory of this incident throughout my life.

While I thank you very much for the same, I take this opportunity to wish you a long, prosperous and happy life.

With my regards,

Very Truly Yours,

MAHESH K. SHAH

181

Response from Mr. J.R.D. Tata to Mr. Mahesh Shah's thank you letter

BOMBAY HOUSE.
FORT. BOMBAY-400001

August 24, 1992

Dear Mr.Shah,

I thank you for your letter of August 11 and was quite touched that you should have taken the trouble to write to me and to publicise in the Mid-Day what I consider to have been a very simple gesture of helpfulness.

With all good wishes.

Yours sincerely,

(J. R. D. Tata)

Mr.Mahesh X. Shah
2/119, Shekhar Apts.,
S.V.Road
Malad (West)
Bombay 400 064

182

ADITYA INVESTMENT

Ref. No. _____   Date   12.8.1992.

To

The Editor
MID DAY
Bombay.

Enclosed please find my letter addressed to
Bharat Ratna J.R.D. Tata. Kindly have this
letter printed in your "Letters to the Editor"
column and oblige.

Thanking you,

Yours very truly,

(MAHESH K. SHAH).

ADITYA INVESTMENT

Ref. No. _____ Date _____

THANKS TO BHARAT RATNA J.R.D. TATA

It was a day of gusty wind and heavy rain on 11th
August 1992, when I was looking for a cab at Churchgate
to leave me at Stock Exchange. As usual all the
taximen were off the roads, and I was helpless.
Incidentally, a car of Bharat Ratna J.R.D. Tata was
waiting at signal, and I saw him in his car and was
appreciating mentally the greatest Indian, who
immediately made a sporting gesture and asked me to
move in his car.

At the same moment, I was so deeply moved by his
gesture that the words are not enough to express my
gratitude to him. With this, I wish him a long and
happy life.

E/119, Sahakar Apts., S. V. Road, Malad (West). Bombay-400 064
Tel. : 690219 / 692318

184

Response from mid-day readers to Mr. Mahesh Shah's letter

HEARTS OF GONE

I WAS thrilled to read Mahesh Shah's letter, 'A noble soul' (MID-DAY, August 19). J R D Tata is no ordinary philanthropist. He truly has a heart of gold.

I am reminded of an incident similar to the one cited by Shah, in 1952. I was strolling with a couple of friends along Marine Drive when suddenly it started raining. The occupant of a passing car offered us a lift.

It turned out to be none other than India's great opening batsman Vijay Merchant. Only someone with a kind and noble heart would care to make such a gesture.

I later sent him a 'thank you' card and requested an autograph, which was promptly despatched to me.

Our country needs more people like Merchant and JRD, who bring cheer to people.

M S KILPADY
Goregaon (East)

J R D Tata... A warm heart, a kind smile for everybody

MAHESH SHARMA'S letter delighted me. J R D Tata is a generous man. I know him since 1939 and have always known him to offer people lifts.

I have often taken up his offer. I can remember him climbing into his car at his residence in 'The Cairn' on Altamount Road, passing Kemp's Corner and stopping at 'Shelamar', residence of Pherozshah J Murzban, on Hughes Road. His chauffeur would then hold the door open while three persons would get in and be given a lift to Churchgate and Flora Fountain. This was a daily routine.

It warms the heart to think of this gentleman extending a helping hand to so many. His kind smile will never fade from my memory.

PERIN M R B JEEJEEBHOY
Peddar Road

185

Yet another example of J.R.D.'s nobility of soul expressing itself through humane gestures follows. This anecdote was narrated to me by my friend, **Mr. Alex Emmanuel**, who retired a few years ago after serving the **Tatas - VP, Human Resources, with Tata Sons**. Currently, Alex is the founder-director of People Plus India Pvt. Ltd. Here is the memory of his earliest interaction with J.R.D., told in his own words.

'It was the mid-seventies. I was a student at the Tata Institute of Social Sciences, where I was also the president of the students' union. During a conversation with the then Director of the Institute, Dr. M. S. Gore, I requested him if it were possible to invite Mr. J.R.D. Tata for the Annual College Day function: an audacious suggestion on my part, indeed. J.R.D. was a legend whom the presidents and prime ministers, kings and queens, yearned to meet. And where, then, was the question of such an icon sparing valuable time to TISS to attend the college day function?

Dr. Gore didn't seem astounded. In fact he asked his secretary to connect him to Mr. R. M. Lala (that is what I remember.) The very next day I received a message that I could go and meet Mr. J.R.D. Tata and invite him. I was dumbfounded. All of just 24-years-old, I stood frozen for a while.

But now I had to go ahead with the invite. I took Bus No. 90 or 92 from our institute to Dadar, and from there another bus to Haji Ali, and then took a taxi to Mr. Tata's house. His house was named "*The Cairns*"; a century-old mansion situated on Cumballa Hill in Mumbai, surrounded by trees; truly a fairy tale environment.

And there I was – a young man alighting from a '*kaali-peeli*' (famed black-and-yellow Mumbai taxi) Premier Padmini taxi, wanting to meet the legendary J.R.D. !! The security guard at the gate was not convinced of my credentials, but finally I was ushered on to the verandah. I was 15 minutes early. Minutes seemed hours. Then, someone asked me to enter the house.

........continued

........*continued*

I went in to what looked like a drawing-room and was about to settle on a chair. **I felt someone courteously pull the chair back a little and then push it forward to make sure I was comfortably seated.** 'How polite even the peons and attendants at J.R.D.'s residence are,' I thought to myself. **BUT TO MY GREAT SURPRISE, I SOON REALISED THAT THE PERSON WHO HAD MADE ME COMFORTABLE ON THE CHAIR WAS NONE OTHER THAN J.R.D. HIMSELF.**

A little later, an attendant brought in some coffee and cookies and left them on the table. **And then yet another surprise. J.R.D. personally got up and served me the coffee and offered me some cookies.**

It was the biggest lesson I learned on humility in my life. The fear and anxiety that had enveloped me till then turned into reverence and adulation, which got multiplied manifold when this icon completely put me at ease by asking my views on population control (as I was a student of social sciences), and I shared my thoughts with him. Fortunately it was relatively easy for me to share my views on this issue as our students' union had conducted a debate just a few days before on this very same subject.

Well, all I can say is this was an unforgettable event, which is etched in memory for all times to come.'

MR. ALEX EMMANUEL

187

LEARNINGS
FOR LEADERS

You can easily judge the character of a man by how he treats those who can do nothing for him

-JOHANN WOLFGANG VON GOETHE

Humility touched with feelings of humanity is the hallmark of a great leader.

We can just imagine if such is the royal treatment Mr. J.R.D. Tata displayed to strangers whom he had just met, would he ignore the welfare of any of his own employees and customers?

It is always observed that the actions of great leaders speak loud and clear, in perhaps 'small' and maybe not in very 'loud' or 'flashy' ways. Yet it is certain that these leaders are able to enhance the world with the glory of **values** of care, concern, humility, and love for humanity.

Such leaders are constantly evolving, focusing every moment of their lives on doing good, and providing pleasurable moments to everyone and anyone they even faintly and temporarily associate with.

Life for such great and evolved leaders is a life of sharing and giving, where they always seek moments of opportunity to silently gift in a world otherwise filled with selfishness and strife. Such leaders are able to spread warmth and generate genuine goodwill, thereby subconsciously but certainly enhancing their own personal brand and the brand of the organisation they represent.

Also, in western nations, care for the elderly is a state responsibility, while in our developing country, parents in their old age hope to be looked after by their children. J.R.D. appreciated, acknowledged and encouraged this **traditionally Indian value** through his thoughtful action outlined in the first anecdote in this learning. **In developed countries, the upkeep of elders is outsourced to professionally managed senior-citizen centres, leading to the development of individualistic tendencies where the society becomes self-centred and based on selfishness. Supreme individualism, which is the by-product of such a philosophy, instils greed and unbridled desire. J.R.D., by appreciating and rewarding the young man's thoughtful gesture, displayed his innate leader-ship attribute of motivating young individuals to care for the elderly, a value sorely needed in our fast-paced society today.**

While these silent gestures of J.R.D. were obviously not undertaken by him for public consumption, word of such noble acts **does** spread. This is what constitutes genuine goodwill. Organisations today are hungry and desperate for what they term as '**Public Relations**' and you will often see photographs in a newspaper of a CEO having lunch with his driver in the office canteen, ostensibly to prove to the world how down-to-earth the CEO in question is. Such photographs and associated articles are often 'planted' stories, in a media which has increasingly sold itself to the highest bidder. Readers are by now aware that what they read in the newspapers and view on television is often paid for and doctored, and thus have little faith in such content.

The original definition of 'Public Relations' was, is, and will remain – 'Unpaid Publicity.' A detailed study of the history of public relations will tell you so. The moment money passes hands for publicity purposes, it ceases to remain public relations and becomes disguised advertising. **Thus, ironically, any organisation which categorises itself as being in the business of Public Relations, is actually in the business of disguised advertising, as genuine Public Relations cannot be PAID for, it has to be EARNED, through altruistic actions.** Definitions of key terms cannot change, however much persons with vested interests may wish them to. **True public relations and the related positive word-of-mouth publicity originate when others speak good of a person or an organisation not with ulterior motive, but from genuine belief in the goodness of that individual or that organisation.**

189

J.R.D. never had any intent of obtaining publicity from his thoughtful gestures, which is what true public relations is all about. Others speak good about him with no vested interest behind their words, because there was no ulterior motive behind J.R.D.'s noble acts in the first place.

Paid public relations exercises can never even hope to come close to achieving the desired publicity as compared with the tremendous goodwill that acts done with noble and selfless intent can generate.

> " There is no SMALL act of kindness. EVERY act creates a ripple with no logical end "
>
> -Scott Adams
> (creator of the Dilbert cartoon-strip character)

POINTS TO PONDER AND PRACTICE

- Often, during the course of your leadership career, you will get opportunities to silently perform good gestures. You may not have the resources or the energy or the inclination to perform a good deed at every chance you get, but once in a while (or maybe twice in a while), it would do you and your heart good to perform these little noble acts

- Do not do these good deeds because you feel others are watching, or because you can gain mileage from them later. Do them so silently, that even your left hand is not aware of the good deeds that your right hand does

- Remember, **SOMEONE**, from above, is always watching

- The three quotients which combine to form the core of a holistic leader are:

    -Intelligence Quotient (IQ)

    -Emotional Quotient (EQ)

    -Spiritual Quotient (SQ)

- Modern leadership thought lays greater emphasis on the parameter of spirituality, which in simple words could be described as doing good when no one on earth is watching. Good leaders owe it to the society in which they live to generate goodness and motivate and encourage the youth in following a path they can be proud of treading on

PRACTICE PLUS PASSION MAKE PERFECT

> **" A great leader's courage to fulfil his vision comes from passion, not position "**
>
> -JOHN C. MAXWELL

WHAT **J.R.D.** BELIEVED IN AND **PRACTICED**

> **" To be successful, the first thing to do is fall in love with your work "**
>
> -SISTER MARY LAURETTA

GROUP CAPTAIN
GEOFFREY LEONARD
CHESHIRE

The foreword to the excellent book – *Aircraft and Engine Perfect: The story of JRD Tata who opened up the skies for his country*, authored by Murad Fyzee and published by Tata McGraw Hill, is written by **Group Captain Geoffrey Leonard Cheshire**, a World War II flying hero of the Royal Air Force.

In this foreword, Group Captain G. Leonard Cheshire (a recipient of the Victoria Cross for exceptional bravery) **outlines the keenness; the passion and zest which he had observed J.R.D. approach any task with.**

Cheshire writes: 'I first met JRD Tata in 1956. He was then at the height of his career....The occasion was the private viewing of a film on IATA's role in making airlines safer and more convenient for passengers which he was introducing. As one would expect from somebody in his position, he spoke with authority, came across convincingly and brought in a happy touch of humour. **But there was much more to it than that.** He clearly was completely steeped in his subject, loved it and wanted us to share his own zest and joy. Looking back, I think that **zest is the key to understanding JRD's remarkable achievements**, zest for whatever he is engaged in, and zest for life in general. That is something we all need whatever our position in life, high or low. Most of us have it in one form or another when we are young, but if we are not careful it can begin to fade as we get older, especially if we let ourselves get too immersed in routine. Zest for life carries over difficulties and setbacks, even over disaster; it carries us forward into new fields and new interests and is a truly life-giving force. But if once it disappears we are in danger of disappearing too. **Look at Jeh (JRD), skiing up to the age of 85, and still vitally and constructively interested in everything around him....'**

Of course, with all the innate passion and zest for life which J.R.D. displayed to a ripe old age, he added to it the vital ingredient of the **'hands-on'** – getting down to the nitty-gritty – and **ensuring that his leadership was based on the winning formula:**

'PRACTICE PLUS PASSION MAKE PERFECT'

> *When love and skill work together, expect a masterpiece*
>
> -JOHN RUSKIN
>
> (After all, passion is a strong form of love, and skill is primarily acquired through practice.)

LEARNINGS
FOR LEADERS

Passion will move men beyond themselves, beyond their shortcomings, beyond their failures

-JOSEPH CAMPBELL

It is often said '**Practice Makes Perfect**.'

But having personally trained many thousands of students of management as well as corporate personnel over the last eighteen years, I have come to the conclusion that '**Practice Makes Perfect**' is only **HALF THE STORY**.

Someone doing a task repeatedly, but routinely and mechanically, with little or no interest, is also getting 'practice' at doing the task.

Until PASSION enters the equation, the man who is merely 'practicing' routinely and mechanically, will be little better than a machine.

This is the reason why many individuals with twenty years of experience do not rise to their expected or desired level in the corporate hierarchy – their 'twenty years of experience' has been so devoid of passion and interest, that in their case, **twenty years experience is nothing but two years experience repeatedly multiplied ten times**.

Because passion is the '**steam which drives the human engine**,' it is important that you take keen interest in whatever you do, so that the time and effort you invest in that activity gives you a ten-fold or even a hundred-fold return.

> *'Don't ask yourself what the world needs; ask yourself what makes you come alive. And then go and do that. Because what the world needs is people who have come alive.'*
>
> -HOWARD THURMAN

195

The renowned Polish pianist, Ignace Paderewski (who, for a few months, was also the prime minister of Poland), was once asked, why, despite he being among the best pianists in the world, still diligently practiced at his piano at least six hours every day.

His response was illuminating. He replied, If I miss **ONE** day's practice, I notice the drop in my performance. If I miss **TWO** day's practice, my **CRITICS** notice the drop in my performance. And if I miss **THREE** day's practice, my **AUDIENCE** notices the drop in my performance.

IGNACE PADEREWSKI

Your work is going to fit a huge part of your life, and the only way to be truly satisfied is to do what you believe is great work. And the only way to do great work is to love what you do. If you haven't found it yet, keep looking. Don't settle. As with all matters of the heart, you'll know when you find it

-STEVE JOBS

For some people, the time they spend at their workplace is the time they love the best. It is in this context that the following is relevant.

One day, when Thomas Edison, the prolific inventor, came home from work, his wife told him, "Thomas, you have worked for many days without a break. You need rest and must go on a vacation."

"But where should I go?" asked Edison, who had never really given much thought to such things.

His wife, rather than name a specific place for him to visit, suggested, "Just decide to go where you would rather be than anywhere else on earth."

Edison smiled and said, "Very well. Tomorrow I will do exactly that."

The next morning found Edison at the place he loved best and was more passionate about than any other place on earth – his beloved laboratory.

THOMAS EDISION

Tomorrow's victory is today's practice

-CHRIS BRADFORD

POINTS TO PONDER AND PRACTICE

- Do not do any task simply for the sake of doing it. Even if you have to perform any task or activity which you have never undertaken before as part of your job, get into the depth of it, understand its subtle nuances and finer elements, so that you do not just get average results, but results which you can be justly proud of. And you will invest time, effort and energy willingly in understanding elements of your work when you truly love and enjoy what you do. As the great sage and philosopher **Aristotle** said over 2,000 years ago:

  "Pleasure in the job puts perfection in the work"

- Most importantly, remember the wise words of Marshal Ferdinand Foch:

  "The most powerful weapon on earth is the HUMAN SOUL ON FIRE"

- And if you follow the advice of Steve Jobs, who said...
  'The only way to do great work is to love what you do'
      ....you can never go wrong

GIFT THOUGHTFULLY –
THOUGHTFUL HOST
THOUGHTFUL GIFTS

" The excellence of a gift lies in its appropriateness rather than in its value "

-CHARLES DUDLEY WARNER

WHAT **J.R.D.**
BELIEVED IN
AND **PRACTICED**

" It's not how much we give but how much love we put into giving "

-MOTHER TERESA

There come many opportunities in the life of a corporate leader when he needs to gift others on special occasions. It could be the occasion of birthdays of employees or key customers, or offering a token to a visiting dignitary, or thanking someone for a favour done.

There are **two** ways in which leaders could possibly select gifts.

ONE – Delegate staff to purchase an expensive gift, giving little thought to what is being gifted, as long as it is expensive and grand.

TWO – Make the gift as personal as possible, customising it so that the recipient gets exactly what he or she wants. This is the ultimate in thoughtful gifting.

J.R.D., a man who always preferred to adopt the personalised touch, opted for the second, **which is why he is not only remembered as a successful leader, but also a thoughtful one**.

An instance of this attribute of J.R.D. will illustrate the point. J.R.D., due to his immense personal contribution to the world of aviation, was elected President of IATA (the International Air Transport Association) for the year 1958-59, the fortieth year of commercial aviation. In his capacity as President, he hosted the first IATA conference to be held outside Europe or America. He hosted it at the Ashoka Hotel in New Delhi.

The IATA delegates came from all over the globe, many of them accompanied by their spouses, and all were truly charmed with the creative efforts that J.R.D. and his team had taken to make the conference a memorable one.

The icing on this beautiful cake was the choice of parting souvenir that J.R.D. had planned for the spouses of the visiting international delegates.

J.R.D. decided that rather than selecting a gift for these ladies, he would let them choose their gift for themselves.

So a room in the Ashoka Hotel was filled with different kinds of presents the ladies could choose from. Articles like sarees, shawls, scarves, simple but tasteful jewellery, were all laid out and THE LADIES COULD THEMSELVES CHOOSE THE SOUVENIR THEY MOST WANTED FROM AMONG THE VAST VARIETY DISPLAYED. What could be a more customised gift than this?

The ladies were obviously thrilled. Many ladies after returning to their homes, personally wrote back to say what a wonderful idea of J.R.D. that was.

A disciple once asked his Guru, **"Why is it that God graciously accepts the offerings of some and apparently rejects the offerings of others? Does the acceptance or rejection depend upon the size of the offering?"**

"Not at all," replied the Guru. **"For God, it is love that matters. It is love that you humbly bring as a gift and an offering to the table of the Lord. If you bring expensive gifts to the altar but leave your heart at home, He will surely spurn your offering, though it may be the most expensive gift in the whole world."**

LEARNINGS
FOR LEADERS

Gift-giving is a true art:

1. *You need to understand the person to whom you intend to give the gift.*

2. *You need to know what they truly want.*

3. *You must be able to give it to them.*

Anything less is a symptom of varying degrees, on your part, of ignorance, distance, or insult. But if you cannot AFFORD the right gift, telling the person what you WOULD gift if you COULD, justifies everything – as you present that not-so-perfect substitute

-VERA NAZARIAN

Leaders are representatives of their organisations, and their duties involve not only strategic, executive, and tactical decision-making, but also building the reputation of the organisation as a thoughtful, generous, and large-hearted one.

Great leaders are also not only recognised by the ideas they generate and implement on the 'big' issues, but also on the 'small' ones, which may be small in name, but huge in impact for their ability to touch the heart.

In December 2013, the Calgary-based Canadian airline **WestJet**, set up electronic **Santa Claus** chat-boxes in their terminals at the Hamilton and Toronto airports. Passengers thought the chat-boxes were put up for fun, and taking this opportunity to speak to 'Santa' live, adults and children alike spoke into the chat-boxes, giggling and telling 'Santa' what they would like most for Christmas. Then they forgot about it and boarded their flights for Calgary, on their way home for the Christmas holidays. **But the chat-boxes had not been erected 'just for fun' by WestJet.**

While the passengers were on their flights to Calgary, 150 WestJet shoppers in Calgary quickly played back the recordings made by the passengers on the chat-boxes, listened carefully to the Christmas wish each passenger had expressed, and then rushed to shop for their passengers' 'wish-list,' get the gifts wrapped, and delivered them to the airport before the flights landed.

When the passengers landed at Calgary and reached the baggage-claim area, the tired passengers saw not only their luggage, but also big, blue boxes with their names on the front, and their dream Christmas gifts inside.

Impressive to the core.

A thoughtful leader such as J.R.D. and a thoughtful brand such as WestJet are the ones who are appreciated by their employees and their customers more than those who are merely clinically efficient and purely profit-oriented. The two qualities (that of 'total thoughtfulness' as well as 'profit orientation') **can** co-exist in one individual as well as in one brand, but that requires a special kind of individual and brand, **one who has trained himself and themselves to think with the head as well as the heart**.

J.R.D. was a shining example of such a superior blend of leadership.

Once a beggar on the roadside stretched out his hands as **Alexander the Great** was passing by. The beggar was ragged and wretched and would apparently have been satisfied with a couple of copper coins which would easily have met his needs. Yet Alexander gave him a handful of gold coins.

A courtier accompanying Alexander was puzzled and queried, "**Sir, a few copper coins would have amply served his need. What need had you to gift him gold**?"

Alexander replied, "**Copper coins would certainly suit the beggar's need. But it is gold coins which suit Alexander's gifting.**"

ALEXANDER THE GREAT

POINTS TO PONDER AND PRACTICE

- As a leader of an organisation, you will often be in a position where you need to offer gifts, momentos and tokens of appreciation to people on vatious occasions on behalf of the organisation. This becomes an excellent opportunity for you to ensure that stakeholders formulate a positive opinion about you and the brand you represent, not on the basis of the monetary value of the gift, but rather on how personal and thoughtful and tasteful and appropriate the gift you selected appears to the recipient

- **In this age of social media, it is relatively easy to identify the tastes and preferences of individuals.** Take that extra effort to search for these on the profiles of people whom you would be gifting, and then select the most appropriate gift

- This will tell the recipients how much you truly care, and how much effort you have taken to understand the likes, tastes and choices of others. **This shows to a good degree the level of emotional intelligence you as a leader possess, and will make people feel the organisation would be similarly thoughtful in other actions as well**

" What is the best gift you ever received? Perhaps you will recall that in each instance, the best gift was one that was tied with the heartstrings of the giver, one that included a part of self "

-WANDA FULTON

204

TRUST PEOPLE UNTIL
THEY GIVE YOU
REASON NOT TO DO SO

" Just like a mind is conditioned to distrust and be suspicious of people, it can be re-conditioned to trust them as well. Trust people unless they give you reason not to trust them, and reap the benefits of this trust by being trusted and loved in return "

-CYRUS M. GONDA

WHAT **J.R.D.**
BELIEVED IN
AND **PRACTICED**

"The best way to find out if you can trust somebody is to trust them "

-ERNEST HEMINGWAY

205

Trust is a key word in the leadership lexicon.

Trust is a two-way process for a leader. He first needs to have trust in his people, and that is when his people put their trust in him. This is a win-win situation for all concerned.

Unfortunately, trust is a rare entity in today's cut-throat corporate environment.

J.R.D. never suffered from a lack of faith when it came to trusting his beloved people. In fact, he held a healthy attitude towards trust. He believed that it was right to trust people. He also felt that to be innately suspicious of others without reason or cause was not correct.

His words on the subject of trust were, "**I like people and trust them unless they show themselves unreliable or incompetent.**"

And J.R.D. was a man who always meant what he said.

 In a mid-sized city in the U.S.A., an apparel store thoughtfully set aside 200 umbrellas for the use of pedestrians passing by who may have been caught unawares in the rain. These people were not even the customers of the store, just casual passers-by, who could walk in and borrow an umbrella without leaving any deposit. All they had to do was just leave their name and address.

Eight months after the store management initiated this policy, they took stock and found they still had 197 umbrellas on hand. One had been damaged in a rainstorm and only two had not been returned. **On the other hand, the store had won many new loyal customers who had gratefully walked in to borrow an umbrella when they had been caught in an unexpected shower.**

LEARNINGS
FOR LEADERS

SANT KABIR

> *Rahiman aap thagaiyo*
> *Aur na thagiye koi*
> *Aap thage sukh upje*
> *Aur thage dukh hoi*

The lovely *doha* (couplet) of Sant Kabir which you read above (and which was brought to my attention by my late and good friend Dr. Vishambhar Saxena), encapsulates everything one needs to know on the subject of trust. A rough translation of this beautiful couplet would be:

O Man, it matters not much if you are cheated

But never make the mistake of ever cheating others

For if you are cheated by others, your loss will be credited to your karmic bank account for which you will be repaid in future

But if you cheat others, suffering to you will result

Of course, this does not mean that you should trust blindly. Nor does it imply that you trust repeatedly, those people who have cheated you in the past. As J.R.D. said: "I like and trust people, **UNLESS** they show themselves unreliable or incompetent."

The American game of **baseball** is quite similar to the game of cricket, with a few marked differences. One such difference is, in cricket, if a batsman is bowled once, he is considered out. But in baseball, a hitter (batsman) needs to be struck out (the equivalent of being bowled out) three times before he is considered out.

This concept has found application in the matter of trust.

The best leaders follow a **'three-strike rule'** when it comes to trusting people.

This means that they do not distrust a person on sight, or operate on the philosophy that people cannot be trusted at all. Rather, such leaders start by trusting everyone they meet. If a person gives the leader reason to distrust him once, the leader gives him a second chance, and often even a third. If after that, the person still betrays the leader's trust, the leader 'strikes him out.' Of course, as explained elsewhere in this book (in the learning on maintenance of infrastructure and safety), a condition applies. There can be no second chance for people who act deliberately irresponsible and put the lives of others in jeopardy. For such individuals, once is more than enough.

But taken on the whole, the 'three-strike rule' is such a sensible and people-oriented way of operating, it is a wonder that more leaders do not adopt it. **It does no good to be suspicious of all people everywhere under the false assumption that everyone is a cheat or a crook.** Rather, trust in people, and even if a few do cheat you, as Sant Kabir beautifully explained, that is ultimately their misfortune, not yours. And the benefit of trusting the rest, the majority who are fine, upstanding and honourable people, who want to be trusted and who want to repay the trust you have reposed in them, is their commitment, dedication, hard and smart work, and everlasting loyalty from their side towards you and your organisation.

The following is modified from an article which appeared in an old issue of the *Church of Scotland's Children's Review*:

Some years ago, an apparel manufacturer of Scotland told the Sunday school teacher of a class of poor boys that he would get them each a new suit of clothes. (Sunday school is a school where classes are held only on Sundays for imparting religious education.) The worst and most unpromising boy in the class was a lad named Bob.

After a few Sundays, Bob stopped coming to school. His teacher went in search of him, and found him, but with his new suit of clothes dirty and torn.

The manufacturer gave this lad a second suit, but yet after attending another couple of Sundays, he again absented himself. Utterly discouraged, his teacher reported to the manufacturer that they must give up on him.

REVEREND ROBERT MORRISON

But the manufacturer decided to give him a third chance, and gave him a third suit after making him promise to attend regularly. Once Bob gave his word, he did begin to attend the classes regularly and faithfully, and became a firm believer in God and in his religion.

The end of the story is that this young boy, Bob, later on in life became the **Reverend Robert Morrison**, the great missionary to China, who translated the Bible into the Chinese language, thus opening the doors of his religion to the millions of that country.

The following interesting piece of news appeared in the *Church of Ireland Gazette* many, many years ago:

'Matthew Henry, the famous scholar, was once accosted by thieves and robbed of his purse. He wrote in his diary: **"Let me be thankful first, because I was never robbed before; second, because although they took my purse, they did not take my life; third, because although they took my all, it was not much; and fourth, BECAUSE IT WAS I WHO WAS ROBBED, NOT I WHO ROBBED."**

POINTS TO PONDER AND PRACTICE

- Think back to all the people you have ever trusted. How many of them have misused or abused your trust? Not more than a handful. Unfortunately, it is this handful which stands out in the mind, as it is human nature to always recall and recollect the negative faster than the positive

- Consider a sheet of white paper with one small black dot on it. Show this sheet to someone and ask him what he sees. The chances are the person will say: **"I see a black dot."** Although the black dot covers not more than one percent of the surface area of the sheet of clean, white paper, this is the answer you will most likely receive. Rarely will a person say: "I see a sheet of white paper with a small black dot on it." This is unfortunate, but this is the reality of human psychology and behaviour

- We have been conditioned since childhood by a cautious society to first watch out for and spot the negative

- And we do this with regard to people as well. We see negatives where none exist. Merely because someone, somewhere, in our distant and unrelated past cheated us, we assume all men to be cheats. Resist the urge to do so. **Practice looking first for the good rather than for the bad.** It is a habit which you can develop over time, and a habit which you as a leader will profit from

MAINTENANCE OF INFRASTRUCTURE AND STANDARDS OF SAFETY MUST NEVER BE COMPROMISED

" *Another flaw in the human character is that everybody wants to build and nobody wants to do maintenance* "

-KURT VONNEGUT

WHAT **J.R.D.** BELIEVED IN AND **PRACTICED**

" *Concern for man himself and his safety must always form the chief interest of all technical endeavours* "

-ALBERT EINSTEIN

J.R.D. laid absolute emphasis on maintenance and safety standards. For him, life and limb of every passenger and crew on-board his aircraft and every manager and employee working in his factories and offices was an aspect that simply could not be compromised, under any circumstances whatsoever. And rightly so.

Bakul Khote of Air India once remarked: "**J.R.D. personified many areas of excellence – maintenance, high utilisation and skilled pilots.**" It is clear from this observation that a healthy obsession with maintenance and safety (skilled pilots), was his priority. Service standards, though vital, came a close second. And that is as it should be.

Even today, few are aware that the primary purpose for an air-hostess and purser being on-board a flight is to ensure the safety and security of the passengers. Service is the secondary aspect of their duties. This is a question which is often asked during the conducting of interviews for cabin-crew positions: "**What is the primary purpose for having a cabin-crew on board an aeroplane?**" The correct answer is: "**To ensure passenger safety.**"

J.R.D. kept himself updated with the latest safety equipment and technology being developed throughout the world, and as soon as such equipment and technology was perfected and available for commercial use and sale, he ensured Air India aeroplanes adopted the same.

―――――――

After J.R.D. left Air India as its most loved Chairman, the staff of Air India wrote on the first page of their Air India journal, the *Magic Carpet* (in fond memory of his exemplary leadership):

'...You, Mr. Tata, signify everything to us that is dedication, loyalty and single-minded devotion to a cause....**constant in your endeavour to have the latest and the most sophisticated equipment for the airline...**'

Thus it is evident that even the employees of Air India had observed and realised this quality of J.R.D. and appreciated him for it.

LEARNINGS ▬▬▬▬▬▬
◼ FOR LEADERS

*" Safety is not an exercise to keep us in work.
It is a matter of life and death. It is the sum of our
contributions to safety management that determines
whether the people we work with live or die"*

> -SIR BRIAN APPLETON (WHEN HE WAS MEMBER OF THE ENQUIRY
> TEAM WHICH ENQUIRED INTO THE PIPER ALPHA OIL-PLATFORM
> DISASTER ON 6TH JULY, 1988, OFF THE COAST OF SCOTLAND)

On the 14th of June, 2014, an article in the *Times of India*, (Mumbai edition), article titled – **DGCA Dilutes Flying Norms for Drunk Pilots** – mentioned how the Directorate General for Civil Aviation (DGCA), the apex body for policy-formulation and implementation pertaining to the aviation sector in India, had now relaxed rules which could negatively impact passenger safety. Up till then, if a pilot was found drunk on duty **TWICE**, his licence to fly was suspended. From now on, the DGCA would only cancel a pilot's licence if he was found drunk on duty **THRICE**.

I personally feel that for such severe violations, one occasion is sufficient to suspend a pilot permanently, as not only does his insensitive and thoughtless action endanger his own life, but also the lives of his fellow-crew members, his passengers, and the aircraft he is responsible for.

Not to forget the fact that his one action could possibly make an insurance company shell out millions of dollars against probable subsequent claims and result in the hike of insurance premiums for the industry as a whole.

A man or a woman who does not have the basic self-control to stay away from the bottle when others' lives are at stake deserves no second chance.

But DGCA, in its 'wisdom,'(or lack of it), has changed the rules, and rather than reduce the second time to just one, has 'generously' increased it to three times before a pilot who is drunk on duty can have his license cancelled. Now, instead of after the second time he commits this gravest of grave offences (which was DGCA's existing rule), DGCA permits a pilot to be caught drunk on duty, twice, and let off with suspensions, and only have his licence cancelled the **THIRD** time he is caught for the **SAME GRAVE** offence.

The article goes on to mention that justifying this move, a senior DGCA official said: **"Pilots are a scarce resource and India is anyway facing a pilot shortage."**

Such can never be the reasoning that a leader with a sense of **values**, a clear understanding of right and wrong, would adopt. **Yes. Mr. DGCA OFFICIAL, PILOTS MAY BE A SCARCE RESOURCE, BUT SO ARE THE LIVES OF PASSENGERS.** After all, for a passenger, his current life is the **only** one he has. **For a passenger who is at the mercy of a drunken pilot, there is no third, nor even a second chance.**

Whether scarce resource or not, there can be no compromise when issues of safety to life are concerned. After all, one must remember that even being drunk when driving a car is considered dangerous, and here we have a senior government official in a leadership position making excuses for a drunkard flying an aeroplane filled to capacity with possibly over 300 passengers trusting their lives to him or to her.

While traffic police get strict on drunken driving, DGCA gets lenient on drunken piloting.

Leaders, please note, the **'Three-strike Rule'** (elaborated in learning 19 in this book) does **NOT** apply to such grave offences where lives could be put at risk simply because an irresponsible person does not have the self-control to forego his/her drink when professional requirement demands.

J.R.D., lenient leader though he was, always ready to give people a second and even a third chance, would have agreed that such violations, which impact safety, cannot be excused or condoned even once.

As a responsible leader, you too should learn to differentiate between those offences or slip-ups which can, and should, be pardoned, even twice or thrice, and those (few and far between such as this one under discussion), where no second chance is permissible. These are severe offences which could have been easily avoided, and which needlessly put lives of innocents at risk.

While the above example of drunken pilots pertained to human carelessness, the one below pertains to **poor maintenance** in areas which are by themselves non-life-threatening, but this aspect too can be **perceived** by passengers as potentially endangering their safety.

The following is an incident involving Air India, (a recent incident, not from J.R.D.'s time), abridged from an article which appeared in the *Times of India*, (Mumbai edition), dated 2nd June, 2014. The article was titled - **Clogged Toilets Force Air India's Frankfurt Flight To Turn Around Mid-Way:** Air India Flight 121 to Frankfurt from Delhi on 31st May, 2014 **returned to IGI airport (New Delhi) three hours later because all four toilets on the aircraft were clogged.** With two full meals, an evening snack and an unlimited supply of beverages awaiting the 214 passengers on board, completing the over eight-hour-long journey was not an option for the Boeing 787 Dreamliner (a very modern aircraft). **The two toilets in the front for business class as well as the two in the rear were all out of order. "The flushes were unserviceable so the plane had to return to Delhi,"** said an Air India official. .....**Some Air India sources said the airline's maintenance needs to do a better job.** Said an Air India official: "AI is the oldest airline of the country. It should know the behaviour of Indian passengers and should maintain toilets accordingly. **The failure to do so has cost the airline dearly, both monetarily and in terms of losing flyer's faith."**

A management concept of immense relevance and import here is the concept of **BROKEN WINDOWS.** Initially devised by law-enforcement authorities in the U.S.A. as a means to proactively identify which apartments and houses would probably be targeted by burglars for break-ins, it was found that apartments which had windows which were cracked and broken and not replaced were the potential first targets of burglars. **This is because the burglars, seeing a window cracked or broken and not replaced, assume that the owner would be a careless and irresponsible individual, and therefore it was likely that this owner would also be careless about aspects such as safety locks, burglar alarms, etc.**

The outcome of this research now finds great relevance in the world of management. If the customers or clients of an organisation find a SINGLE ASPECT of that organisation to be defective (such as non-functioning flushes in aircraft toilets, for example), they would naturally assume that the leadership of that organisation is careless and irresponsible in general, and that many or possibly even all other aspects of the organisation could possibly be defective as well.

Thus, it is possible and natural for a person reading the article about lack of maintenance of on-board toilets to perceive – **'If ALL FOUR TOILETS of an aeroplane which has just taken off can SIMULTANEOUSLY FAIL TO FUNCTION DUE TO POOR MAINTENANCE, then my immediate reaction as a potential passenger is that ALL FOUR ENGINES OF THAT AEROPLANE CAN ALSO FAIL SIMULTANEOUSLY FOR SIMILAR REASONS.'**

Whether the customer perception is right or wrong is not the question. What is important is that it is the customer's perception and he will act upon it. As Kate Zabriskie has rightly said:
– **'THE CUSTOMER'S PERCEPTION IS YOUR REALITY.'**

Similarly, in every industry there are unique infrastructure related maintenance issues, none of which should be even slightly overlooked by the leadership, let alone blatantly ignored, nor given step-motherly treatment.

The concept of **Six Sigma**, originally a statistical concept, has now become a useful management tool to identify defects and errors in all aspects of operations. Six Sigma scientifically assists organisations that are systems-inclined to understand where they currently stand on key identified parameters as far as level of errors and defects are concerned. Once the current status is identified, prioritisation can be undertaken as to where management attention and focus needs to be invested with immediate effect, and how improvement on these parameters can take place. Generally, these parameters are ones which would be of maximum importance to customers. In simple terms, Six Sigma is a method of measuring and setting targets for reducing and minimising defects or errors in product or service that are directly connected to customer requirements and expectations.

Under J.R.D.'s stewardship, his personal involvement with operational issues ensured that maintenance as well as standards of safety was given top priority, as it is a factor key to passenger well-being and convenience. The beauty of J.R.D.'s style of leadership was that he created the time and devoted the energy to focus on **all** aspects of the organisations which he led, even focusing on shades of fine detail. **He did not centre his attention on big issues alone and let smaller matters pass him by.** For example, he did not just focus on multi-crore contracts for purchase of aircraft, but he also gave equal importance to aspects of day-to-day maintenance and safety.

The following example pertaining to leadership focus on safety standards is extracted from *The Bamboo Principle* authored by Ken Lodi: 'In the  1950s, the CEO of **Volvo** had a passion for **safety**. He lost a relative in a car accident and resolved to make vehicles safer. His primary motivation was **innovation in the context of life-saving technology**. He recruited Nils Ivar Bohlin, an engineer who developed ejection seats

SAAB Fighter Aircraft for SAAB fighter aircraft in the 1950s.

Bohlin's task was challenging. After working with four-point harnesses found in fighter jets, he understood their value and their limitations for automobiles. However, together they engineered a simple solution still used in cars today: the three-point safety restraint. Volvo introduced it in 1959, and it soon became the (safety) standard with all brands (of automobiles). Millions of lives have been saved since its inception. The three-point safety restraint is a classic example of what happens when people with **SIMILAR VALUES** and complementary talents collaborate to change the world.'

The job of a leader is to constantly raise the barrier and tighten and improve standards in areas where it matters; never to relax standards and lower them under flimsy grounds.

The **San Francisco Golden Gate Bridge** is a marvel of engineering. The *Frommer's* travel guide describes the Golden Gate Bridge as "possibly the most beautiful, certainly the most photographed, bridge in the world." It opened to the public in 1937 and was, until 1964, at 4,200 feet, the longest suspension bridge main span in the world.

The bridge was constructed in two phases, and for reasons of economy, during the construction of the first phase, very little safety equipment or devices were put in place, and as a result twenty-three men working on the bridge fell to their deaths in the deep waters below. Then in the construction of the second phase, the persons in charge of the project decided to invest in installing for the safety of the workmen, the greatest safety net in the world at a cost on over $100,000. (Back in the 1930s, this was a huge sum of money.)

This safety net worked wonders, as it saved the lives of at least ten men who fell into it without injury. But this was not the only advantage the safety net offered. The work in the second phase carried on at a 15 to 25 per cent faster rate than in the first phase, as the workmen were now relieved from the possibility of falling to injury and death. The knowledge that they were safe ensured that the men now devoted their full attention and energy to the task at hand.

POINTS TO PONDER AND PRACTICE

- As a leader or as a manager, or even as a supervisor, there will be certain aspects of organisational infrastructure which will be under your broad purview, even if they are not your direct job responsibility. Focus on them and ensure that you develop and use a scientific method to measure any defects and errors in such infrastructure (whether physical or virtual), which could lead to a negative customer perception or experience. Then act swiftly and decisively to minimise or preferably eliminate these errors and defects. Develop policies which will ensure maintenance of infrastructure and adherence to safety is always given top priority by all throughout the organisation

- **Remember, FIRE-PREVENTION is always a superior leadership approach as compared to FIRE-FIGHTING**

- As a leader, at all times keep in mind the concept of **Broken Windows** and ensure that as far as possible, not a single 'Broken Window' exists within your organisation which could give an eagle-eyed customer a reason to doubt his reason to do business with your organisation

- Instil in your people the thoroughness and attitude of **zero-tolerance** when it comes to matters which deal with safety issues of any kind

FOCUS ON THE INDIVIDUAL AS WELL AS ON THE ORGANISATION

> *The Sun, with all the planets revolving around it, and depending on it, can still ripen a bunch of grapes as though it had nothing else in the Universe to do*

-GALILEO GALILEI

WHAT **J.R.D.** BELIEVED IN AND **PRACTICED**

> *Never ignore individual people for the sake of the organisation, nor ignore the organisation for the sake of the individuals. A leader has to walk this constant tight-rope, as his responsibility lies both towards the organisation, and the individuals who constitute it. Experience will teach you the correct blend in which to divide your time, attention, and energy; but the starting point is to first recognise that both segments deserve a judicious allocation of your valuable time and attention*

-CYRUS M. GONDA

219

Despite leading an overall workforce of well over a few hundred thousand employees, J.R.D. as head of the Tata group found time to look after and resolve the needs and concerns of individuals within the organisation.

Although he had multiple responsibilities at the apex level of the entire organisation and in its many entities, whenever he could do something for an individual employee at any level, he took great pleasure in helping out.

The following anecdote is illustrative of the **personal touch** which was the hallmark of J.R.D.'s leadership.

There was once a young man employed with a Tata company, whose parents and brothers were settled in Canada. As he was residing alone in India, he was deliberating whether to permanently move to Canada and join his family, or stay on in India and continue his job and further his career with the Tata group.

This young man's dilemma somehow came to J.R.D.'s notice. He called the young man over to have a talk and advised him in a fatherly manner as to how to take a decision which he would profit from. He suggested that the young man join his family in Canada as he (J.R.D.), felt that the young man should be with his family and would benefit from doing so in the long run.

As the young man was thanking J.R.D. for his advice, J.R.D. told the young man, "Why didn't you come to me earlier? **Why don't you use me while I am still there?**"

This is true leadership. Giving as much importance to the personal dilemma of an individual, as one gives to dilemmas facing the organisation as a whole.

After all, without individuals, there IS no organisation.

Many years ago, the then King Edward of England visited the English city of Norwich to lay the foundation stone of a new hospital. Many school-children had gathered to welcome the king and they also sang for him. After the king had left, one of the school-teachers present noticed a little girl crying, and asked her, "**Why are you crying? Did you not see the king?**" The little girl sobbed and replied, "**Yes, teacher, I did. BUT THE KING DID NOT SEE ME.**"

LEARNINGS
FOR LEADERS

JULIA WARD HOWE

Julia Ward Howe, a human-right activist, was one day having a word with renowned American senator, Charles Sumner. Julia requested Sumner to help her by taking time out to provide his assistance to a person in need of help. Senator Sumner answered, "**I would love to help, Julia. But I've become so busy that I can no longer concern myself with individuals.**"

Julia sarcastically replied, "**Why Charles, that's REMARKABLE. Even God hasn't reached that stage yet where he is too busy to concern himself with individuals.**"

CHARLES SUMNER

Seasoned leaders know they have a responsibility towards their stakeholder segments as a whole, but they never forget that their stakeholder segments are ultimately made up of individual people. Such seasoned leaders judiciously allocate their time between addressing larger organisational concerns as well as the professional troubles and personal problems of their people.

This also serves as a reminder to their subordinates that their leader considers individuals sufficiently important to concern himself with their personal issues and dilemmas. These subordinates in turn will also devote a certain amount of time to addressing concerns of other individuals (customers, suppliers, subordinates), and thus the leader ensures through leading by example that any individual of any stature who falls within the scope and purview of the organisation's sphere of activities will not be ignored.

221

THE STAR THROWER

A beautiful story which is relevant here was originally written by Loren Eiseley, an anthropologist and animal lover, who hoped through his work to motivate others to be kind to creatures of all kinds and of all shapes and sizes. But although the story may refer to a non-human creature, the message for human-beings is the same, for we are all God's creations.

Here is the story, lovingly retold by Peter Straube:

Once upon a time, there was an old man who used to go to the ocean to do his writing. He had a habit of walking on the beach every morning before he began his work. Early one morning, he was walking along the shore after a big storm had passed and found the vast beach littered with starfish as far as the eye could see, stretching in both directions. Off in the distance, the old man noticed a small boy approaching. As the boy walked, he paused every so often and as he grew closer, the man could see that he was occasionally bending down to pick up an object and throw it into the sea. The boy came closer still and the man called out, **"Good morning! May I ask what it is that you are doing?"**

The young boy paused, looked up, and replied **"Throwing starfish into the ocean. The tide has washed them up onto the beach and they can't return to the sea by themselves. When the sun gets high, they will die, unless I throw them back into the water."**

The old man replied, **"But there must be tens of thousands of starfish on this beach. I'm afraid you won't really be able to make much of a difference."** The boy bent down, picked up yet another starfish and threw it as far as he could into the ocean. Then he turned, smiled, and said, **"It made a difference to THAT one!"**

Giuseppe Garibaldi was an Italian general and politician, known as one of the 'fathers of modern Italy.' Garibaldi once met a shepherd who was upset as he had lost one of his small lambs. Garibaldi did not pass the shepherd by, but rather instructed his soldiers to search the surrounding hillside and countryside for the lost lamb. Since night had fallen, the soldiers scoured the area with lanterns, but returned empty-handed.

The next morning, Garibaldi slept on later than usual, and when at last his servant approached Garibaldi to waken him, he found Garibaldi asleep with the lost lamb, which Garibaldi then instructed his servant to restore to the shepherd. Even after all the other soldiers had given up the search, Garibaldi had not given up till he found that one lost lamb and brought it to safety.

GIUSEPPE GARIBALDI

> *I know there are thousands and thousands of poor, but I think of only one at a time. What we do is nothing but a drop in the ocean. But if we didn't do it, the ocean would be one drop less. I never look at the masses as my responsibility. I look at the individual. I can love only one person at a time. I can feed only one person at a time*

MOTHER TERESA

POINTS TO PONDER AND PRACTICE

- Your organisation/department/team may be small, mid-sized, or large. **But one thing is for sure – it is made up of individual people**

- It is these individuals, who, when together blended as a motivated team, ensure success for you and your organisation. Do not consider only the overall team as important, but focus on the individuals who comprise the team. Just as a team has concerns which need to be solved, so do individuals have their own personal concerns. If these concerns are not resolved, the output of the team suffers. Thus a wise leader gives importance to even resolving the personal problems that individuals on his team may be facing

OFFER
CONSTRUCTIVE CRTICISM

" Every human being is entitled to courtesy and consideration. Constructive criticism is not only to be expected but sought "

-MARGARET CHASE SMITH

WHAT **J.R.D.** BELIEVED IN AND **PRACTICED**

" A pure heart does not demean the spirit of an individual. It, instead, compels the individual to examine his spirit "

-CRISS JAMI

As elaborated in a later learning in this book, J.R.D. was a firm believer in a 'hands-on' style of management.

Even in the years after Air India was well established and J.R.D. was still its Chairman, he frequently flew by Air India as a passenger and would closely observe aspects such as levels of cleanliness and hygiene, housekeeping and upkeep, decor, service levels, and the like. Not only would he observe these things with a critical eye, he would take down detailed notes, and after his flight had landed, he would send memos and reports based on what he had experienced and observed during the course of his flight to the Managing Director or to the concerned General Manager of the airline for further action.

In one particular memo, with regard to a flight he had flown by from Bombay to Paris, he wrote a very detailed letter to the General Manager of Air India, outlining his various observations during the course of the flight.

He commenced the memo by clarifying that the suggestions and comments he provided were offered with the sole purpose of helping and assisting the management to do its job of serving the passengers better. He specifically mentioned that his suggestions, observations, and comments should not be taken as complaints or instructions from the Chairman, nor should they be used for harassing the concerned staff members of the airline.

And it was not only corrections and constructive criticism with the intention of improvement that came from J.R.D.'s pen and lips. **He was generous with praise as well.** As Bakul Khote, who had the privilege of initiating the Customer Service department of Air India says, "Every time 'Jeh' (J.R.D.) travelled by Air India or any other airline he kept long notes on everything he had noticed. **If done well, he was quick to praise. When he went through a group of people, even the humblest felt that he was noticed.**"

On another occasion, in 1972, this is what J.R.D. wrote to the then Director of Engineering of Air India, Mr. K.G. Appuswamy, congratulating him and his team for a job well done. He wrote: 'I travelled back from Geneva last week on Everest (an Air India aircraft), which I believe is by now one of our oldest ships (aeroplanes are also called airships, or ships), and was most impressed by its spotless condition. I do not know whether it had recently come out of overhaul (complete maintenance), but it looked as if it had just been delivered brand new from the factory.'

Such deserving praise from the Chairman, who observed and appreciated good work on behalf of his team, went a long way in ensuring that **operational staff remained motivated and continued to put in their best efforts, secure in the knowledge that their good work was being observed and appreciated and their efforts were not in vain. And they realised that even when criticism did come their way, the intention behind it was always positive and healthy, which made them put in efforts to improve the outcomes of their jobs in line with realistic leadership expectations.**

LEARNINGS ███████████
FOR LEADERS

> **One who utters speech that isn't rough**
> **But instructive and truthful**
> **So that he offends no one,**
> **Him I call Brahmin**
>
> -THE DHAMMAPADA

Criticism as a neutral concept could be defined as the identifying and mentioning of something which is not being done right, or something which could be improved upon.

By itself, there is nothing wrong with the concept of criticism, as looking at the definition, its aim would be to improve upon an existing outcome.

The problem often associated with it lies in the intent and type of criticism being applied. There is something called as 'constructive criticism' and then there is the type I would term 'malicious,' 'destructive,' 'vindictive,' or 'mindless criticism.' It is this second category which is the dangerous one.

Malicious criticism is that which is done for the sake of primarily belittling the other person, or done with negative intent. No solution for improvement or betterment is offered, and the tone of the critic in this case is negative, rather than positive.

Most individuals with a healthy attitude would welcome positive or constructive criticism, which is done with the intent to better things, or to guide and show the recipient a better, an improved, or the right way.

Henry L. Jordan writes: 'I was coaching my son in tennis. He tossed up the ball, swung his racquet and his first serve landed right in the net. "You're hitting into the net," I called. He shifted his stance, took a different grip on the racquet handle, and tried again. Same result. "It's going into the net," I told him again. He glared at me and made another try. "Still going into the net," I said pleasantly. He flung his racquet to the ground. "Look," he told me. "I can see that its going into the net as well as you can. You don't need to sound like a broken record about it. **Tell me what to do to keep it from going into the net.**"

A leader who observes that things are not being done correctly should first identify if a better way is possible within the available resources provided to the concerned staff. If yes, then he could first commend and praise the person on the positive aspects of performance observed, and later show the person the areas where improvement is possible, how this improvement could be made, and why this improvement, if made, would be better for all concerned.

A true leader would, when offering suggestions for improvement, take time and effort to clarify to the person being corrected that the observations and suggestions being made and provided should be taken in the right spirit. This would result in win-win for all concerned.

The leader needs to identify areas which are praiseworthy as well as areas where he needs to constructively criticise. People like to be recognised for the good they are doing. Praise at least twice as often as you criticise. That is a thumb-rule for good leaders to adopt.

Thomas Carlyle was a Scottish philosopher who lived in the 1800s. One Sunday morning, he was getting dressed to deliver a speech to a large audience. His mother asked him, "**And where might you be going, Thomas?**"

Thomas replied, "**Mother, I am going to tell the people what is wrong with the world.**"

His mother tugged gently on his sleeve and said, "**Yes, Thomas. But are you going to tell them what to do about it?**"

POINTS TO PONDER AND PRACTICE

- How often do **you** compliment others as compared to how often you criticise? Make it a ratio of at least two-is-to-one in favour of complimenting as compared to criticising. This will be a sure way of ensuring your team views you in a positive light. **It will also make them more open to accepting criticism when you do give it, as they know you are also capable of giving praise where and when it is due**

- Never merely criticise without following up by showing an improved way. If possible, demonstrate or at least explain in detail that improved way yourself, so that the person being corrected knows exactly what is to be done. Also, **ensure that the person you are correcting has the resources and the time to do the tasks in the way you tell them they should be done**. Only then could it be termed as constructive criticism.

- Remember the wise words of **Abraham Lincoln**:
  "He has a right to criticise, who has a heart to help"

EVOLVED LEADERS KEEP THEIR DOORS (AND HEARTS) OPEN TO ALL

> *When I look at a person, I see a person – not a rank, not a class, not a title*
>
> -CRISS JAMI

WHAT J.R.D. BELIEVED IN AND PRACTICED

> *Rational thought is knowledge without bias*
>
> -UNKNOWN

In the late 1980s, or in the early 1990s (I forget which), I had attended a talk given by J.R.D. Tata at a Parsi colony in Mumbai. Many Parsi community youth were present, attending the talk. J.R.D., the grand old man, clearly told the Parsi (the community to which J.R.D. himself belonged) youth that the doors of his organisation were as open to them as to anyone from any other community. Merit in all regards would be the sole criteria, and that if the youth of the Parsi community felt that they stood an edge in employment simply because of the fact that they belonged to the same community, it was not quite right for them to think so.

At that moment this may have sounded harsh to some present, but it also reminded many of the proverb – **Give a man a fish, and feed him for a day. Teach a man to fish, and feed him for a lifetime**. By stating what he did, **he indirectly encouraged and motivated the youth to study hard, acquire professional qualifications, develop and sharpen essential career-enhancing skills, and thus ensured that they equipped themselves to face all challenges of life in a confident manner.**

J.R.D. believed in equal opportunities for all – irrespective of caste, creed and gender.

But this does not mean that Mr. J.R.D. Tata was not religious or spiritually inclined.

Indeed, in his personal life he had a deep love for his religion, and he valued his religion more than any business deal, as the following anecdote will amply demonstrate.

Pope Paul VI

In the book *J.R.D. - As Air Indians Remember*, (conceived and compiled by M. S. Kohli); it is narrated how Nari Dastur, a senior executive with Air India during the Tata days, recalls the time when he (Nari) was Manager – Italy, for Air India, when **Pope Paul VI** was to visit India in 1964. The Air India staff in Rome were working hard to ensure that the Pope would consent to fly from Rome to India with Air India, as the Pope had previously flown only Alitalia (the Italian national carrier) and by no other foreign airline.

After a long and hard corporate struggle, Nari Dastur 'won,' and the Pope travelled by Air India from Rome to Mumbai (then Bombay).

J.R.D. congratulated Nari on this achievement and was curious to find out how it had been achieved. **Nari said it was a hard battle, and jokingly remarked to J.R.D. that even if he (Nari), himself a Parsi like J.R.D., had to convert and become a Catholic to get the Pope to fly by Air India, he would have done it**. On hearing this J.R.D. got genuinely upset and angry and said to Nari, **"How dare you say that! You! A Dastur!** (A *Dastur* is a member of the Parsi priestly class.) I would have never believed it to be possible. **I don't want to hear such words from you ever again!"**

232

The above reveals just how much J.R.D. valued his religion in his personal life, but yet when it came to recruiting staff for the Tatas, he was professionalism personified.

J.R.D. was a firm believer in God and spiritual power, as the following quote by him will testify:

**'When you WORK, work as if everything depends on you.
When you PRAY, pray as if everything depends on God.'**

When J.R.D. passed away in Switzerland, it was Nari Dastur who arranged for a Parsi priest (a *Dasturji*) to come over from Germany and recite the Parsi prayers over his earthly remains. (That Parsi priest, Mr. Erach R. Gonda, is the younger brother of my late father, Mr. Minoo R. Gonda.)

The Tatas have always been primarily patriotic. Even later, after J.R.D.'s time, when the Tata Group was identifying a successor for Ratan Tata, who was voluntarily stepping down as Chairman on attaining the age of 75, Ratan Tata himself said, **"My successor will not be anti-Parsi or pro-Parsi, but will be the right person. The Tata Group is an Indian group and we should not be looking at it as a Parsi group."** Thus once again displaying the high levels of patriotism displayed not only by J.R.D. as an individual but by the Tatas as a family philosophy.

(Photo – kind courtesy – *Jame-Jamshed* newspaper)

In the above photograph - J.R.D. Tata (right) with Eruch Desai (left), J.N. Guzder (centre left) and Dr. (Ms) Mehroo Bengalee (centre right)

This photo shows Mr. J.R.D. Tata in full traditional Parsi outfit being felicitated at a function by Mr. Eruch Desai and Mr. J.N. Guzder, (both former Bombay Parsi Panchayat Chairpersons), along with Dr. (Ms) Mehroo Bengalee (former Bombay Panchayet trustee and former Vice Chancellor – Mumbai University)

LEARNINGS
FOR LEADERS

" Great vision without great people is irrelevant "

-JIM COLLINS

At a time when many management institutes around the country are laying claim to 'Number One' position on the strength of the job-placements they offer, it would be an eye-opener to delve a little deeper into this whole rigmarole of their placement 'game.'

Most of the institutes which offer the best placements proudly claim that they do so because of their **strongly entrenched alumni network** currently employed in the corporate world. What does this actually mean? A management institute, which has been in existence for many years, already has its former students (alumni) well placed in decision-making positions in corporate houses, and makes use of them to place their current students in these corporate houses, primarily playing on their sentiments as they belong to the same institute.

This entire exercise comes under a human resource activity broadly termed as 'selection.'

In management colleges, when the topic of 'selection' is taught, one of the sub-topics under 'selection' is 'Errors made by Interviewers.' **An error obviously means a fault or a defect in the process.**

If the objective of the process of selection is to select the most suitable candidate from those available, anything which prevents this from happening would be an error and needs to be corrected.

One common error made by many interviewers has been identified as 'bias' or 'partiality.' This means, if an interviewer selects a candidate for reasons other than merit and suitability to job profile; maybe on the basis of a common hometown, mother-tongue, or a common college attended, it results in incorrect and erroneous selection, as these factors have no role to play in merit and job suitability, as far as the organisation is concerned.

Thus the leading management institutes which proudly proclaim that it is their well-placed alumni network which is primarily responsible for their good placement record, are actually propagating and perpetuating a common, primary error in the selection process.

This happens despite the fact that the management students are taught in class to **NOT** be biased while selecting.

J.R.D. Tata actually practiced unbiased selection, keeping merit as a criterion, and not favouring members of his own community at the cost of another.

If all corporate houses practiced this philosophy of equitability, merit in the corporate sector would truly reign supreme.

POINTS TO PONDER AND PRACTICE

- Ensure that you encourage your subordinates to constantly hone and upgrade their work-related skills by encouraging them to volunteer for and participate in optional training programmes, by inculcating the reading habit, and also if possible by enrolling for relevant evening, weekend, or correspondence certificate or diploma courses. Making this a practice ensures win-win, as when the employees are armed with needed skills, it gives your organisation a competitive edge, as well as secures the future career prospects of these individuals

- If you wish to offer the best quality offering to your customer base and thus build a strong and lasting brand, select people who are deserving, meritorious and honest. These would be the prime criteria on which your selection policy should be based

EVERY LEADER NEEDS TO BE A GOOD HUMAN RESOURCE PERSON

> " *To be a leader, you have got to lead human beings with affection* "
>
> -J.R.D. TATA

WHAT J.R.D. BELIEVED IN AND PRACTICED

> " *The growth and development of people is the highest calling of leadership* "
>
> -HARVEY S. FIRESTONE

The term 'Human Resources Management' evolved in the 1980s, when enlightened organisations and their leaders realised the supreme importance of the human factor as a key positive organisational differentiator. Until then, the human factor (in general) had been considered the mere equivalent or even less important than other resources such as land, money, machinery, market, and all the rest.

J.R.D. as a leader was far ahead of his time, and realised and appreciated the importance of the human factor in organisational success far before the 1980s, which was when it became popularly fashionable to believe so.

He genuinely liked and trusted people, and that was vital as it made him first and foremost a good man manager.

When it came to the all-important issue of labour welfare and people relations, J.R.D. had established very clear and fair principles in these matters, which he implicitly followed and practiced.

The **first principle** which he felt was imperative for getting along with people was **frank, open,** and **on-going communication**. In fact, the smooth relationship established between the management and the workers at Tata Steel, Jamshedpur, which is considered a model case-study in superb labour relations, is largely based on **continuous communication and dialogue**, where all major as well as minor issues of concern and importance were discussed thread-bare till both sides understood all issues and reached common ground before proceeding together on the road ahead.

The **second principle** J.R.D. implicitly believed in and practiced when it came to dealing with people was the **practice of absolute honesty and genuine sincerity**. This prevented misunderstandings and mistrust, which are so often the cause of otherwise great teams and organisations collapsing by the wayside.

And the **third principle** of leading people which J.R.D. believed in was **having trust in and also liking the people who had the good fortune to be led by him**.

J.R.D. was a firm believer in the cause of employee welfare. He espoused the philosophy and practice of an eight-hour working day, thus ensuring the concept of work-life balance for his employees. He also initiated for his employees free medical aid and a workman's accident compensation scheme as well as a worker's provident fund scheme, at a time when these were not mandatory requirements according to Indian labour laws.

So advanced and globally renowned were J.R.D.'s genuine efforts in improving employee welfare and enhancing labour relations, that on 11th August, 1953, the *National Association of Foremen of USA* announced that its annual **"international management man award will go this year to J.R.D. Tata of Bombay for his work in developing modern and humane industrial relations in Indian plants and factories."**

In 1979, TISCO, under J.R.D.'s stewardship initiated a **revolutionary, previously unheard of practice in India** – that of deeming a workman to be on duty from the moment he left home for work till he reached home from work after completing his duty. Thus TISCO would take full financial responsibility for the worker in case of any unfortunate mishap to or on his way back from work.

J.R.D. was always practically innovative, not only in ensuring his customers and passengers were offered the best quality of product or service, but also in keeping his employees comfortable and at peace with win-win human resource practices and offerings.

Indeed, a leader cannot be considered a great leader, unless, like J.R.D., he truly **values** his people.

> *There are no business problems, management problems, leadership problems, or profit problems. There are only PEOPLE problems*
>
> -DAN WALDSCHMIDT

LEARNINGS
FOR LEADERS

> *Human resources are like natural resources; they're often buried deep. You have to go looking for them, they're not just lying around on the surface. You have to create the circumstances where they show themselves*

-KEN ROBINSON

I t is said that every manager, irrespective of the function he heads, whether it be marketing, sales, finance, operations, or any other, is primarily a human resource manager. The reason for this is clear. The definition of the term *manager* itself encompasses motivating others to perform their best, getting the individuals to perform as a team, and ensuring that people want to do a good, creative, error-free job, by channelising their energies and efforts in the right direction.

Once a manager or leader can achieve this, his organisation can be a force to reckon with, and can overcome larger players with superior resources who have failed to utilise their manpower in an optimum manner.

Men can never be PUSHED or PULLED into doing a good job. They need to be LED.

A brief history of the human resource function follows, and makes interesting reading.

First came the concept of **labour relations**, which evolved to **personnel** and then to **human resources** and now again in India it is back to labour and industrial relations which is becoming the 'in-thing' when it comes to acquiring qualifications and work experience for people-handling jobs.

The manufacturing sector in India (and world-wide), is witnessing a boost and a much-needed revival, and along with the thrust on manufacturing comes a focus on blue-collar and factory workers and labour laws and legislations and the understanding and application of various acts such as the Factories Act and so on.

People-handling is a skilled activity – an art as well as a science, and requires the development and sharpening of hard-skills as well as soft-skills. Relevant knowledge of minimum pay, compensation structure and packages, labour laws, domestic inquiry committees, and the like is as important as involving oneself with the functions of recruitment, employee appraisal, training and development, counselling, chalking-out career paths, and so on.

Of course, despite acquiring all the above knowledge, if the three principles for effectively handling and leading people as espoused by J.R.D. are not practiced, good human relations between management and the workforce will remain a distant dream.

We often hear so much about the phenomenal success of *Google,* which is primarily due to its unique brand of leadership. But if you study this leadership style in-depth, what emerges is that Google's resounding success is strongly based on its excellent people management policies, which in turn give Google its technical superiority and leading edge.

" *It all comes down to this: If you want one year of happiness, grow grain. If you want ten years of happiness, grow trees. If you want hundred years of happiness, grow people* "

-HARVEY MACKAY

POINTS TO PONDER AND PRACTICE

- Treat others as you would yourself like to be treated. That would seem to be a simple, and golden rule for effective people handling. Of course, the needs of the organisation and its other stakeholders should be kept in mind while also ensuring your people are well looked after

- In most cases, if you select the right set of people, if you focus on their development and well-being and honestly and transparently share with them your organisational objective and define their roles clearly, motivating them in the right manner and maintaining healthy two-way lines of communication, all will be well in your organisation in the long term

Good human relations not only bring great personal rewards but are also essential to the success of any enterprise

-J.R.D. TATA

LEADERS NEED TO CONTINUOUSLY WORK ON FINE-TUNING THEIR COMMUNICATION SKILLS

> *The basic block of good communication is the feeling that every human being is unique and of value*
>
> -UNKNOWN

WHAT **J.R.D.** BELIEVED IN AND **PRACTICED**

> *You can have brilliant ideas, but if you can't get them across, your ideas won't get you anywhere*
>
> -LEE IACOCCA

The Tata group has always been renowned for being an open and transparent organisation.

J.R.D. carried forward the on-going Tata tradition of being a proactively communicative leader.

He was always anxious that the channels of communication between him and his people should remain open and transparent, thus preventing needless misunderstandings. He did his best to ensure that staff relations never deteriorated, and put in his best efforts to ensure that he remained close to his people.

In a message to his staff at Air India in 1967, he said:

"My only regret is that the growth of the airline has made it difficult for me to keep in touch with any but a few of you. This, I suppose, is inevitable in large organisations such as ours, but even so, I have increasingly felt that communications between members of the top management, including myself, and the bulk of our staff have become too tenuous, and in some places actually non-existent. **This inevitably results in a lack of understanding of each other's problems, motives and feelings, and leads to misunderstanding and mistrust. I am anxious, therefore, to find ways and means of improving communications between top management and all categories of our officers, staff and workers.**"

Not only did he convey this heart-felt message to his people, but to prove that he was genuinely concerned about maintaining two-way channels of communication, he invited suggestions from staff as to how this could be achieved.

I have yet to personally hear of a current-day CEO of a large Indian conglomerate feeling so strongly from the heart about wanting to improve staff relations, and focusing on simple, old-fashioned, but highly effective personalised communication as the primary tool for doing so.

LEARNINGS FOR LEADERS

" There has never been a better time for people in business to reconnect through meaningful communication to what matters most to them and to each other for the greater good "

-Miti Ampoma

Unfortunately, the emphasis on communication in most organisations today is merely cosmetic.

The content for most training programmes for effective communication reads more like the syllabus of a public speaking course.

But public speaking is only one small part of the entire gamut of leadership communication.

The vital ingredient of interpersonal and face-to-face communication in the corporate success recipe is rarely given the importance it deserves.

When it comes to communication, leaders must not merely focus on improving and perfecting their accent, grammar, vocabulary, and body language, but also strengthen the vital elements of:

- Honesty
- Transparency
- Willingness to be corrected
- Receiving and providing feedback

Organisations where leaders communicate to their people regularly, conveying both good news as well as not-so-good-news, invite and welcome inputs from people down the line and actually listen to such inputs, and communicate a sense of oneness in terms of a clear corporate objective, are the organisations where success is assured.

Jeffrey Bleustein, the charismatic CEO of **Harley-Davidson**, was almost fanatical about making himself approachable and available to all his stakeholders. He believed in mingling and mixing with customers, employees, investors and even suppliers. He preferred face-to-face meetings as that way he could grasp the feelings and emotions of the stakeholders he met. This led to him intimately understanding their needs so Jeffrey could then proceed to erect strong, trustful, mutually beneficial relationships.

Not only him, but also his wife Brenda, attended around a dozen Harley Owners Group rallies annually, with each such rally being attended by over a hundred thousand Harley-Davidson enthusiasts. Jeffrey and his executives did not merely sit on a stage at these rallies, but mingled and even rode bikes with customers and encouraged the rally participants to share their problems and ideas.

From the information secured at these rallies, many profitable products and training programmes for Harley dealers and customers were developed. Jeffrey Bleustein said there was no way such strong personal relationships could be developed by sitting in an office. As he put it, **"You need to spend time together, to develop relationships so that you really get at the heart of what's important to the relationship."**

With such leaders at the helm, no wonder Harley-Davidson till today remains an iconic brand with a huge cult following.

POINTS TO PONDER AND PRACTICE

- Regularly communicate corporate vision, ethical standards expected by the organisation, changes in strategy and tactics, goals, plans and financial figures to people throughout the organisation

- Explain clearly to individuals their exact job responsibilities, expectations in terms of deliverables, exactly and on what parameters their performance will be appraised, remuneration methodology and systems, and other essentials, so they are able to focus on getting their work done and do not have to worry about whether they are doing their job right and how they will be rewarded for it

- One thing is for certain. The more you sincerely work on improving practical communication skills, you will be recognised and appreciated as a better leader

J.R.D. TATA
IN PICTURES

(Images are kind courtesy of Tata Central Archives, Pune)

254

A GOOD LEADER IS ABOVE ALL A KEEN LISTENER

> *Wisdom is the reward you get for a lifetime of listening when you'd have preferred to talk*
>
> -DOUG LARSON

WHAT J.R.D. BELIEVED IN AND PRACTICED

> *A good listener is not only popular everywhere, but after a while he gets to know something*
>
> -WILSON MIZNER

Nari Dastur, Air India's Regional Director for Europe during J.R.D.'s tenure as Air India chairman, recalls an instance when a conference had been organised by the Indian Government in Frankfurt to identify ways and means to encourage European tourist traffic to be diverted to Indian destinations. The conference was attended by the then Indian Minister for Tourism, the Indian Director-General for Tourism, and other concerned dignitaries. J.R.D. was also invited to and was present at this conference.

All the delegates were enthusiastic and talked in glowing terms about India's most obvious tourist attractions – Goa, and the beaches of Kerala. **Everyone TALKED, but one man LISTENED.**

That one man was J.R.D.

As often happens, the excitement of the conference died away for most of the delegates as soon as the conference concluded, and they forgot what they had so eagerly discussed as they returned to office and went about their other work.

But the man who had spoken little at the conference and who had truly listened, absorbing all that was said, and analysing it in his active mind, returned to India with the lessons of the conference intact, and immediately initiated the construction of two premier hotels in prime locations in Goa, named the **Fort Aguada Hotel** and the **Taj Village**. Today, these two hotels are prime destinations for international tourists visiting India and wishing to sample the delights of Goa. These two deluxe hotels, which provide five-star deluxe hospitality to their delighted guests, saw the light of day, because J.R.D. like the others not only attended the conference, but unlike the others, genuinely listened.

Fort Aguada Hotel - GOA

258

LEARNINGS FOR LEADERS

> *Growing organisations in any field must constantly evolve, accept or even seek new ideas, new visions, and new enthusiasms*

-J.R.D. TATA

Every leader will agree that communication is one of the most important of leadership traits and responsibilities.

But while communication in general is given due importance by most leaders, that vital part of communication, **listening,** which forms more than fifty percent of practical communication, is rarely given the importance it deserves.

Communication is often assumed to consist almost entirely of speaking. **It is incorrectly assumed by most of us that listening will happen anyway.** It does not. Although we have two ears, and only one mouth, and the ears are placed at a higher level on the human body than the mouth (perhaps Mother Nature's way of subtly indicating their superiority), **for most of us our assessment of our communication skills consists almost entirely of how well we speak or write, not how intently and productively we listen**.

This is a tragedy, as we never really learn anything while we speak – we only learn while we are listening.

And leaders, in this highly fast-paced and competitive era, need all the learning they can get.

Always be aware and alert of your surroundings. Let nothing distract you from your ability to listen, especially when you are in an environment and situation where you need to keep your eyes and ears open and focused on the work at hand.

While waiting in a shipping company office to be interviewed for a job as a wireless operator, a group of applicants filled the reception area with such a steady buzz of conversation that they were oblivious to the dots and dashes that began coming over a loudspeaker placed high on a wall in that room.

Around that time, another man entered the reception area and sat down quietly by himself. Suddenly he stood to attention, walked into the private office through a door in the reception area, and a few minutes later came out smiling, telling the other applicants to leave, as he'd got the job.

"How'd you get in ahead of us? We were here first," called out one of the applicants indignantly.

"One of you would have gotten the job," the successful applicant replied, **"if you had listened to the message from the loudspeaker."**

"What message?" they all asked in surprise. They had been too busy chatting with one another to have actually listened to anything else around them.

"Why, the message in **Morse Code**," the man answered. "The message in Morse Code (which is shipping language and works by beeping sounds in a series of dots and dashes), which said:

'The man I need must always be on the alert. The first one who gets this message and comes directly into my private office through the door in the reception area will be placed on one of my ships as wireless operator.'"

Amelita Galli-Curci was a famous Italian opera singer. Once, while she was resting in her dressing room after a stage performance, she heard a knock on the door. Used to receiving visits from aspiring singers and musicians hoping to use her influence to climb the ladder of success in the music industry, she was surprised to see at the door a shy young girl holding a bouquet of flowers.

Having invited her young admirer in, Amelita asked her, "**Do you sing?**"

"**Oh, no,**" said the girl.

"**Then do you play any instrument?**" asked Amelita, probing further.

"**Oh, no,**" said the girl again, "**I JUST LISTEN.**"

Galli-Curci was touched and embraced the young girl, saying –

"**I had quite forgotten that there were still people left who ONLY listen.**"

Today, there is an oversupply of speaking, and a corresponding short-supply of listening. People who can listen to others are actively needed.

Take time to listen.

Invest energy in listening.

Real listening is probably much harder to do than speaking for most people.

We are social beings, and we need others to listen to us as much as we need others to speak to.

Things to do to be a better listener:

- Use facial expression, body positioning and eyes to show you are truly interested

- Don't interrupt while the person is speaking

- Ask questions to show you are on track and interested

- Use words and phrases such as – "Go ahead, tell me more"

- Avoid phrases such as – "That was wrong of you", "You shouldn't have done that", "You shouldn't feel that way", "You're making an issue out of nothing"

Real listening has great value.

The problem with listening is that the more we listen to others, the more we are likely to react – or even overreact – to what they have to say. Resist the temptation to react and just listen without judging. People want to be heard, and until they are heard, they will fight to be heard. The key is hearing them out. Listening is risky, as it may make us hear things we don't want to or are not comfortable with. As you understand their perspective, slowly you will feel your resistance drop. Listening does not mean you have to agree with what the other person says. But if we are truly interested in learning more about ourselves and about others, about being better connected to others, about strengthening our relationships and solving problems and conflict areas that exist between us, there is nothing else as good as listening to clear the air.

> **" A pair of good ears will drain dry a hundred tongues "**
>
> -Bob Phillips

Jack Welch, the CEO of General Electric once told his workers, "Real communication is an attitude, an environment. It's the most interactive of all processes. It requires countless hours of eyeball-to-eyeball back and forth. **It involves more listening than talking.** It is a constant, interactive process aimed at creating consensus."

AN EFFECTIVE EXERCISE – Next time you are with a client or with a colleague, and they are yearning to tell you something which obviously matters a lot to them, try this. See how long you can listen with full focus to what they have to say, without interrupting or adding your own points. All you should allow yourself to say are things such as 'hmm,' 'what happened next?' 'that's interesting,' and so on. See how long you can keep the person speaking. It is a good exercise to develop your discipline to truly listen.

> **" If speaking is silver, then listening is gold "**
>
> -Turkish Proverb

Sensei Terry Dobson, a pioneer of the sport of Aikido, tells a slightly lengthy but lovely tale in his book *Safe And Alive*:

'The train clanked and rattled through the suburbs of Tokyo on a drowsy spring afternoon. Our car (train compartment), was comparatively empty, - a few housewives with their kids in tow, some old folks going shopping. I gazed absently at the drab houses and dusty hedgerows. At one station the doors opened, and suddenly the afternoon quiet was shattered by a man bellowing violent, incomprehensible curses. The man staggered into our car. He wore labourer's clothing and was big, drunk and dirty. Screaming, he swung at a woman holding a baby. The blow sent her spinning into the laps of an elderly couple. It was a miracle that the baby was unharmed.

Terrified, the couple jumped up and scrambled toward the other end of the car. The labourer aimed a kick at the retreating back of the old woman, but missed as she scuttled to safety. This so enraged the drunk that he grabbed the metal pole in the centre of the car and tried to wrench it out of its stanchion (upright fixture that provides support). I could see that one of his hands was cut and bleeding. The train lurched ahead, the passengers frozen with fear. I stood up. I was young then, some twenty years ago, and in pretty good shape. I'd been putting in a solid eight hours of Aikido (a Japanese martial art) training nearly every day for the past three years. I liked to throw and grapple. I thought I was tough. The trouble was, my martial art skill was untested in actual combat. As students of Aikido, we were not allowed to fight.

"Aikido," my teacher had said again and again, "is the art of reconciliation. Whoever has the mind to fight has broken his connection with the universe. If you try to dominate people, you're already defeated. We study how to resolve, not start conflict."

I listened to his words. I tried hard. I even went so far as to cross the street to avoid the *chimpira*, the pinball punks who lounged around the train stations. My forbearance exalted me. I felt both tough and holy. In my heart, however, I wanted an absolutely legitimate opportunity whereby I might save the innocent by destroying the guilty.

........continued

264

"This is it," I said to myself as I got to my feet. "People are in danger. If I don't do something fast, people will probably get hurt."

Seeing me stand up, the drunk recognised a chance to focus his rage. "Aha!" he roared. "A foreigner. You need a lesson in Japanese manners!"

I held on tightly to the commuter strap and gave him a slow look of disgust and dismissal. I planned to take this turkey apart, but he had to make the first move. I wanted him mad, so I pursed my lips and blew him an insolent kiss.

"All right!" he hollered. "You're gonna get a lesson!" He gathered himself for a rush at me. A fraction of a second before he could move, someone shouted, "**HEY!**" It was earsplitting. I remember the strangely joyous, lilting quality of it – as though you and a friend had been searching diligently for something, and he had suddenly stumbled upon it. "Hey!" I heard it again.

I wheeled to my left; the drunk spun to his right. We both stared down at a little old Japanese man. He must have been well into his seventies, this tiny gentleman, sitting there in his immaculate kimono. He took no notice of me, but beamed delightedly at the labourer, as though he had a most important, most welcome secret to share.

"Come here," the old man said, in an easy vernacular, beckoning to the drunk. "C'mere and talk with me." He waved his hands lightly. The big man followed, as if on a string. He planted his feet belligerently in front of the old gentleman and roared above the clacking wheels. "Why the hell should I talk to you?" The drunk now had his back to me. If his elbow moved so much as a millimetre, I'd drop him in his socks.

The old man continued to beam at the labourer. "What'cha been drinking?" he asked, his eyes sparkling with interest. "I been drinkin' *sake* (Japanese rice wine)," the labourer bellowed back, "and it's none of your business!" Flecks of spittle spattered the old man.

........*continued*

"Oh, that's wonderful," the old man said, "absolutely wonderful! You see, I love *sake* too. Every night, me and my wife – she's seventy-six, you know – we warm up a little bottle of *sake* and take it out into the garden, and we sit on an old wooden bench. We watch the sun go down, and we look to see how our persimmon tree is doing. My great grandfather planted that tree, and we worry about whether it will recover from those ice storms we had last winter. Our tree has done better than I expected, though, especially when you consider the poor quality of the soil. It is gratifying to watch when we take our *sake* and go out to enjoy the evening – even when it rains!" He looked up at the labourer, eyes twinkling.

As he struggled to follow the old man, his face began to soften. His fists slowly unclenched. "Yeah," he said. "I love persimmons too...." His voice trailed off.

"Yes," smiled the old man, "and I'm sure you have a wonderful wife."

"No," replied the labourer. "My wife died." Very gently, swaying with the motion of the train, the big man began to sob. "I don't got no wife. I don't got no home. I don't got no job. I'm so ashamed of myself." Tears rolled down his cheeks; a spasm of despair rippled through his body.

As I stood there in my well-scrubbed youthful innocence, my 'make-this-world-safe-for-democracy' righteousness, I felt dirtier than he was.

Then the train arrived at my stop. As the doors opened, I heard the old man cluck sympathetically. **"My, my,"** he said, **"THAT IS A DIFFICULT PREDICAMENT INDEED. SIT DOWN HERE AND TELL ME ABOUT IT."**

I turned my head for one last look. The labourer was sprawled on the seat with his head in the old man's lap. The old man was softly stroking the filthy, matted hair.

As the train pulled away, I sat down on a bench in the station. What I had wanted to do with muscle had been accomplished with kind words. I had just seen Aikido in action, and the essence of it was love. I would have to practice the art with an entirely different spirit. It would be a long time before I could speak about the resolution of conflict.'

266

POINTS TO PONDER AND PRACTICE

- How would you honestly rate yourself as a listener?

- Do you pay full attention when others are speaking?

- While others are speaking, are you already formulating your response as to what to say next?

- Have you often been checked and corrected for interrupting others?

- Do you respect and pay attention to others' points of view even if they do contradict with your own?

- **The above questions are worth investing time over.** Formulate your responses to these questions honestly, and if you feel you are not up to the mark on any of these vital parameters, seek the help of someone who you feel is good at listening and can help you improve on the same

- If you already are a good listener, you, like J.R.D., must have benefited from it. If you have not actively focused on improving your listening skills, then practice true listening by implementing the few action points mentioned above. Like most other skills, improved listening is not difficult to understand, but requires discipline to acquire

- But, after all, for a leader, discipline in all respects is also a must. So instil the self-discipline to become an effective listener. You will need this skill to succeed in your leadership role

" I make progress by having people around me who are smarter than I am – and listening to them. And I assume that everyone is smarter about something than I am "

-HENRY KAISER
(INDUSTRIALIST – KNOWN AS THE 'FATHER OF MODERN AMERICAN SHIPBUILDING')

DIGNIFIED LEADERS DISPLAY
'A SENSE OF OCCASION'

> " *Because you believed I was capable of behaving decently, I did* "
>
> -PAULO COELHO

WHAT **J.R.D.**
BELIEVED IN
AND **PRACTICED**

> " *The ABC's are*
>
> • *Attitude*
>
> • *BEHAVIOUR*
>
> • *Communication skills* "
>
> -GERALD CHERTAVIAN

There are those occasions where pure celebration is the motive, some occasions where solemnity is required, and some are simply occasions for quiet reflection.

J.R.D. had an instinctive sense of adopting the appropriate behaviour for the occasion.

This anecdote pertains to Bobby Kooka, the legendary marketing and public relations man who had headed the public relations function for Air India for many decades. He also edited the in-house Tata magazine, and retired from the services of the Tata group in 1971.

At his retirement function, J.R.D. began addressing those gathered to felicitate Bobby with the words, "**First of all, let me remind you all that you haven't been invited here to enjoy yourself. This is a farewell function. As I have often remarked before, a French poet has said, 'To depart is to die a little.' The appropriate behaviour at a farewell party is therefore like at a funeral.**"

These solemn words from J.R.D. reminded those present that while for them it could possibly be an occasion to eat, drink and make merry, for Bobby it was a sweetly-sad occasion, marking the end of a long, fruitful and memorable career with the Tata Group.

It is vital that leaders learn to play this important role – that of setting the appropriate tone for any event or occasion, which, as leaders, they will often be called upon to do.

LEARNINGS FOR LEADERS

Since leaders, by the very nature of their role, are often called upon to preside over occasions of various types, it is important that they perfect the art of appropriateness, as all eyes at any event would inevitably be tuned towards them.

Often, nowadays, we see 'leaders' behaving inappropriately even at solemn occasions, not even realising what behaviour or dress-code would be considered as suitable.

At the funeral of South African statesman Nelson Mandela, President Barrack Hussain Obama of the U.S.A. and a few other world leaders were seen laughing and joking and taking 'selfies' (self photographs) at the funeral. Their actions were widely publicised and highly criticised.

And on the sober occasion of the 70th anniversary of the World War II D-Day landings at Normandy in France in June 2014, during solemn ceremonies to mark the anniversary of the day where thousands sacrificed their lives to gain freedom for the world, again it was President Barrack Hussain Obama who was observed casually chewing gum while the French national anthem was being played. Queen Elizabeth II of England and other world leaders were also present on this solemn occasion and were all standing at attention while President Obama casually chewed gum like a teenager. Observers vented their feelings on Twitter denouncing Obama's **gum-chewing** during the ceremony as **'shameful'** and **'vulgar,'** with one Twitter user even labelling him a 'lout'. Another user tweeted 'Obama do you want a Coke too while chewing gum?' While yet another tweeted 'The Queen arrives and you have Obama chewing gum.'

People notice these things about their leaders more than they do about others.

Leaders not only need to set the tone by themselves behaving appropriately at all occasions, but also need to instruct, request and ensure that their fans, followers, and employees behave accordingly. **Even if it is a celebratory occasion, leaders need to send a message to people that they should enjoy themselves, but not in a manner which causes a disturbance to others.** As a recent example, in May 2014, the Bollywood actor Shahrukh Khan and some people in Kolkota were celebrating the IPL victory of Shahrukh's cricket team, the *Kolkota Knight Riders,* in a manner so disturbing to the general public that riot police had to be called in to bring the situation under control.

It is convenient for a 'leader' to evade responsibility for the behaviour of his fans and followers by saying:

"I never told them to behave in this manner."

But as a leader, it is important that you **SHOULD** guide your people to **NOT** behave in an inappropriate manner.

Leaders need to learn a sense of appropriate decorum and also instil it among their people and their followers. That is one of the reasons, after all, they are called leaders.

Remember, the world is watching, and your leadership brand depends upon it.

Leadership is a matter of having people look at you and gain confidence, seeing how you react. If you're in control, they're in control

-TOM LANDRY

A few centuries ago, when U.S.A. was a very young country, John Winthrop was the governor of the Massachusetts Bay colony. As he and his people faced the daunting task of building a new government in a new land, he addressed them with these words:

"We must always consider that we shall be as a city upon a hill......the eyes of all people will always be upon us."

JOHN WINTHROP

POINTS TO PONDER AND PRACTICE

- Identify the various types of occasions and events which you as a leader would be called upon to preside over. Categorise them into celebratory, formal, solemn, reflective, and any other category that you can think of

- Practice the type of speeches you would make, decide the attire you would wear, the facial expressions and the tone you would adopt, and most importantly the message you would pass on to your people on these occasions. The best leaders plan and practice these things before they appear in public

- Be on your best behaviour at such occasions, as you would by default be the centre of attention at such times. **Make sure you are not a mere spectator to rowdy or inappropriate behaviour indulged in by your people, but rather take the lead in guiding them to behave in an appropriate, dignified and mature manner as befits the disciplined followers of evolved leaders**

THE POWER OF A
KIND WORD AND A SMILE

> *You are never fully dressed without a smile*
>
> -Martin Charnin

WHAT **J.R.D.** BELIEVED IN AND **PRACTICED**

> *A smile is an inexpensive way to improve your looks*
>
> -Charles Gordy

J.R.D. always had a kind word and a smile for all those he came in contact with, whether he knew them or not.

He believed in the positive power and impact that a smile and a few words of genuine praise and appreciation could have on other people.

J.R.D. said: **"The trouble is, we don't smile enough. When I am driving in the car, and a person appears to recognise me, I look at that person and smile. This makes him happy and does not cost me anything."**

The 'J' in the initial of his name could well have stood for '**Jolly**' or '**Jovial**.' (It actually stands for Jehangir.)

Such was his humility, that he held no ego, and smiled and uplifted the spirits of every human being fortunate to cross his path.

ADIL C. BHESADIA

The following was narrated to me by Mr. Adil Coover Bhesadia, a hotelier, a noted caterer, and my good friend. Many years ago, Mr. Bhesadia was seated in the lobby of the Taj Mahal Hotel, Mumbai, with his wife, Yasmin. Adil noticed J.R.D. seated nearby and wanted to approach and have a word with him, but Yasmin felt J.R.D. might not like being disturbed by strangers. Adil was however adamant and did not want to pass up the opportunity to meet J.R.D., and coaxed his wife to accompany him to where J.R.D. was seated. **Adil asked J.R.D. if he could speak with him, and introduced himself and his wife as the proprietors of a small hotel located at Juhu, Mumbai.**

J.R.D. courteously stood up, shook hands with the couple, exchanged small talk, and then uttered words of wisdom and motivation, saying, **"Mr. Bhesadia, never consider yourself small. You will grow big from wherever you have started. Work hard and work honestly, and you will grow in whatever business you are in. All the very best." Adil and Yasmin were touched and their spirits rose at J.R.D.'s honest and genuine efforts at motivating them, a couple whom he had never met before.**

Not only did J.R.D. himself sport a serene smile on his face, he ensured that those he interacted with left him with smiling faces and happy hearts as well.

If you can't do anything else to help along, just smile

-ELEANOR KIRK

A FORMER AIR INDIAN REMEMBERS

Armin Dutia Motashaw, whose poem 'An Ode To JRD' appears in the initial pages of this book, is a former Air Indian who had an opportunity to observe J.R.D.'s unique style of functioning at close quarters. The following are some of her observations on J.R.D. in her own words.

'Such a great man, my hero was. I would love to share a few instances I cherish.

When boarding or deplaning an aircraft, as the commander, he would carry his own bag and never let a loader do so. He would always stand in the queue for the lift and let the ladies go before him. Wow, such discipline! Such chivalry!

At customs he would open the bag for examination, avoiding embarrassing the officer, who would definitely hesitate to ask JRD to open it. (Those days there was no electronic screening.)

He had instructed the Air India staff that whenever Mother Teresa travelled on Air India, she should be upgraded. He had also instructed that all the sweets, candies and toffees that were left in stock on the aircraft at the end of the journey should be given to her for the little children she looked after and lovingly tended to. Think, How very thoughtful and loving JRD was.

There were many such instances in this great man's life. Truly a great son of India. I wish him Garothman Behesht (which is the Highest Heaven in Zoroastrianism.)'

LEARNINGS
FOR LEADERS

> ## " *A smile is a curve that sets everything right* "
> -Phyllis Diller

An extremely interesting and profitable anecdote is narrated in a book on the importance of being a 'nice' person in the corporate world. The gist of it is as follows:

Two leading advertising agencies are competing for a million-dollar contract from a leading brand. The person from the brand's end, who will be the decision-maker as to which advertising agency his brand will award the contract to, is in a dilemma. The two competing agencies are both top-notch, both have successfully developed winning advertising campaigns for their existing clients, and both are the winners of numerous advertising industry awards.

Unable to choose between the two, this decision-maker decides to visit the offices of both these advertising agencies to see if he can identify some differentiator among them on their own respective home grounds. After visiting the offices of both these agencies, he makes his choice, and decides to award the contract to the first agency he visited.

The people from the second agency are naturally disappointed, but sufficiently mature to realise that there is some learning to be taken from this incident. So they approach the brand person who made the decision and say they appreciate his decision, but ask him if they could know on what basis he made his choice. The brand person tells them that it was indeed a difficult decision to make. There was very little to choose from between the two agencies as far as parameters such as professional credentials, quality of previous output, their ranks of creative people, and so on were concerned. Which is why he felt the need to personally visit the offices of the two agencies to identify some difference between the two.

He adds that when he visited the office of the first agency, it was on a hot, humid, sultry day. He felt the sweat seeping from him as soon as he alighted from his air-conditioned vehicle to step into the office. **Yet, the doorman who stood at the entrance of this advertising agency, who must have been on duty for the past few hours in this same humid, hot weather, greeted him with a warm, broad, genuine smile, while politely holding the door to the entrance of the office open for him. THIS SMILE, SAID THE BRAND REPRESENTATIVE, IS WHAT MADE UP HIS MIND FOR HIM. That the doorman, after spending hours in such oppressive heat, could still be sufficiently motivated to smile and welcome a visitor to his office, spoke volumes about the positive work environment and healthy working relationships prevalent in that agency.** And, for the most productive and creative output to flourish, such an environment was a vital pre-requisite. It did not mean, the brand representative hastened to add, that the creative output of the second agency was under question or doubt. **But all else that was visible being equal among the two agencies, the smile of the doorman became the deciding factor for the awarding of a million-dollar contract.**

A friend of mine recently interacted with a senior banker who professed a counter-view – "Remain aloof, don't smile too much. It makes you appear more knowledgeable and wise. Don't appear too friendly, or you won't be taken seriously," is the advice he had.

This is just – not – true.

Such thought processes stem from an inherent, perhaps a sub-conscious, inferiority complex. Where to appear natural and friendly is thought of as a weakness. **Where it is assumed that in order to project power and self-worth, one must appear deliberately nasty, or at least cold and distant.** Such facades rarely work over a period of time, for the simple reason that no facade can ever work in the long run.

J.R.D. was natural. He was warm. He was a 'people-person.' He had a beautiful smile which he used often. And he was loved because of the warmth and concern he exuded.

The very basic differentiator between a leader and a manager is that a LEADER is a PEOPLE-PERSON, and a MANAGER is a NUMBER-PERSON. The smile, then, is a natural part of a leader's persona. See J.R.D.'s photographs on the cover of books and elsewhere. He is always wearing a lovely, natural, gentle smile.

There is a story about a little girl who lived in a small house in a dark back-alley in the slums of London. But she yet managed to win first prize in a flower-growing contest. The judges were curious and asked her to explain how her flower had managed to survive in such a dark and cheerless spot. The little girl explained her 'secret': a little ray of sunlight came into the dark alley in which she lived and as soon as it appeared, she put her flower-pot right in its path. And as the ray of sunlight kept moving along the alley through the day, she kept moving the flower along with it so that the flower stayed in the sunshine all day long. **So though darkness and shadows surrounded it, the ray of sunlight constantly bathing it with a warm glow made the flower blossom into a prize-winning one.**

'There is no truth to the maxim, "Nice guys finish last." I was once told it is not important to be liked, it is important to be respected. The two are not mutually exclusive. Some people think they are respected when they actually are feared. Be yourself. Be secure in your knowledge, your beliefs, your sensitivity to others, and your morality. Role models are important, but don't try to emulate someone whose style and values are not compatible with yours. It's true that many a***oles get to the top, but you don't have to be one to succeed.'

– **Simon M. Kornblit**
(Former EVP, Worldwide Marketing, Universal Pictures)

DO PRAISE – IT PAYS

Appreciating and praising people for genuine efforts and tasks done well has always been known to motivate people to perform even better in the future. **But are you aware that simple praise has the same effect and impact on people as does a financial reward?**

In fact, although offering praise and recognition costs nothing, studies indicate it can even be as effective as giving employees monetary compensation.

- In 2008, strategy consultancy firm *White Water Strategies* reported that **being praised can have the same impact on job satisfaction as being awarded a one percent pay rise.**

- The *Japanese National Institute for Psychological Sciences* has undertaken research on the neurological impact of praise, discovering that **being paid a compliment activates the same part of the brain as receiving cash.**

- A study by online career site *Glassdoor* revealed that **more than 80 per cent of employees say that they are motivated to work harder when their boss shows appreciation for their work**, as compared to less than 40 per cent who work harder simply because their boss is demanding or because they fear losing their job.

It is not that appreciation and praise should be showered for profit alone. But in the corporate context, where profit plays such an important part, it would be folly for a leader to miss out on using a tool which not only makes you a leader or manager to be admired and loved by your subordinates and team mates, but which would also make your employees feel the impact of financial reward at no extra cost.

And nothing plays a greater role in motivating others than does the simple act of appreciating their efforts through a few kind words.

There is more hunger for love and appreciation in this world than for bread

-MOTHER TERESA

POINTS TO PONDER AND PRACTICE

- Remember, every person is born with a warm heart

- **Circumstances may have changed you into someone like whom the senior banker described – cold, aloof, distant. If so, now is the time to change. Regain your natural warmth. Let it glow and make the people you meet feel happy they came in contact with you**

- And step one to regaining this warmth is to practice your natural smile as often as you can with as many people as possible. Everyone loves and trusts a person who behaves naturally and not artificially. So go ahead, let your inner warmth not remain buried, but let it burst out in the form of a broad, genuine smile with which you can win the world

- Whichever field of work you may be in, always remember the ancient Chinese saying, '**A man without a smiling face must never open a shop**'

- Practice what the ancient Greek sage, Bias of Priene, said: '**If you see a person without a smile, smile first**'

Kind words can be short and easy to speak, but their echoes are truly endless
                                                        -MOTHER TERESA

LEADERS LOVE BOOKS –
READ–LEAD–SUCCEED

> **You cannot open a book without learning something**
>
> -Confucius

WHAT J.R.D. BELIEVED IN AND PRACTICED

> **There is more treasure in books than in all the pirate's loot on Treasure Island**
>
> -Walt Disney

In his enlightening book: A *Touch of Greatness*, Mr. R. M. Lala touches upon J.R.D.'s deep and enduring love for books and reading. J.R.D. was a voracious reader and he read studiously after office hours, catching up on the higher formal education he had missed out on since he had not attended university.

In J.R.D.'s humble home was a study-room of which he was justly proud. This room contained a shelf of books devoted to aircraft and aviation, another shelf of books containing works on sports cars and motor racing, and yet another shelf of books devoted to military strategy. Apart from these books on work-related areas from which he learned and implemented a great deal, J.R.D. was also fond of light reading such as crime fiction.

283

In the classic work: *Aircraft and Engine Perfect* authored by Mr. Murad Fyzee and published by Tata McGraw Hill, the author writes about J.R.D.'s love for reading and the benefits which accrued therefrom as follows: 'With no formal background or training in engineering, JRD had a natural talent for things mechanical. He was an excellent motor-car driver, with sure hands. He liked to take things apart to see how they worked. **He read technical magazines, papers and books ceaselessly.** In the years to come he would be able to follow the most technical of details of aircraft and aviation technology. He would be able to enter the world, or the workshop, of the engineer, the mechanic.....with confidence and understanding. **The technicians in turn soon came to know and respect him for his professionalism.** He was not only a boss, he was also a professional.'

Mr. Murad Fyzee also wrote about J.R.D.: 'Reading voraciously, JRD had devoured everything that had ever been written about most of the early, heroic pioneer pilot-constructors, the Wright Brothers, Bleriot, Farman, Curtis, Latham, Breguet and others, with their strange contraptions of wood, wire, canvas and bicycle wheels! Then also the legendary fighter pilots of World War I. Men such as Richthofen (the Red Baron) and Boelchke of Germany, Ball and MacCudden of Britain, Guynemer and Fonck of France, Rickenbacker of the USA (who was to found Eastern Airlines), and Bishop of Canada, in whose careers and exploits JRD had delighted.'

Mr. Fyzee further writes: 'Ever since World War I, JRD had been reading every book he could get hold of on flying and aviation. But there was one man, a French aviator, who became more than just an author, a philosopher-writer, who was and still remains JRD's hero. This was, of course, Antoine de Saint Exupery....It was his first book *Courier Sud* which undoubtedly made an indelible impression on JRD. **It must have lain dormant in JRD's subconscious to surface in his subsequent ideas and plans to form an airline.'**

Thus it is obvious that reading and learning played no small role in the professional and personal brand success that Mr. J.R.D. Tata achieved.

LEARNINGS
FOR LEADERS

You may have tangible wealth untold,
Caskets of jewels and coffers of gold.
Richer than I you can never be,
I had a mother who read to me

-STRICKLAND GILLIAN (1869 – 1954)

The more you read, the more you know.

The more you know, the better equipped you are.

The better equipped you are, the more genuinely confident you will feel to interact with people, put forward your ideas and suggestions, accept and think over the ideas and suggestions of others.

For it is reading which sharpens the intellect; broadens your mind by making it aware of the fact that other opinions can and do exist apart from your own.

The following is a contribution from the popular *Reader's Digest* magazine which tells us precisely this:

'Comedian David Brenner came from a poor family. When he graduated from high school, he was given an unforgettable gift. "Some of my friends got new clothes, a few rich ones got new cars," he remembers. "After I had my diploma in my hand, my father came over, congratulated me, and reached into his pants pocket and took something out. I extended my hand palm up and he let his present drop into it – a five cent coin called a nickel." Then he said to me, '**Buy a newspaper with that. Read every word of it. Then turn to the classified ad section and find yourself a job. Get out into the world. It's all yours now.**' I always thought that was a great joke my father had played on me....until a few years ago in the Army, I was sitting in a shelter thinking about my family and my life. It was then that I realised that my friends had gotten **ONLY** new cars, or **ONLY** clothes. **My father had given me the whole world. What greater gift could there be?**"

An extremely important point for leaders to ponder:

The Director of the *Xavier Institute of Management and Research,* Mumbai, **Dr. Vaidyanathan**, a very good and true friend, and one who in my humble opinion is among the most brilliant strategic thinkers in the country today, feels strongly on the subject of the importance of intensive and exhaustive reading for executives and leaders. He observes that the leadership and top management of Japanese and Korean companies rarely, if ever, resort to using the services of high-priced external management consultants. **The reason for this, believes Dr. Vaidyanathan, is that the CEOs and top leadership of these companies literally immerse themselves in reading voluminous amounts of material, thereby developing a strong personal knowledge base. They soak in relevant and much-needed information like a sponge from what they read. They take regular sabbaticals to refresh, rejuvenate, and update themselves, where they invest up to eighteen hours a day in meditation and reading.**

Truly, leaders need to voraciously read if they wish to succeed.

A few stimulating and highly motivating examples of leaders BENEFITING TREMENDOUSLY through the love of books and the power of reading follow:

Henry Knox, who served as George Washington's (the first president of the USA) commander of artillery, was an amateur soldier, who learned artillery usage reading military books in his Boston bookstore. He could communicate like an expert on practical artillery based on the strength of his reading. As Rivarol, the French author rightly wrote: **'The printing press is the artillery of thought.'**

Although **Thomas Jefferson** (the third president of the USA) was already a well-educated man, in 1769, when he was elected to the Virginia Assembly, one of his first acts was to **order and read 14 books, authored by experts on the theory and practice of governance. He used the information he obtained through these books to create and communicate efficient policies for effective governance.**

Bill Gates of *Microsoft* is a voracious reader. While on the way to a new destination, Gates devours books and magazine articles about the location he is about to visit. Once he reaches his destination, he asks a lot of follow-up questions about what he's read on the way to the people he meets. **On the way to India, he discovered India had 14 distinct languages, and realised that Microsoft's products had to be much more localised and customised to cater to the Indian market. This was done, and it immediately increased the sales of Microsoft.**

287

Howard Schultz, the founder of *Starbucks*, is a voracious reader, and the busier he gets the more he reads. He carries at least three books with him when he boards a flight to ensure he doesn't run out of reading material before the flight lands. **When he reads something he really appreciates and finds useful, he orders hundreds of copies and hands them out to his employees, encouraging them to read and learn and profit from it as well.** He often reads material to strengthen his recent experiences. For example, after visiting Japan, he read *Memoirs of a Geisha* and after himself undertaking a spiritual journey, he read *The Haj* by Leon Uris, the story of a man's spiritual journey. **He feels such reading helps keep his personal experiences alive and helps him gain a holistic perspective.**

"

So please, oh please; we beg, we pray,

Go throw your TV set away,

And in its place you can install,

A lovely bookcase on the wall

"

-ROALD DAHL

A *Gallup Poll* showed that **high-income people read an average of nineteen books a year.**

A question for **YOU** to answer - How many do **YOU** read?

HARI KRISHNA EXPORTS –
A TRUE LEARNING ORGANISATION

Not only do leaders need to read voraciously, they also need to encourage the habit of reading among their people.

I was privileged to recently be invited as a keynote speaker at the annual day of *Hari Krishna Exports*, and was pleasantly surprised to find that they gift books to their employees on every possible occasion. Such an approach by the leadership shows the organisation to be a growing and learning one.

I was also pleased to learn that the leaders of this organisation are great admirers of Mr. J.R.D. Tata, and noticed that J.R.D.'s portrait adorns the wall of their elegant corporate headquarters in Mumbai at a very prominent place.

This organisation (a leader in its field – **it being the world's leading diamond and diamond jewellery conglomerate**) commenced business operations in 1992, and celebrated its silver jubilee year in 2017, one year before this book first went into print.

MR. GHANSHYAM DHOLAKIA

The young and dynamic Dholakia brothers (namely Mr. Savji Dholakia, Mr. Ghanshyam Dholakia, Mr. Himmat Dholakia and Mr. Tulsi Dholakia), who are the promoters of this organisation, had very little formal education.

However, the brothers realised the importance of reading, education, and the power of knowledge; and this philosophy inspired them to start a few initiatives which they believe have been primarily responsible for their sustained success. One of the primary initiatives being – **the commencing of a culture of book reading and knowledge sharing** which they started way back in 2007.

........*continued*

With this philosophy firmly entrenched in mind, they set a policy which required all the employees in their organisation, across levels, to invest at least 30 minutes every week, during working hours, to read some book of their choice on the topics of self-development / sales and marketing / spirituality etc., which are available in their well-stocked company library.

Besides this, every employee is encouraged to set his / her own target to read a certain number of books within the year. All the employees of the organisation are gifted an appropriate book, in addition to a box of sweets on their birthdays, so that the family of the employee can also benefit by developing the habit of reading.

The organisation also gifts books to its valuable clients on their birthdays, wherever in the world these clients may be located. It is a small gesture and token of esteem from the organisation's end to express appreciation to its loyal customers. After all, as the Dholakia brothers so aptly put it, 'a good book can enlighten and enhance the knowledge of every person who reads it.'

Another noble activity which Hari Krishna Exports undertakes is the organising of Blood Donation Camps thrice a year. Every donor of blood in these camps is gifted a book in a language of his / her choice, namely English, Hindi, Gujarati, Marathi, or any other.

Apart from all this, any visitor who pays their first visit to the organisation's office is gifted with a photo of his / her visit as a memoir, along with a book relevant to their taste and choice of subject.

It is worth noting that since 2007, **more than 12,000 books** have been gifted by this organisation to staff, customers, well-wishers, as well as to family members of the company's management and employees. **No wonder the organisation has seen such rapid growth in such a relatively short span of time, with such an enlightened leadership at the helm.**

(I would like to take this opportunity to extend my gratitude to my former student, **Mr. Siddhartha Shanker**, who is now the Head – Emarketing, with Hari Krishna Exports. He is the one who extended an invite to me to address the employees of this fine organisation.)

POINTS TO PONDER AND PRACTICE

- Reading gives you ideas and develops your thinking process. These two elements are essential for you to become a better, well-rounded communicator, which is a very essential leadership skill

- In order to communicate effectively, you need to improve:

  1. Vocabulary

  2. Grammar

  3. Knowledge, both profession-specific as well as general

  (Reading helps you improve all of the above three areas)

- In the wise words of Ron L. Smith:

  'Some good book is usually responsible for the success of every really great man'

'HANDS-ON'
LEADERSHIP ALWAYS
WORKS WONDERS

" *A leader is not an administrator who loves to run others, but someone who carries water for his people so that they can get on with their jobs* "

-ROBERT TOWNSEND

WHAT **J.R.D.**
BELIEVED IN
AND **PRACTICED**

" *There is a connection between the HEAD, the HEART and the HAND. It is this connection that enhances your leadership* "

-ANYAELE SAM CHIYSON

This learning relates to how much of the piloting J.R.D. took upon himself during the early days of the airline he founded with great love.

In fact, the original pilot strength of Tata Airlines consisted of just three individuals – Nevill Vintcent, Homi Bharucha, and J.R.D. himself. And in those early days, J.R.D. personally took on a lot of the flying workload.

Even the first commercial flight of Tata Air Lines, which carried precious and much awaited airmail from Karachi to Bombay on 15th October, 1932, was piloted by J.R.D. himself.

And on 4th November, 1945, after completing a flight from Dum Dum airport to Jamshedpur, J.R.D.'s flight log book showed his time in air as having completed 1006 hours and 50 minutes of piloting time, most of which involved carrying airmail for his fledgling but rapidly growing airline.

To a large extent, the stupendous later success of Air India under J.R.D.'s able stewardship can be traced back to the fact that J.R.D. knew and thoroughly understood the nerves and very pulse of the airline so well, having himself taken the 'hands-on' approach in its earlier days.

Sheila Murray Bethel said: "**If leadership serves only the leader, it will fail. Ego satisfaction, financial gain, and status can all be valuable tools for a leader, but if they become the only motivations, they will eventually destroy a leader. Only when service for a common good is the primary purpose are you truly leading.**" J.R.D. epitomised this special brand of leadership, and the Tata group was the resultant and happy winner.

Many, many years ago, some soldiers were attempting to move a heavy tree trunk without much success. Their immediate superior was standing by their side, watching his men struggling, but not lifting a finger to help his men. Then a man on a horse came by, and asked the superior why he wasn't assisting his men. The superior said with dignity, "**I am the corporal. It is my job to give orders.**"

The man on the horse dismounted, rolled up his sleeves, and went to help the struggling soldiers. After some time, and with his help, the soldiers succeeded in their task. The man then quietly mounted his horse, rode up to the corporal, and said, "**The next time your men need help, send for the commander-in-chief,**" and silently rode away.

That man on the horse was **General George Washington**, himself the commander-in-chief of that army, and soon to become the first president of the U.S.A.

LEARNINGS
FOR LEADERS

> *Leaders aren't born, they are made. And they are made just like anything else, through hard work. And that's the price we'll have to pay to achieve that goal, or any goal*
>
> -VINCE LOMBARDI

Linda Ray defines what exactly hands-on leadership is all about, and also what it is not. She writes: 'Hands-on leadership often is misconstrued to mean micromanagement. This generalisation reduces the presence and participation of leaders to a nuisance and an obstacle to productivity – something best to be avoided. True hands-on leadership, however, does not mean being bossy. It means fully assuming a leadership role, steering from the front, and working side-by-side with employees to achieve the goals of the company.'

What Linda Ray writes defines J.R.D.'s hands-on brand of leadership perfectly.

As another outstanding corporate example, **Sam Walton**, even after he became head of the largest organisation in the world (Wal-Mart), regularly dropped in unannounced at any of his multiple stores, stood behind the counter with a trainee salesperson, conversed with customers, and even gift-wrapped parcels for his customers, demonstrating to the trainee the best way to gift-wrap a parcel and not waste paper either, at the same time keeping his conversation with the customer flowing. He would then accompany the fortunate customer to the check-out counter, wait in line alongside, and see how efficiently the cashiers were functioning and how much time it took for a customer waiting in line to settle his bill. Many improvements in the billing system were then made by Sam, including the adoption of new technology to speed up the billing process.

Then he would grab a sack of doughnuts and some flasks of coffee, get into a helicopter, and drop in at any of the Wal-Mart farms, and help the employees pick fruit from the trees. Taking a break, he would sit down with them, share the doughnuts and coffee, and engage them in light conversation, also soaking in invaluable first-hand inputs from these front-line employees of his.

And as Linda Ray further writes: 'One of the most obvious benefits of a hands-on leadership style is that it allows you to make sure that everything is done correctly. This does not mean that you should agonise over the details if your employees are getting good results. What it does mean is that you are familiar with the bigger picture of your company's daily workings. By occasionally showing up on the front-lines, you have the opportunity to lead by example. **It's one thing to announce to your employees that they need to meet a goal. It is far more effective to show them how the work is to be done by doing it beside them.** Leading by example is one of the ways to apply a hands-on approach to leadership.'

Doesn't this apply so well to what J.R.D. as well as Sam Walton both demonstrated in their own inimitable way?

As an unknown wise person once said, **'No matter what you've done or accomplished in the past, you're never too good to roll up your sleeves, get dirty, and do the 'grunt' work. No job is ever too menial, no task ever too unskilled or boring. Remarkably successful people never feel entitled – except to the fruits of their labour.'**

Any leader, in order to be truly successful, must know the functional aspects of the industry he is part of in a hands-on manner. For this, he needs to spend substantial time performing the grass-root element functions associated with his industry, so that he knows them inside-out, top-to-bottom. In short, success in a leadership role requires a hands-on leadership style and approach.

In fact, research proves that so-called 'Eureka' moments are not spur-of-the-moment random thoughts, but accrue to an individual who has spent years, if not decades, deeply involved in a particular field of study or endeavour. Contrary to popular belief, **Sir Isaac Newton** did not randomly dream up the **Law of Gravity** simply because an apple fell on his head. His discovery was in fact the culmination of years of intense research into the field.

Sir Isaac Newton

As James Clear clarifies: 'The story of the falling apple has become one of the lasting and iconic examples of the creative moment. It is a symbol of the inspired genius that fills your brain during those "light bulb moments" when creative conditions are just right. What most people forget, however, is that Newton worked on his ideas of gravity for nearly twenty years (after the apple struck him in 1666) until, in 1687, he published his groundbreaking book, *The Principia: Mathematical Principles of Natural Philosophy*. **The falling apple was merely the beginning of a train of thought that continued for decades..... Creativity is a process, not an event. You have to work through mental barriers and internal blocks. You have to commit to practicing your craft deliberately. And you have to stick with the process for years, perhaps even decades like Newton did, in order to see your creative genius blossom.'**

So now you have yet another reason to be motivated and practice a hands-on brand of leadership. Not only does it set an example for your people, it also is a route to enhancing your latent creativity.

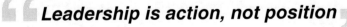

Leadership is action, not position

-Donald H. McGannon

Once you attain that desired position of leadership, never forget what the legendary actress and fine human being, **AUDREY HEPBURN**, had to say on the subject: '**As you grow older, you will discover that you have two hands, one for helping yourself, the other for helping others.**'

And who better can you help with that second hand than the people who are striving to make your organisation a success?

The story is told of a former Indian prime minister who once suffered from sudden weakness and was immediately escorted to one of the best hospitals in our capital city. The most senior doctor in the hospital rushed to assist him. Unfortunately, this doctor had since many years renounced active medical practice and served in an administrative capacity.

To take a blood sample of this prestigious patient, this doctor kept poking the needle into the forearm, but, having lost practice to effectively carry out this basic procedure, ended up puncturing the skin in several places, attempting to find the right spot with the needle. The prime minister was upset. A relatively junior doctor who was still a hands-on medical practitioner took over, and the required blood sample was extracted with ease.

ASK YOURSELF: Are you, as a senior leader, still in touch with the base skills which your subordinates need to have and which you yourself were skilled in when you commenced your career? You need to constantly practice these skills before you lose your edge, and with it, possibly also a part of the admiration and respect of your subordinates. It wouldn't be difficult. After all, you would already have been proficient at these skills in the past. The key word is 'practice.'

A young, highly successful businessman with upwardly mobile aspirations, knew not a thing about sailing or seamanship, but bought himself a magnificent yacht.

On 'day one' of his new acquisition, he proudly took his mother to see the sparkling new ship. As they boarded the vessel, he put on a captain's cap lined with the traditional insignia of gold braid and anchors and said, **"See, I'm now the captain."**

Since his mother made no comment, the young businessman asked, **"What's the matter? Aren't you impressed?"**

His mother's response quickly brought him down to earth. She said, **"You want me to be impressed? Okay, I'll act as though I'm impressed if that will please you. To yourself, you're a captain. To me, you may be a captain. BUT TO REAL CAPTAINS, YOU'RE NO CAPTAIN."**

POINTS TO PONDER AND PRACTICE

- Follow what John C. Maxwell says: `

  '**A leader is one who knows the way, goes the way, and shows the way**'

- Do not change jobs too often. And even more important, do not change industries too often, as in order to get into the crux of any activity, the important element of time cannot be speeded up. Take career decisions after sufficient thought and after developing skills and insights in a field of choice. It is relevant to note that J.R.D. did not commence with an airline on a whim or an impulse, nor because it became the 'flavour-of-the-season.' He developed his concept over a long period of time. Ever since a young lad, he had been thrilled by exploits of the early aviators in France, where he spent a substantial part of his growing years. **He also was flying from a very young age, being the first Indian ever to secure a pilot's license**

- **Any leader who has not invested sufficient time mastering the grass-root aspects of the industry in which he hopes to make a mark, will be a superficial leader in the best of times, and in all probability a liability to the organisation he leads in times of crises**

- In fact, too many start-ups are failing today because they are initiated by individuals who know very little about the industries they have set up shop in. They initiate ventures in fields simply because they see 'opportunity,' abundant funding, and the field being the 'flavour-of-the-month' and others doing well in it.

" " *The real reason I always succeeded in my own campaigns is because I was always ON THE SPOT* " "

-ARTHUR WELLESLEY, DUKE OF WELLINGTON
(The General who defeated Napoleon at the Battle of Waterloo)

LEARNING #31 QUALITY AND NOT QUANTITY SHOULD BE YOUR PRIORITY

> *Quality is first engineered, only then is it inspected*

-J.R.D. TATA

WHAT **J.R.D.** BELIEVED IN AND **PRACTICED**

> *Leadership is not magnetic personality – that can just as well be a glib tongue. It is not 'making friends and influencing people' – that is flattery. Leadership is lifting a person's vision to high sights, the raising of a person's performance to a higher standard, the building of a personality beyond its normal limitations*

-PETER DRUCKER

When Air India came into being with J.R.D. at the helm, he was realistic and knew that there were many existing, well-established international airlines which were far older and having resources and reach far greater than the fledgling Air India. He was aware that Air India could not hope to compete with these existing airlines in terms of reach and size.

He never even attempted to do so, realising that his organisation's strength lay in the quality of its equipment, the superior level of maintenance, and the attractive decor. He ensured that these vital elements were second to no other airline. **He also took great care to excel in an area which passengers found most important – quality customer service.** This is where he knew Air India could make its mark and compete on an equal footing with established airlines around the globe. As J.R.D. was fond of saying, "**Common people have an appetite for food, uncommon people have an appetite for service.**"

He told his employees, "**I want that the passengers who travel do not have occasion to complain. I want to establish that there is no airline which is better liked by passengers, where the food and service is better and which sets a better image than Air India.**" And while J.R.D. was in charge of Air India, this became a reality.

For J.R.D., it was imperative that his organisation constantly moved in a forward direction so as to be recognised in the minds and hearts of customers as being the best, at least as far as quality was concerned. His efforts paid off, in an almost a 'Believe-it-or-Not' fashion.

It would be impossible for us today, observing as we are the current abysmal depths to which the image of Air India has plunged, to believe that **in J.R.D.'s time, (in 1968 to be precise), Air India headed the list of international airlines surveyed by quality expert Julian Holland in an article cum survey published in the 'Daily Mail,' London.** Julian noted – 'I left some chocolates on my seat while the plane was delayed in Rome for an hour. When I returned, they had not been moved, but the (curtain) blinds had been drawn (closed) at the window to keep the sun off them and prevent them from melting.'

While credit for such razor-sharp observation and quality service action definitely goes to the concerned cabin-crew on duty on that flight, the **ultimate credit must belong to J.R.D., as he was the man who ignited the spark and provided the inspiration through his own values for providing super-service to all passengers** of the airline.

302

This also demonstrates the superior levels of quality of service which India and Indians are capable of, with the right men at the helm of affairs. It is a reaffirmation of what we can achieve, provided we have the right men in leadership positions. It is a lesson for any organisation based on Indian soil, that our people possess the expertise and the wherewithal to excel and be second to none in the world on quality parameters, as long as they are driven by a leader with the right set of values.

Although Air India was nationalised and taken over by the Government at a very early stage 'in the national interest,' J.R.D. stayed on as its Chairman until 1978. The year 1978 was a sad year for Air India, as the year J.R.D. left the airline was the year Air India's quality standards started seeing a visible and marked decline.

Nari Dastur, who was a key member of J.R.D.'s team, and who rose to be Regional Director for Air India for Europe, had this to say about J.R.D. – "**He loved Air India and it would have hurt him if there was anything which was not of a high standard and he did that by example. Whatever he wanted of others, he was doing much more himself.** Of course, we had our conflicts yet all worked together for a common purpose. **If your chief lives, dreams, talks only of one thing (quality and high standards), it is infectious.**"

An example from TELCO, which had a tie-up with **Benz** of Germany to manufacture trucks is also instructive of J.R.D.'s focus on quality standards. The Germans as a people are known to be obsessed with quality, and so was J.R.D., as was also Mr. Moolgaonkar, who headed TELCO at that time. German technicians stationed in the TELCO factory at Jamshedpur identified defective parts and components with an eagle eye, and kept them to one side. Then, on a weekly basis, these rejected parts were inspected to identify why the defect arose in the first place, and what lessons for improvement could be learned even from these defective parts. **At first, the Indian engineers, not used to such perfection, found the entire exercise a tedious one. But gradually they realised its importance as a vital step towards becoming a quality manufacturer, and this is one reason why TELCO's standards rose and so did the reputation of the products it manufactured.**

This proves once more that employees orient themselves towards working in a quality manner if their leaders set an example and create the necessary environment.

LEARNINGS ▮▮▮
▮ FOR LEADERS

"Cleanliness is the hallmark of perfect standards and the best quality inspector is the conscience"

-J.R.D. TATA

The values the leader possesses and lays stress upon will decide and determine the choices he will make and the path his organisation will follow.

Today, in general, the corporate focus is on growth.

There is nothing wrong with that. But it is unfortunately an unhealthy focus on growth to the exclusion of almost everything else that matters. As someone wisely put it, '**Growth for the sake of growth is the ideology of a cancer cell.**'

Today's corporate focus is on being 'Number One' in terms of size, volume, customer base, or market share. But rarely is the thrust on being 'Number One' in the eyes of the brand's existing customers on the parameter of quality.

Many organisations, in their rush and urgency to expand, end up growing too fast, without correspondingly developing the infrastructure, or hiring and training the right manpower to service and satisfy the increased client base they have gained through aggressive selling tactics. Then when new customers realise that the quality offered in terms of product, service, or after-sales-service is not up to the mark or as promised in advertisements, they delink from the organisation and spread the negative word. All the efforts and **expenses** (I will not use the word '**investments**'), incurred in attracting new customers then go down the drain, as corresponding efforts and investments have not been made for retaining the existing customers, who form the bread, butter, jam and cheese of any organisation's revenue and profitability model.

It is QUALITY of product and service deliverables which need to be focused on first. Then QUANTITY and volume of sales, or share of customer votes, will follow by default.

A few international examples will serve to drive this point home.

Consider **Switzerland**, a small, land-locked nation, with very few natural resources in terms of mineral wealth. **It leads the entire world in a myriad of industries – watch-making, high grade writing-instruments, banking, chocolates, cheese, hospitality, tourism, hotel-management education**, and a few more. They manage to do this, and retain their leading position in these industries while competing against approximately two-hundred-odd other countries of the world, primarily because the Swiss are **literally positively obsessed with quality, accuracy, and punctuality**.

Or consider two other nations – **Japan** and **Germany**. Both of them absolutely, utterly, and thoroughly destroyed, their cities flattened, their resources and people almost decimated and demolished, due to the ravages of World War II, which ended in 1945. These two countries were the worst impacted by the War. Yet, within a period of a mere twenty-five years, by 1970, they were both back on their feet and giving industrialised nations with vast resources such as the U.S.A. a run for their money.

In fact, Japan and Germany are among the top five economies of the world today, despite their comparatively small size. **Japan in particular has almost no natural resources, is unfortunately prone to and plagued by tsunamis, earthquakes and floods, and has very little land it can use for agricultural cultivation.**

But by playing to their strengths, **by focusing on quality rather than on quantity, Japan, as well as Germany**, have become world-beaters in the field of heavy-machinery, consumer electronics, high-grade steel, household equipment, automobiles and even in the arena of tourism, hospitality, financial services and banking.

THAT – IS THE **POWER OF QUALITY**.

> **Once again, J.R.D. had his priorities right.**
> QUALITY FIRST – QUANTITY SURELY FOLLOWS.

A visitor to the studio of the famed master painter and sculptor Michelangelo critically remarked, "**I cannot see that you have made any progress on this painting since I visited here last month.**"

Michelangelo pointed out, "**I have retouched this portion on the top, softened the facial expression on this person, developed the muscle-tone on that individual in the right corner, given more energy to the limb here, and reddened the lip of that woman to make it more natural.**"

The visitor was not impressed, and said, "**But those are merely small things.**"

MICHELANGELO

Michelangelo smiled and countered, "**That may be, but small things make perfection, and perfection is by no means a small thing.**"

If a man is called to be a street sweeper, he should sweep streets even as a Michelangelo painted, or Beethoven composed music or Shakespeare wrote poetry. He should sweep streets so well that all the hosts of heaven and earth will pause to say, 'HERE LIVED A GREAT STREET SWEEPER WHO DID HIS JOB WELL.'

-MARTIN LUTHER KING, JR.

POINTS TO PONDER AND PRACTICE

- As a leader, one crucial decision you need to take – is whether to focus on improving quality, or playing the quantitative number game

- Remember and practice what J.R.D. said:

  'If you strive for perfection, you will surely get excellence'

- Unfortunately, you cannot focus on **both** quality as well as quantity at the same time. **The trick, and the beauty of the solution to this riddle is that by focusing on quality; quantity in terms of sales, satisfied customers and business growth will be attained by default. But by focusing on quantity, you lose out on quality as well as on quantity**. This is a lesson from history, and no one has been able to prove it to be wrong. As an intelligent leader, having your own, your people's and your organisation's interests at heart, focus on improving quality. You will not regret it. You and your organisation will ultimately be the winners on all counts

HAPPINESS IS THE ULTIMATE GOAL – A GOOD LEADER GETS HIS PRIORITIES RIGHT

> " *I don't want India to be an economic superpower. I want India to be a happy country* "
>
> -J.R.D. TATA

WHAT **J.R.D.** BELIEVED IN AND **PRACTICED**

> " *A primary function of leadership is to ensure a happy, motivated and committed workforce. A highly paid, qualified and experienced employee can still be unhappy, unproductive and disloyal if the working environment is not conducive. But a happy and committed employee is always putting in his best, is attached and devoted to his colleagues, his superiors and his subordinates, uses his mind, heart and hands to good effect, and becomes the key organisational asset* "
>
> -CYRUS M. GONDA

309

Once, an American economist analysed and announced that India had tremendous potential and could be an 'economic super power' in the next (the twenty-first) century. J.R.D.'s response to this was his famous and incisive quote – **'I don't want India to be an economic superpower. I want India to be a happy country.'**

He did not say this just because it sounded good and politically correct. J.R.D. was a man who always spoke his mind. If he said something, he sincerely meant it.

What a beautiful sentiment, simply yet eloquently expressed: "I want India to be a happy country."

It is understood by people who have experienced life in its truest form that happiness is not dependent upon wealth alone. Happiness as a human goal lies beyond the scope of what material wealth can deliver.

J.R.D. practiced what he preached. He always strove to primarily make the organisations he led as places where his employees could be happy. Of course, his employees' economic well-being and material needs were also well looked after.

Ask any individual with reasonable experience of working in Corporate India and they will tell you that many organisations today exist which offer stupendous remuneration, and then proceed to make the lives of their employees utterly and absolutely miserable. Such organisations, despite offering the best monetary compensation in the industry, are unable to hold on to talented and creative employees, who primiraliy require a happy and conducive working environment to function at their productive best.

The 'Happiness Index' is today considered by leading economists as an important parameter while mapping the progress and evolution of a nation and its people. While most 'leaders' are bent on crying themselves hoarse about developing on financial parameters such as GDP, Stock Market Indices, Gross Growth, Net Growth, and so on, J.R.D. displayed true vision by focusing on the parameter that truly mattered – happiness.

Understanding that happiness mattered most, J.R.D. initiated the development of a culture of joyful working within his organisation as a priority. His philosophy, which he put into practice, was that **happiness and peace should abound among his people so that goodwill and good fortune would follow as a natural consequence.**

Here is what **ROBERT KENNEDY** had to say on the subject while delivering a speech to students at the *University of Kansas* on March 8, 1968:

"Even if we act to erase material poverty, there is another greater task, it is to confront the poverty of satisfaction– purpose and dignity – that afflicts us all.

Too much and for too long, we seemed to have surrendered personal excellence and community values in the mere accumulation of material things.

Our Gross National Product, now, is over $800 billion a year, but that Gross National Product, if we judge the United States of America by that – that Gross National Product counts air pollution and cigarette advertising, and ambulances to clear our highways of carnage.

It counts special locks for our doors and the jails for the people who break them. It counts the destruction of the redwood (forests) and the loss of our natural wonder in chaotic sprawl.

It counts napalm and counts nuclear warheads and armoured cars for the police to fight the riots in our cities.

It counts Whitman's rifle and Speck's knife, and the television programmes which glorify violence in order to sell toys to our children.

Yet the Gross National Product does not allow for the health of our children, the quality of their education, or the joy of their play.

It does not include the beauty of our poetry or the strength of our marriages, the intelligence of our public debate or the integrity of our public officials.

It measures neither our wit nor our courage, neither our wisdom nor our learning, neither our compassion nor our devotion to our country.

It measures everything in short, except that which makes life worthwhile. And it can tell us everything about America except why we are proud that we are Americans.

If this is true here at home, so it is true elsewhere in the world."

Robert Kennedy

Profound words indeed from Robert Kennedy.

J.R.D., just like Robert Kennedy, had his priorities right, and that is one of the the first rules of sound leadership.

LEARNINGS
FOR LEADERS

" *Most of our troubles are due to poor implementation.... wrong priorities and unattainable targets* "

-J.R.D. Tata

A very important leadership and management theory, which has a humongous practical ramifications, is the *Maslow's Theory of Need Hierarchy*. Abraham Maslow opined that human needs evolve in a hierarchy, with basic human needs which need to be satisfied first lying at the lowest level, going up the chain to higher level needs. These higher level needs are the ones which mature and evolved individuals aim to satisfy, once their basic needs have been sufficiently met.

The crux of this theory is that at the middle level of the need hierarchy, lie the needs which are oriented towards money and status. There is no upper limit to money and status, which, after achieving, the needs for money and status can be satisfied. **The quantum of money and status needed to satisfy these needs differs from individual to individual, and is related to greed, not need.** We have super-wealthy individuals in our poor country, who are listed among the richest men in the world, who stay in housing complexes with their nuclear families in a space which could easily accommodate thousands. Yet, their need for money and status has apparently not been satisfied, and they aim for more.

At the highest level of the need hierarchy are the self-actualisation needs, where individuals who are truly evolved, lie. These needs are not linked to monetary gain, economic achievement and attainment of social status and standing, but are tuned towards a **sense of inner fulfilment** which can be achieved by doing something truly worthwhile. Something which these individuals feel adds value to the world and to the lives of others.

Reaching the level of self-actualisation is the ultimate goal of all mankind, and J.R.D., himself being an evolved soul, realised this and instinctively wished the same for his fellow countrymen.

In fact, J.R.D. was a man far ahead of his time. Today, studies are focusing on the 'HAPPINESS INDEX' to evaluate the true state of advancement of a nation. The Happiness Index is being given higher priority by those who matter (even the United Nations), as compared to defunct and outdated concepts such as GDP, which as Robert Kennedy so sagely pointed out, rely on dollars, dimes and cents, and rupees, annas, and paise alone, totally ignoring the intangibles which matter the most in human happiness.

J.R.D. talked of happiness as being the key factor to measure human growth many decades ago. But the *United Nations* General Assembly released its second annual World Happiness Report as recently as September, 2013. This report measures happiness and well-being in countries around the world and is helpful in guiding decisions at the apex level with regard to formulating public policy.

According to this report, Denmark, with a high personal taxation rate of over 60 per cent, and the relatively poor people of some South Sea Islands in the Pacific Ocean were found to be among the happiest people living on our planet, proving that happiness does not depend on wealth and low tax rates alone. These people are the happiest because of certain non-monetary factors present in their lives; human factors, such as:

- A sense of respect for their environment

- An involvement in art, music and literature

- A sense of humility and equality widely spread in their society

- Leaders who actually listen to, genuinely understand, and who are truly one with the common people

Many other countries and their peoples listed high on the Happiness Index are nowhere near the top nor even in the middle as far as per-capita income or other traditional indicators of wealth are concerned.

Why does happiness matter?

Happiness, it is proved, helps people live longer, lead more productive and fulfilling personal and professional lives, earn higher wages, and be better citizens in general. By focusing on improving levels of happiness, rather than focusing on material rewards and monetary measures alone, societies and organisations can enable their citizens and their employees to raise themselves up in a holistic manner – materially, emotionally, and spiritually.

There is little doubt that the employees of Tata companies would be rated very near the top of the list on the Happiness Index if a corporate survey on this crucial parameter were to be carried out for leading organisations across India.

And isn't happiness what really matters in the end? **And if happiness is what really matters in the end, does it not make sense to focus on it right from the beginning?**

J.R.D. focused on his people's happiness, and that is so important for the people and for the organisation they represent and are part of.

Fortunate indeed, are those organisations and nations which have at their helm of affairs, men of the evolved stature of J.R.D. Tata, who know exactly what's best for their people and who place human happiness at the apex of their leadership endeavours.

Some strive for power
But often in vain.
Some thirst for Glory
So hard to attain.

Some crave possessions
That wealth alone brings
But these, alas, are
Transitory things.

The wise are they
Who while on earth's sod
Seek first in their lives
The Kingdom of God.

- SISTER MARY GEMMA BRUNKE

In September 2016, Madhya Pradesh became the first state in India to officially set up a **HAPPINESS DEPARTMENT**. This progressive step was announced by Madhya Pradesh Chief Minister **Shivraj Singh Chouhan**, who said: "Besides the basic necessities of *Roti*, *Kapda aur Makaan* (food, cloth and shelter) people need something more to be happy in their lives....Normally, happiness is measured with economic growth rate which is not entirely correct as our country for ages believed otherwise. There is something more which can bring happiness in the lives of people..."

Mr. Shivraj Singh Chouhan will himself be heading this department.

This new Happiness Department will define parameters of happiness and efficiency. It will also work towards policy-making and the implementation of the concept of happiness. It will provide an action plan and activities for experiencing happiness and also assess the mindset of the people of the state on this vital parameter of happiness from time to time. This department will serve as a 'knowledge resource center' to give suggestions to ensure happiness by infusing positivity in the lives of the people.

POINTS TO PONDER AND PRACTICE

- Are you as a leader of your team or of your department or of your organisation, focusing on the 'Happiness Index' of your people, in conjunction with other parameters you may be using to measure your organisational growth?

- The importance of attracting and retaining the best talent by giving equal importance to non-monetary motivators is now being understood and practiced by mature and evolved organisations. It would be good to add this parameter to your leadership repertoire

- Money can only motivate and retain your best people up to a point. Beyond that, what matters is a healthy working environment, effective leadership, open two-way communication, good relations with superiors, colleagues and subordinates, and an opportunity to allow inner talents to blossom into visible output to achieve personal goals in conjunction with the goals of the organisation

- Remember what Dennis Wholey said: "Happy people plan actions, they don't plan results." Thus being happy is the more practical option for a leader as well as for the people he leads

- As an enlightened leader, an understanding of this basic truth of human nature will take you a long way down the road to superior leadership

SECTION THREE - VALOUR

INTRODUCTION TO THE
VALOUR SECTION

> *It's not the size of the dog in the fight, it's the size of the fight in the dog*
>
> -MARK TWAIN

Bravery comes in different colours and varied shades.

There is **physical bravery**, mostly associated with men in uniform, who perform daring deeds for the flag and country, often sacrificing their lives for their comrades and for a cause they believe in.

Then there is **moral courage**, typically associated with a certain class and calibre of statesmen, such as **Mahatma Gandhi**, **Abraham Lincoln**, **Nelson Mandela** and **Martin Luther King, Jr.** (All these gentlemen also displayed great physical courage – the Mahatma, Abraham Lincoln and Dr. Martin Luther King, Jr., being assassinated for their just and righteous beliefs, and Nelson Mandela spending decades imprisoned in solitary confinement.)

And then there is **spiritual valour**, demonstrated by human saints such as **Mother Teresa**. Once, the story is told, when she was washing the feet of a leper, a Westerner observing her marvelled and said, "Mother, I wouldn't do that for a million dollars." Mother Teresa smiled her serene smile and replied, **"Even I wouldn't do this for a million dollars. I do this for the love of God."**

The following true story amply demonstrates the type of courage needed in today's corporate world – **the courage to speak up and to speak out when needed**.

The U.S.A. in its long and chequered history has often coveted and encroached aggressively on the territory of its neighbours. Many wars have been fought by them with Mexico, and much Mexican territory has been unjustly annexed by the Americans. Fortunately, in this dubious past, there were still men in the U.S.A. with moral convictions and a strong sense of right and wrong.

HENRY DAVID
THOREAU

One such man was **Henry David Thoreau**, the famed naturalist, philosopher and author. He opposed the American war with Mexico, as he believed it to be an attempt by U.S.A. to expand its slave-holding territories. As an American citizen, he refused on moral grounds to pay his taxes, since he felt the tax money was being used to help the war effort. He was jailed both for his beliefs and for his refusal to pay his taxes.

While in jail, his friend, the philosopher and author **Ralph Waldo Emerson**, who was also opposed to the war and to slavery, came to visit Thoreau.

Emerson asked Thoreau:
"Henry, why are you in prison?"

RALPH WALDO
EMERSON

Thoreau, from behind the bars of his prison-cell, looked Emerson straight in the eye and replied:
"Waldo, why are you NOT in prison?"

The lesson on valour for leaders is clear. From now on, you have a fresh set of choices to be made. Forget the past. It is now the future that matters. Will **YOU** now decide to take the right and courageous choice at every future crossroads you come across?

As **Maria Robinson** said: '**Nobody can go back and start a new beginning, but anyone can start today and create a new ending.**'

Valour is a most admirable quality, and if you put it to use at the right time for the right reasons, as J.R.D. most certainly did, it can greatly enhance your organisation's repute and your personal leadership standing.

J.R.D. amply displayed **all three forms of valour**: the **Physical**, the **Moral**, as well as the **Spiritual**.

The lessons which follow in this section demonstrate J.R.D.'s valour, courage and bravery in the corporate context.

NEVER MIND MY STATUS – YOU FOLLOW THE SYSTEM AND DO YOUR DUTY

> ***The people follow the example of those above them***
>
> -CHINESE PROVERB

WHAT **J.R.D.** BELIEVED IN AND **PRACTICED**

> **He who has never learned to obey cannot be a good commander**
>
> -ARISTOTLE

The following anecdote about J.R.D. was narrated to me by my good friend and former Air India staffer, **KIRTI SHRIVASTAV**.

KIRTI SHRIVASTAV

Once, in the 1980s, when J.R.D. was the chairman of Air India (India's national carrier), he came to Mumbai airport, unfortunately having forgotten to carry his identity card with him. Because of this innocent lapse on his part, he was stopped at the entrance to the airport by a security guard, who was new to the job and who didn't recognise J.R.D.

J.R.D. did not get upset with the guard, did not raise his voice in typical 'Indian VIP' fashion and yell, "**Do you know who I am**?"

He realised he had erred in not carrying his identity card with him and was quietly and humbly turning back from the airport entrance, when other staff on duty recognised him, rushed up, explained to that security guard who J.R.D. was, and he was let into the airport complex.

Once inside, he called over the security guard who had stopped him at the entrance for not carrying his identity card, thanked the guard for doing his job efficiently, and handed him a Rs. 100 note as a tip for good work done and an encouragement to keep doing so in future. (Rs. 100 was a decent sum back in the 1980s and would probably be the equivalent of the guard's weekly salary.)

Why did J.R.D. not get upset with the guard?

Why did he silently turn around and begin to walk away?

Why did he praise and even reward the guard later?

Because, for J.R.D., it was paramount that all individuals, including himself, '**follow the system.**'

During his stewardship of the organisation, it was primarily due to the emphasis he laid on adherence to processes that the airline could compete on an equal footing with more older and larger international airlines that enjoyed healthy support from their country of origin.

———————

This humility and adherence to systems and the adoption of a disciplined approach was not only unique to J.R.D. but is visibly embedded in the Tata philosophy, as the example which follows demonstrates.

A former MBA student of mine did his summer internship training with a Tata company at Bombay House (the Tata group headquarters). After returning to college for his second-year MBA, he narrated the following incident he had witnessed during his internship.

He explained how he was taken to the common canteen in Bombay House for lunch by his superior. While waiting in queue to be served lunch, he casually turned around to observe the surroundings, and saw **MR. RATAN TATA**, the towering personality, patiently waiting his turn behind the star-struck trainee in the lunch queue.

The young lad offered to let Ratan Tata in the queue ahead of him, but Ratan (the Jewel) politely smiled, declined, and said gently – '*I'll wait my turn, thank you*'. He is now a fan of Ratan Tata and the Tata group for life.

I am sure any other employee of Bombay House will vouch for this innate display of etiquette through personal observation. It speaks volumes of the *sanskaar*, the values, the upbringing, of the Tatas and the culture percolating from the top of adhering to systems and processes, which the leadership has ensured is positively percolated throughout the length and breadth of the organisation.

And who could be a better authority on the importance of structure, systems, and processes than the greatest scientist of them all – **Albert Einstein.**

Not only did Einstein say: '**Setting an example is not the main means of influencing others; it is the ONLY means.**'

Einstein also wisely observed: '**You have to learn the rules of the game. And then you have to play better than anyone else.**'

And once again, it was Einstein who sagely remarked: '**More the knowledge, lesser the ego. Lesser the knowledge, more the ego.**'

Not only did J.R.D. set a sterling example to all present that no one is above the law, he showed that he had understood and indeed mastered the rules, and that he could play the game better than anyone else – a true sportsman to the very end.

325

LEARNINGS
FOR LEADERS

" A system-driven organisation, where the leader is the first to follow the rules rather than break them, grows stronger and faster, without developing the flaws and cracks which make other organisations vulnerable to collapse "

-CYRUS M. GONDA

Christian Archibald Herter had been the governor of the state of Massachusetts in U.S.A. from 1953 - 1957 and he was campaigning hard to get re-elected for a second term in office.

One day during his campaign, after having had a busy morning and missing his lunch, he arrived at a church barbecue. He was famished. As he moved down the serving line for his share of the meal being offered, he held out his plate to the woman serving chicken. She put one piece on his plate and then turned to serve the person waiting next in line after Herter.

"Excuse me," Governor Herter said, "do you mind if I have another piece of chicken ?" "Sorry," said the woman. "I'm only supposed to give one piece of chicken to each person." "But I'm starved," the governor said. "Sorry, only one to a customer," replied the woman politely. **The governor was normally a modest man, but he was also hungry, so he decided to throw a little weight around. "Lady, do you know who I am?,"** he said loudly. **"I'm the governor of this state."**

The lady was not impressed. She responded to the governor by telling him, **"Do you know who I am? I'm the lady in charge of the chicken. Now, move along, mister."**

A majority of VIPs and VVIPs in India are apparently allergic to following laid-down systems and procedures.

An online article titled '**Do you know who I am?! VIP checkpoint tantrums are causing security threats at airports as officers get specialised training to handle ugly outburst from celebrities and elites**' authored by Ankur Sharma and published on 10th March, 2014, in the *Daily Mail* makes for interesting reading. Among other things, Sharma writes: 'Very very important persons are usually on a short fuse. Nobody knows this better than Central Industrial Security Force (CISF) personnel on security duty at airports across the nation (India) where the tantrums of privileged people are a never-ending nightmare.....VIP rage is now an accepted job hazard for these airport security officers, and they are being conditioned and trained for dealing with the unruly behaviour of elite passengers....'

Captain G.R. Gopinath, who founded the erstwhile Air Deccan, is honest enough to write on the NDTV.com blog: '....This urge to throw one's weight around and drop names, to seek special privileges, then flaunt those privileges to show others how ordinary they are, to jump red lights in red-beaconed cars – all this has been standard practice in India for too long. Not just MPs, but judges, famous Supreme Court lawyers, media honchos, celebrity God-men who preach spirituality and simplicity are guilty of strutting in VIP mode at airports, greatly inconveniencing other passengers. **Even I am guilty of it. And I've seen airline CEOs doing the same, ignoring the rights of the passengers who are their customers.**'

As we can clearly see, the rot has set in deep.

As a leader, demonstrating VIP status at the drop of a hat is not a thing to be proud of, but rather tends to demotivate others around and lower down in the hierarchy.

Abraham Lincoln once wisely remarked: **"I would rather be a little nobody, than to be an evil somebody."**

Once people observe the leader act arrogantly and challenge the system successfully, they too, start feeling that rules are there to be broken if one is 'strong' enough to break them and get away with it; that systems and procedures are meant to be bypassed by those who have the power to do so. **The result is chaos, anarchy and mismanagement, leaving the door wide open for any individual with mala fide intent to take advantage of the overall laxity which results from the leader's capricious and boorish behaviour.**

The wise words of Ally Carter are relevant:

'Rules exist for a reason. Rules exist because when people don't follow them, people get hurt.'

On the other hand, the **advantages of leaders like J.R.D. personally adhering to systems and shunning the VIP culture are multiple. Such a positive example ensures that your people do their job diligently. The gatekeepers (whether to physical or online spaces) will not feel insecure. Rather, they will be able to do their job with honour, secure in the knowledge that they are backed by their leadership in the discharge of their duties**. If the leader takes the lead in ensuring that he takes the time and effort to follow the system, so will others. The organisation as a whole and all associated stakeholders will benefit as a result.

A great example of the way that individuals down the line can do their job well if they know that the leadership will be supportive of their honest actions, was narrated to me by the father of my good friend Dr. Kalim Khan. His father, Mr. Abdul Karim Khan, once mentioned how he witnessed an incident in Dubai where the driver of a judge halted the car outside the gate of the court to allow the judge to alight and walk into the court building. As soon as the judge had left the car, the driver noticed that the judge had left his brief-case in the back-seat. The driver picked up the briefcase, left the car where it was at the entrance to the court building, rushed after the judge, handed over the briefcase, and was back at the car in less than a minute. In that short period, he found a traffic policeman was busy writing out a traffic ticket as penalty for wrong parking. The driver pleaded that he had just left the car for a minute, that the car belonged to a judge of the court, and that he had briefly parked as the judge had forgotten his official briefcase in the back-seat of the car. All to no avail. The traffic policeman rightly pointed out that the driver could have driven ahead until he found a legal parking spot, left his car there, and then walked to court with the briefcase.

The policeman confidently discharged his duties and levied a penalty even upon the car of a judge, because he was fully aware that he would be supported by his superiors in this action.

When the top leadership sets a positive example by being governed not only on paper, but also in practice, by the same set of rules which they expect subordinates to adhere to, the result is nothing short of pleasing perfection.

Leaders at the top **NEED** to demonstrate their adherence to systems and processes, even when it impacts them negatively, just as J.R.D. did. This is vital as it then sets an example down the line, and leaders at lower levels such as regional heads, department heads and the like will also realise that systems are paramount. If the leader himself does not set the right example, then chaos and anarchy will prevail.

We often see our elected leaders and celebrities breaking the queue, the traffic signal, entering hotels without undergoing the mandatory security check and so on at many occasions, and we take it for granted that this is the 'done thing' and attempt to emulate them whenever and wherever possible.

This learning is all the more important for us, as we Indians are often brilliant as individuals, but in general we lack a disciplined and process-driven approach. We love taking short-cuts, by-passing the laid down procedure whenever possible. We take pride in the fact whenever we manage to 'beat the system.' We take pride in the fact that we are experts at *jugaad* (manipulating and beating the system.) But by glorying and revelling in this narrow-minded approach, we unfortunately overlook the fact that it is this shortcoming alone which has prevented us from taking our rightful place at the apex level among leading nations in the global arena.

The very practical advantage of this action of J.R.D.'s is that it instills confidence in security guards and other personnel in the organisation that they can politely question and prevent all those who attempt to secure entry without valid identity, and not get cowed down or bullied into submission when some person with a designation attempts to barge his way in where he is not authorised. **As mentioned, in this electronic age, it is not only physical entry barriers which need to be secured, but also computer gateways which have passwords and other security measures which are developed at great cost to safeguard the organisation's and its clients' interests.** Too often, bosses have been known to ask their subordinates for their passwords and misuse them, or bully the information technology people to grant them access to information which they are not authorised to view.

Dr. Deming, the Quality Guru, who has also been quoted elsewhere in this book, was a genius when it came to matters regarding quality, systems, and common sense. **It was his firm belief, backed by research, that 90 percent of the problems an organisation faces are system-related problems and NOT people-related problems.** He elaborated by saying that if some problem occurred in an organisation, the probability was high that the root-cause of the problem was a shortfall or failure in some system or process or in the application of some system component somewhere. **The front face of that problem could be an individual, but by replacing the individual with another one, you were unlikely to get rid of the problem.** The same problem would in all probability recur even with the new person in place, because the root cause of the problem would lie in the system lacunae. The person appearing to be at fault would just be representative of the systemic defect.

For example, in the learning being discussed, if the security guard failed to question an important-looking individual or a person high-up in the organisational hierarchy about his identity documents and just let him through unchallenged, the chances would be high that it had little to do with the inefficiency of the guard. The greater problem would lie in the fact that someone in the organisational leadership had sent across a written or unwritten signal that important persons in the hierarchy and persons close to them were to be let through without asking for proof of their identity, even though the rules said otherwise. Until this systemic deficiency is removed and a strong message from the top leadership, backed by personal example, reaches the security guards, that **NO ONE** is exempt from by-passing the rule, no change of guard with an apparently more efficient and dedicated individual would make any difference.

Observe and analyse for yourself. In most cases where organisations falter and lose out, the root cause can be traced back to some failure in some system design, or someone failing to follow a well-designed and laid-down system.

If you salute your duty, you need not salute anybody. But if you pollute your duty, you have to salute everybody

-Dr. A.P.J. Abdul Kalam

MR. ASHWANI LOHANI SHOWS THE WAY

On the 29th of September, 2017, a terrible tragedy took place at the Elphinstone suburban railway station in Mumbai. Unexpected rain, heavy rush-hour crowd, unfounded rumours, all compounded to cause panic on a narrow railway foot overbridge, causing a stampede which led to the loss of 23 innocent lives, and injured many more.

Railway Board chairman, Mr. Ashwani Lohani, flew down to Mumbai in the aftermath of the tragedy, and was shocked to see at least 20 high-ranking railway officials waiting to receive him at the airport. He admonished them for wasting their time in coming to receive him, when they should have been helping the victims and the families handle the aftermath of the crisis at the hospital and assisting them with necessary formalities for claiming compensation and with other paperwork.

Although Mr. Lohani had specifically instructed the officials not to come to receive him at the airport, as per their habit – 'protocol,' as they called it – they still turned up in large numbers. Mr. Lohani then asked for a list of the officials who had come to receive him despite his orders not to do so, as he wished to initiate action against them. When no names were forthcoming, he then said that if he were not given the list voluntarily, he would access the CCTV footage from Air India at the airport and personally identify each official who had turned up to receive him.

Even when he had taken over as Railway Board chairman in August 2017, he had warned that the practice of giving bouquets and the overall culture of sycophancy and bootlicking would be done away with.

Truly, Mr. Ashwani Lohani is a government official we can be proud of – one, who like J.R.D., passes on the strong message of – "Never mind my status. You do your duty."

331

Once upon a time (that is how most stories with a message begin), there was an arrogant armchair general who had risen to this high rank based more on who he knew rather than what he knew. This general loved issuing orders, and one day he issued an order (quite a sensible one, really) that no vehicle, meaning **NO VEHICLE**, was to be allowed to either enter or leave his sensitive military base without displaying its official identity seal. If the driver of any vehicle attempted to do so without having the requisite identification seal, the sentry on duty was empowered to take suitable action.

The very next day after this order had been issued, a keen young soldier was on guard duty at the entrance to this base when the general's car rolled up to the gate. The car did not have the required identity seal on it, so the young soldier followed the orders he had been given and refused to let it pass.

 This made the general furious, and he got down from his vehicle and bellowed at the staunch young soldier, **"Young man, do you have any idea who I am? I am the top-ranking officer on this base. Move aside and let my car go through."**

The soldier refused to budge or let the car go through without seeing the required identification seal.

Then the general tried a different tactic. In a softer voice, he said, **"I'm the general who issued this order. I'm glad you're doing your duty well. Now let my vehicle go through."**

The young soldier once more refused.

Then the general lost his temper and shouted, **"I'm the officer in charge of this base and I'm giving my driver orders to drive right through. Do you understand that? Do you have any questions?"**

The young soldier replied:

"YES SIR, JUST ONE. WHO DO I SHOOT FIRST, YOU OR YOUR DRIVER?"

Unfortunately today, there is increasing appreciation being showered on what is wrongly termed the 'Indian way of working' - *Jugaad* or manipulation. Jugaad is a word which means resolving issues by bending the rules, and is a word which has absolutely negative connotations. In an era where ethics lie secondary to the ability to get quick results, it is seen as an intelligent by-passing of laid-down rules by those who prefer to take short-cuts (and by doing so, put the entire system and everyone who relies on it in jeopardy).

But J.R.D. never resorted to *jugaad* to get his or his organisation's work done. J.R.D. showed us by personal example that the disciplined way was always the best way in the long run. The least we can do to respect his legacy is to follow the path he bravely outlined and illuminated.

POINTS TO PONDER AND PRACTICE

- **Leadership is not a position or a title; it is action and example** – Unknown

- Many of the rules we tend to ignore and often break are in fact very practical and sensible as they ensure the safety, security and convenience of all stakeholders. It is the leader's duty to encourage all concerned to follow the rules and the laid-down system by setting a positive example himself

- **Leaders are always on the lookout for tools they can use to enhance their leadership effectiveness. But the most effective and powerful tool they could hope to use is available to them free of cost. It is the strength of their own personal example. Why not use it to the fullest?**

- This learning is best summed up by the ancient yet relevant Latin proverb:
  '*Absurdum est ut allos regat, qui seipsum regere nescit*'
  (It is absurd that a man should rule others, who cannot rule himself)

STAND UP FOR YOUR PEOPLE WHEN THEY ARE IN THE RIGHT

> *Always stand up for what you think is right, even if you are the only one standing*
>
> -UNKNOWN

WHAT **J.R.D.** BELIEVED IN AND **PRACTICED**

> *First they came for the Socialists, and I did not speak out –*
>
> *Because I was not a Socialist.*
>
> *Then they came for the Trade Unionists, and I did not speak out –*
>
> *Because I was not a Trade Unionist.*
>
> *Then they came for the Jews, and I did not speak out –*
>
> *Because I was not a Jew.*
>
> *Then they came for me – and there was no one left to speak for me.*
>
> -MARTIN NIEMOLLER
>
> (Speaking as a victim of Adolf Hitler's Nazi regime)

There are many instances where J.R.D. fearlessly stood up for his people in front of government officials, when these officials felt they could take arbitrary decisions simply because they had the power to do so.

As an example, take the case of Mr K.G. Appuswamy, who was an early employee of J.R.D.'s airline, and who steadily rose to be a Board member of Air India. Mr. Appuswamy recalls how in 1975-76, Sanjay Gandhi indicated he would have him removed from the Board of Air India, not because Appuswamy had done anything wrong, but simply because Sanjay wanted to prove some political point.

Rather than face the humiliation of being sacked for no fault of his own, Appuswamy told J.R.D. that he would prefer to resign before the official letter terminating his services reached him.

J.R.D. firmly stated that Appuswamy would do no such thing. J.R.D. even wrote three letters to Prime Minister Indira Gandhi about this, and when he received no response, Appuswamy says J.R.D. even telephoned the Prime Minister about this case.

J.R.D. also sought an appointment with the Prime Minister to discuss Appuswamy's unfair removal, where he told the Prime Minister that Appuswamy was going to leave and Air India would suffer as a result, and that he (J.R.D.), too, may have to consider quitting if this was the way his people were going to be mistreated.

A quality which a leader needs to develop is the quality of ensuring that the men he leads have complete and utter faith in him, and that his men are always willing to support him, **because he always stands up for them when needed**.

"**Whether right or wrong, they are my men, and no one has the right to correct them except me**," is what a true leader of men develops as a matter of honour, whether in the armed forces or in the corporate world.

'**Always defend and praise in public. Strip and punish in private if need be**,' should be the philosophy of the evolved leader.

LEARNINGS ▬▬▬▬
FOR LEADERS

> *"Courage is what it takes to stand up and speak; courage is also what it takes to sit down and listen"*
>
> -Sir Winston Churchill

One of your primary duties as a leader is to stand up and support your people when they are being victimised without cause. If you fail to do so, your leadership position will be under serious cloud.

The situations could vary. You could be a department head standing up to your CEO to support your staff when they are in the right. It could be that the CEO has been given an incorrect picture by someone in which your staff member has been painted as being in the wrong. If such is the case, it is your duty to meet the CEO and set the record straight, in a polite but assertive way.

Or you could be a supervisor standing up to your department head to support a staff of yours who is being treated unfairly by an unreasonable customer or supplier for no fault of his.

Or possibly, like J.R.D., you may be in a very senior position and may be defending one of your senior executives in front of a highly-placed government official. As just noted, when it came to supporting his staff, J.R.D. even reached out to the Prime Minister and had his say.

In such situations, do not worry too much about your reputation or how standing up for your staff could negatively impact your relationship with your seniors. **Your role in such situations is not to aggressively oppose and have a dispute with your seniors.** Your job is to set the record straight; to present your staff's side of the story. In most cases, the senior person may not be behaving unnecessarily vindictive with your subordinate, but he too may have certain compulsions, or he may be having some misunderstanding with regards to your subordinate. This, in most such scenarios, is what you would need to speak up about and clarify and sort out.

I was recently having a career-related discussion with a former student currently employed with a leading manufacturing firm in the paints industry. I asked him how things were, especially since his reporting structure had just changed and he now reported to a new boss. He responded that while the new boss was more intelligent and more dynamic to work with, he still preferred the previous boss.

I asked him the reason, and his answer was, **"While this new boss appears better on almost all parameters, I get the impression that he does not stand up for his subordinates when needed. That is where the old boss scored better and that is why I would rank him higher on the leadership scale."**

Not only is standing up to defend your subordinates when they are in the right, the correct and proper thing to do, but it also increases your standing as a leader, as this is a step which builds your personal trust factor among your other subordinates also.

Sometimes, bosses need to stand up for their employees in front of unreasonable and extraordinarily rude and arrogant customers as well. Jim Belosic, the CEO of *Shortstack*, offers some advice in this regard, the gist of which is encapsulated in the following four points:

1. Employees will be loyal to you if you are loyal to them

2. You can tactfully tell exceedingly arrogant customers that such behaviour towards your staff is not acceptable

3. You **CAN** work out middle-path solutions that work both for your customers as well as your employees

4. Sometimes, the unreasonable customer **HAS** to go

Richard D. Edler, an advertising professional and former managing director of *McCann-Erickson*, New York, wrote:

"It's okay to fire your customer."

'The above quote from a *Wall Street Journal* editorial that impressed me in March 1992. The Journal put a unique twist on good business relationships. In the advertising business there is probably nothing you can do to build morale faster than to resign a client – even when the employees know it might mean hard times and even layoffs.

You see, it always goes the other way. The trade press each week headlines the firing of this or that agency by a client, and the inevitable announcement of a new agency review. Agencies always seem the spineless victim of client whims.

After a while, you start to think this is the way things are supposed to be. But truly great agencies – or any great company serving customers – have their own standards too.

And there ought to be customers you really don't want and wouldn't take, regardless of revenue. Your employees need to know that abusive behavior by any customer will not be tolerated, no matter how important that customer is. That way you and your employees can truly love the customers you have – because you have mutually selected each other. It just changes how you think about everything. And it raises everyone's head up a notch in the process.'

Field Marshal Sam Manekshaw was probably India's most admired and respected military leader. He is also credited as being the brains and the motivation behind India's swift and decisive victory in the 1971 Indo-Pak war.

One among the many beloved traits that Manekshaw possessed was that he always believed that no one, not even senior politicians superior in designation to Manekshaw himself, should mistreat or misbehave with his subordinates.

FIELD MARSHAL
S.H.F.J. MANEKSHAW

He always made it a point to strongly stand up for his men in such situations, which is one of the reasons why his men loved him dearly.

One such example where Manekshaw stood up for his subordinate officer follows:

On a rather warm day, the then Defence Secretary, Mr. Harish Sarin (a powerful civil servant), when entering the Defence Ministry's conference room, is said to have told a Colonel already seated near the window, "**You there, open that window!**"

As the Colonel was getting up to obey this senior civil servant's order, came a sharp "**Sit down**", from Sam Manekshaw, who had just entered the same conference room from another door.

Turning to the Defence Secretary, Sam said politely but assertively, "**Mr. Secretary, don't you EVER address my officers in that tone of voice. You may however say, 'Sam, would you please open that window,' and I will open the window for you. That officer you called out to is a Colonel, and not 'You there.'**"

Harish Sarin, suitably humbled, mumbled something to the effect that he did not mean it that way, to which Sam replied, "**I don't care how you meant it. I heard it and didn't like it.**"

No wonder Sam was beloved by all his men, even the legendary *Gurkhas* affectionately referring to him as Sam *bahadur* (Brave).

The following material is modified from *John Ive – The Genius Behind Apple's Greatest Products* by Leander Kahney (Portfolio-Penguin)

JOHN IVE is the behind-the-scene British-born designer who strongly collaborated with Steve Jobs to develop some of the world's most iconic products – including the iMac, iPad, iPod and iPhone.

He is regarded as the world's leading technology innovator, has been awarded a place on the 2013 Time 100 list, and has even been knighted for his immense contribution to design and enterprise.

Sir John Ive is not only a great developer, but an outstanding leader as well. He headed the design team at Apple, and was extremely protective of the people he led.

Here is what Gautam Baksi, a former Apple product design engineer, had to say with regard to the fiercely protective manner in which Sir John Ive led his team: "He'll take the blame personally for screw-ups. He'd fall on the sword (himself take the blame) for the weakest part of the design. If it's something not up to stuff (up to the mark), he'd personally say it was his fault. I never felt like he threw any of the team members under the bus (never let others take the blame)."

And Doug Satzger, another design team member, proudly stated that Ive was never afraid to bypass his executive colleagues and speak to Steve Jobs directly if someone challenged any of his team members.

No wonder Sir John Ive is highly regarded as the world's leading technical designer today.

POINTS TO PONDER AND PRACTICE

- These are delicate situations, and need to be handled, but handled with care

- The absolutely first thing to do when you feel your subordinate is being unfairly victimised, is to get your facts thoroughly and completely right. This fact-gathering should preferably be done from more than one source so as to eliminate bias or a one-sided story

- Once you are convinced of your subordinate's innocence, or at least partial innocence, seek an appointment with the concerned senior at the earliest. Meet him with all the facts. Listen to what he has to say. Then firmly present your case, also bringing out the good aspects of the track record of the concerned subordinate and how he or she has been an asset to the organisation

- Your word will carry weight, and seeing how you are personally standing up to defend your subordinate, will, in most cases, resolve the matter

- Once the matter is resolved, explain to the concerned staff member that whenever he is in the right, you will always be firmly behind him, but if in the situation he was partially (though not completely), at fault, you could point out how he could modify his behaviour or approach to avoid similar situations from arising in future

MOTIVATE YOUR PEOPLE THROUGH CONCRETE AS WELL AS THROUGH SYMBOLIC GESTURES

> *Whatever makes men feel old is mean – an empire or a skin-flint shop. Whatever makes men feel young is great – a great war or a love story. And in the darkest of the books of God there is written a truth that is also a riddle. It is of the new things that men tire – of fashions and proposals and improvements and change. It is the old things that startle and intoxicate. It is the old things that are young*
>
> -G.K. CHESTERTON

WHAT **J.R.D.** BELIEVED IN AND **PRACTICED**

> *Human beings are complex creatures. They do not live on bread alone. They need to be inspired and motivated by acts which are out of the ordinary, to rekindle in them the belief that they, too, can aspire to and reach great heights. Symbolic gestures, especially those taken at great personal risk by a leader who is loved and trusted, inspire a whole new generation of employees and induct them into the corporate philosophy much more effectively than the most rigorous induction programme devised by any Human Resources Department ever could*
>
> -CYRUS M. GONDA

Of course, in all concrete and material matters, J.R.D. more than took care of and adequately compensated his people, both through monetary as well as non-monetary means.

But he also rose beyond the ordinary, and motivated them by the force of powerful, symbolic gestures, which encapsulated the founding philosophy of the Tata group and encouraged his employees to replicate this philosophy in their personal and professional lives.

On October 15th, 1932, J.R.D. Tata piloted the inaugural flight of Tata Aviation Service (as the airline was then named), carrying a precious load of air-mail in a single-engine Puss Moth plane from Karachi to Bombay (as Mumbai was then known). In the plane was J.R.D., all by himself, and in the rear compartment behind the pilot's seat was the bag of mail he was ferrying from Karachi to Bombay. The tiny aeroplane flew that inaugural flight at a maximum speed of 92 miles per hour. **J.R.D. was then twenty-eight years old**.

On October 15th, 1962, the **thirtieth anniversary** of that first flight, J.R.D. re-enacted the flight from Karachi to Bombay, again in a similar plane – a De Havilland Leopard Moth, as a Puss Moth was not available. Asked why he re-enacted his original flight, J.R.D. said to the staff of Air India (by 1962, the airline had been renamed Air India), **"I re-enacted the inaugural flight, not for sentimental reasons alone, or for the pleasure of doing it. I hoped that to those of you who had never even seen a Leopard Moth in the air, it would bring home the fact that the great airline which we all serve today could be, and was actually built from the smallest beginnings, with little more to sustain it at first than the love, the sweat and the devotion of those who worked for it. If my flight helped to bring this message to you, its purpose has been fulfilled."**

This was done and said by J.R.D. on the thirtieth anniversary of his inaugural flight of the airline, **when J.R.D. was aged fifty-eight**.

Lead and inspire people. Don't try to manage and manipulate people. Inventories can be managed but people must be led

-ROSS PEROT

Stunningly, **another twenty years later, at the age of seventy-eight**, on the **fiftieth anniversary** of that historic first flight, J.R.D. once again re-enacted the flight from Karachi to Bombay in a Leopard Moth. **The waiting crowds cheered as his plane landed, little realising that just three weeks earlier, J.R.D. had suffered a heart attack. His cardiologist Dr. F.E. Udvadia, reluctantly gave him permission to undertake the flight, saying, "Had I tried to stop him he may have gone ahead in any case."**

This time, **J.R.D.'s message to the audience which received him at the airfield was**, "I wanted to dedicate a gesture to those, at first in handfuls, then in hundreds, and finally in thousands, the men and women who ..... have helped me to build up Air India and Indian air transport. I wanted to express in some way my gratitude and pay tribute to them and I did not know of any other way of dramatising this event.....I also had another reason. As I get older, I feel distressed that in recent times there is a growing sense of disenchantment in our land, that the hopes, the aspirations, the enthusiasm, the zest, the joy with which freedom was received in our country some years ago, the achievements that we participated in, including the creation of Air India, had faded. So I thought that perhaps this flight would rekindle a spark of enthusiasm, a desire to do something for the country....This flight of mine today was intended to inspire a little hope and enthusiasm in the younger people of my country that despite all the difficulties, all the frustrations, there is a joy in having done something as well as you could and better than others thought you could."

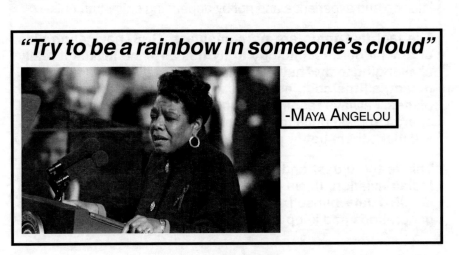

"Try to be a rainbow in someone's cloud"

-MAYA ANGELOU

FLYING A PLANE THAT JRD FLEW

On 19th December, 2016, the *Mumbai Mirror* carried an article wherein the president of the Bombay Flying Club, Captain Mihir Bhagvati, penned his thoughts on piloting India's oldest flyable plane – the Piper Super Cub PA18. Captain Mihir's thoughts went as follows:

'The Piper Super Cub PA18, imported in the 1940s, was one of the most modern aircraft of its time, during the end of World War II days. All the other aircraft then were biplanes, i.e. they had four wings. I consider myself a very fortunate aviator to fly this era of aircraft which a legend like JRD used to fly back in his youth in the 1940s.

This aircraft was restored to its former glory by foreman Eric Lobo and his technicians in 2010. This was a very ambitious project in itself and took six years and over 6,500 man hours to complete.

Flying this aircraft puts you in a different time zone – this aircraft has no steerable nose wheel and it is very challenging to steer her on the ground. The brakes on this aircraft are intentionally weak so that the aircraft wouldn't cartwheel (overturn) when the pilot applied hard brakes. The centre of gravity of the aircraft is so far back that it is really difficult to make a landing in a cross-wind scenario. This aircraft can only be flown by "the seat of your pants," i.e. using intuition and experience and not by depending on instruments.

The fact that there are no computers, GPS, navigation aids or any modern technology to fly this airplane makes it really challenging to fly. That's what I love about flying this tail plane. In fact, all the cool, aerobatic planes the world over are tail planes. I always recommend that newer pilots fly a tail-wheel aircraft at least once to experience the old era of aviation. This will make them better pilots.

This is the oldest and the most precious piece of history in Indian aviation, flown by the father of aviation, Bharat Ratna Mr. JRD Tata himself. We need to preserve it for the future generations and keep her flying.'

LEARNINGS ▬▬▬
FOR LEADERS

> *"The future belongs to the young. We must not only trust them with responsibility but must thrust it upon them while they are still young and full of energy, zest, hope and even illusions. However heart-breaking it may be to ourselves, we must make way for the new generations even when we feel we are still in our prime"*
>
> -J.R.D. TATA

Leaders must strive above all to **INSPIRE**. That, say many experts on leadership, is their primary role. To be a guiding star.

Symbolic gestures are not mere tokens. They are much more than that.

Symbolic gestures are food for the soul.

Often, these symbolic gestures on the part of the leader would involve great courage in one form or another. In J.R.D.'s case, it required great physical courage. In other cases, such gestures may require the demonstration of moral courage, especially if it is a gesture which could be taken negatively by certain powerful segments that may be having their own vested interests. Whatever the situation may be, **leaders should not pass up any opportunity to enact such gestures to genuinely motivate their people and inform them, preferably through demonstration by personal example, about the rich history and founding philosophy of the organisation which they represent.** Once people are motivated from within by the passion and zeal demonstrated by their leader, it sets in motion a sequence of events which on their own steam can take the organisation to previously unattained heights.

Consider the global importance given to the opening and closing ceremonies of a FIFA World Cup or an Olympic Games. Or, within a country, the ceremony of the raising and lowering of a national flag and also the flying of a flag at half-mast on solemn occasions.

These gestures may not have material value. They may be purely symbolic in nature, but without them, life as we know it would not exist.

A story is told of a Frenchman in olden days who had earned the wrath of his king. He was locked up alone in a dungeon. He was there for a long time and it seemed that even his friends and family had forsaken him. In utter loneliness and frustration, he picked up a stone lying on the floor of the dungeon and scratched out on the wall – '**NO ONE CARES**.' A few days later, a small green shoot appeared through a crack in the damp floor of the dungeon. It slowly grew and reached out to the sunlight coming in from the small window on the ceiling of the dungeon. The only thing the prisoner had as an occupation was to watch the growth of the shoot each day. Even though he was given an extremely limited ration of water every day, he saved a little water from that to pour over the shoot till it grew strong and a small blue bud blossomed on it. As the sunlight touched the bud and its petals gradually opened to form a beautiful flower, tears of joy and gratitude streamed down the prisoner's face. He picked the stone, crossed out the words he had initially written, and in their place carved out – '**GOD CARES**.'

POINTS TO PONDER AND PRACTICE

- As a leader, your focus definitely needs to be on the practical elements that go into running an organisation. Things such as cost reduction, pricing policies, the entering of new markets, coming up with new lines of products and services, customer satisfaction scores, and the like. Without a leader's focus on these important organisational parameters, an organisation loses focus and drifts aimlessly

- But at the same time, **your job as a leader requires you to rise above the mundane and to inspire**. In this role, you need to take the driver's seat. You need not fly an aeroplane solo at the age of seventy-eight as J.R.D. did, but there are other symbolic gestures you as a leader can perform to keep your employees' motivation at levels where they are inspired to reach out and do their best

- Remember, you cannot do everything by yourself. One thing, though, which you **CAN** do by yourself, is the all-important function of being a motivator and an inspiration to your people. Do this well, and your people will do the rest of the work on your behalf

TAKE INPUTS FROM
SUBORDINATES AND COLLEAGUES
BEFORE TAKING
CRUCIAL DECISIONS –
(ALSO, TAKE QUICK DECISIONS)

❝ *A genuine leader is not a searcher for consensus, but a moulder of consensus* ❞

-MARTIN LUTHER KING, JR.

WHAT **J.R.D.** BELIEVED IN AND **PRACTICED**

❝ *Leadership is based on inspiration, not domination; on cooperation, not intimidation* ❞

-WILLIAM ARTHUR WOOD

J.R.D. witnessed the cruel stroke of the Indian government snatching away the airline he had painstakingly and lovingly built from scratch and having it 'nationalised.' **After this move, the government offered J.R.D. the chairmanship of the airline, though under government control.**

It was a crucial decision whether to accept this position or decline the offer, not only for J.R.D. personally, but also the whole Tata group, towards which J.R.D. had ultimate responsibility.

The **negative impact** of taking on the chairmanship offered by the government was that it could have possibly encouraged the government to repeat the process of nationalisation in other industries and possibly with other Tata companies, as J.R.D. accepting the chairmanship could indicate surrender to government policies. On the **positive side**, accepting the chairmanship would ensure that the high standards set for Air India when it was controlled and managed solely by the Tatas would continue with J.R.D. being at the helm as Chairman.

J.R.D. did not take this monumental decision by himself, but called a meeting of eighteen of his heads of department from the Tata group and various Tata companies, and sought their inputs on whether he should or not take up the position which the government had offered him.

He explained the situation and then requested each of the eighteen present to give their individual views.

A majority of those present felt he should accept, and that is what he ultimately did, although his initial personal reaction had been to refuse the offer. A condition he insisted upon before accepting was to ensure that existing shareholders of Air India should be fairly compensated by the government.

———————

J.R.D. was a largely self-taught man, as his entry into the Tata group at an early age meant sacrificing a university education. But he never let a lack of formal higher education make him feel envious or antagonised towards those who had an opportunity to avail of it.

In fact, whereas some self-taught CEOs resent qualified subordinates and tend to belittle them at every opportunity they get, J.R.D. valued and prized his qualified team and ensured that whenever he took a decision which a subordinate would have to execute, he consulted the concerned subordinate and sought his inputs before taking the decision. He felt this was essential as it would be they who would be executing it, and they must be convinced about the soundness and appropriateness of the decision, and not merely execute it half-heartedly because J.R.D. had said so. **He always loved to seek insights and inputs from experts in a field, and after having secured that knowledge and having personally understood the issue, he would then take a decision on a consensual basis.**

J.R.D. was also a sound and quick decision-maker, who never let his ego get in the way of taking decisions which would benefit the organisation.

Nari Dastur, the manager of Air India for Germany in the 1950s, recalls an intense discussion he once had with J.R.D. at Dusseldorf airport in Germany. Dusseldorf was then the centre of operations in Germany for Air India, but Dastur, having sound knowledge of local conditions, explained why he felt Air India would benefit if they shifted their centre to Frankfurt airport in Germany. J.R.D. felt the suggestion was ridiculous, as ninety-nine percent of passenger traffic for Air India in Germany originated in the Dusseldorf area and not in Frankfurt. Dastur was persistent and gave logical and technical reasons for his suggestion. But J.R.D. left the meeting, apparently unimpressed by Dastur's reasoning.

However, the very next day, Dastur received a call from the Air India manager in Bombay, telling him that J.R.D. had ordered the move from Dusseldorf to Frankfurt, in line with Dastur's suggestion.

J.R.D. had given heed to Dastur's inputs, and realising that Dastur being the man on the spot, and an intelligent one, and also having the good of the organisation at heart, felt that his opinion made sense. Once J.R.D. realised that, he wasted no time in conveying his decision to support Dastur's views and secure an advantage for the organisation.

It makes little sense if you as a leader hire the best of people, place them in strategic positions, and then fail to listen to or act upon their advice, of course; after giving quick but sufficient thought to their inputs. Quick should never mean rash or insufficiently thought out.

LEARNINGS
FOR LEADERS

> *" It doesn't make sense to hire smart people and then tell them what to do; we hire smart people so THEY can tell US what to do "*
>
> -STEVE JOBS

Though some leaders have preferred a dictatorial style of functioning, and it does appear to work in certain cases, over a period of time it is the consensual style of leadership which produces the best results.

Most leaders have their key team of advisors in place. A majority of these advisors would be experienced and qualified individuals, sufficiently well-versed with the handling of various situations which could arise in the course of business.

It would only be of help for a leader to seek their valuable inputs and consider their advice seriously, before taking crucial decisions which would impact the organisation and stakeholders. But of course, this requires **courage** on behalf of the leader to suppress his ego and to not take advantage of his elevated position.

It is very difficult for an individual who has a high opinion of himself to summon up the discipline and courage to suppress his arrogance and listen to what others have to say, especially if these others are in subordinate positions to him. But it is essential that this be done if the true essence of leadership is not to be diluted.

Besides, if members of the key team are not consulted, and their inputs and advice often ignored, they could feel disgruntled and not wanted. These are **knowledge workers**, and their motivation needs to be constantly kept at peak levels. They need to feel **involved** in the functioning and decision-making of the organisation. After all, that is what they are being handsomely compensated for.

I am aware of some owner-driven organisations where a team of highly qualified individuals have been recruited, but are never even consulted on vital decisions. They are there in the position of '**rubber stamps**.' Why, then, are they hired? Because it is simply a matter of prestige for certain CEOs to have highly qualified people reporting to them.

A similar situation arose a few years ago in the organisation – *Home Trade*, which was a financial advisory organisation that resorted to fancy advertising, using the services of paid, high-profile celebrity brand endorsers. After attracting large sums from gullible investors through high-pressure sales tactics, the money was siphoned off, never to be seen again. In that organisation too, the promoter had hired highly qualified individuals from premier institutions to soothe his ego, and also as an advertising gimmick to lure investors into believing that the organisation was being handled by a team of experts.

Such gimmicks serve little purpose in the long-term or even in the middle-term.

A sensible leader realises the importance of his core advisory team and knows that many heads are better than one, especially when it comes to sound decision-making.

A leader who wishes the best for his people and his organisation would do well to follow the advice of **General Douglas MacArthur,** who with great insight said: '**A true leader has the confidence to stand alone, the courage to take tough decisions, and the compassion to listen to the needs of others. He does not set out to become a leader, but becomes one by the quality of his actions and the integrity of his intent.**'

NAPOLEON BONAPARTE

Decision-making needs to be given more importance than it currently is being given in the scheme of leadership.

For as **Napoleon Bonaparte** observed: '**Nothing is more difficult, and therefore more precious, than to be able to decide.**'

POINTS TO PONDER AND PRACTICE

- As a leader, you should ensure that your core team consists of a healthy mix of experts in multiple disciplines, so that a wealth of expert advice is always available to you when you need it. **Do not appoint individual experts who merely duplicate talent which is already available.** On your team, try and **include** an **industry-related expert**, an expert on **quality**, an expert on **customer service**, an ace in **people management**, a **finance** and **tax** man, a **legal** advisor, a person with expertise in **information technology**, a **communication** specialist. These are disciplines essential for the functioning and success of any organisation today

- Your task as a leader would be to synergise the efforts of these mercurial individuals, encourage them to function at peak performance, motivate them to retain their talents with the organisation, and of course, learn from and benefit from their expertise

- **Never let your ego come in the way of accepting valuable inputs from your subordinates, even if their views differ from your own**

- The debate to identify the **difference between a manager and leader** has produced some interesting observations. One of the best thoughts on this subject was brought forward by Warren G. Bennis, who said: '**The MANAGER asks HOW and WHEN; the LEADER asks WHAT and WHY?**'

- Keep the words of Warren G. Bennis in mind when practicing your leadership role. Before taking decisions, ask more questions that begin with 'what' and 'why,' rather than questions that begin with 'how' and when.' **Leave the questions which begin with 'how' and 'when' to your subordinates to ask and to answer**

- Apply what a wise man once said on the subject of leadership: **LEAD MORE, MANAGE LESS**

MATURE LEADERS NEVER HOLD GRUDGES

> " Heaviest thing to carry..... a grudge "
>
> -UNKNOWN

WHAT J.R.D. BELIEVED IN AND PRACTICED

> " People who forgive and move on are far happier people. They are also more productive, as they can now channelise their energies into positive arenas, rather than waste precious energies in self-destructive and negative thoughts of hatred and revenge "
>
> -CYRUS M. GONDA

After the government-enforced nationalisation of the Tata Airline, it was split into two by the government – Air India (for international operations), and Indian Airlines (for domestic operations).

J.R.D. was offered and graciously accepted the Chairmanship of Air India. He was also asked by the concerned minister, Mr. Jagjivan Ram, as to whom J.R.D. would recommend for the post of Chairman of Indian Airlines, from a list of people the minister had short-listed.

The first and second choice of names that J.R.D. suggested from the list provided to him were not considered by the minister. Instead, the minister appointed a man called Mr. B.C. Mukharji as Chairman of Indian Airlines, who right from the start, without cause, rhyme or reason, behaved in a very hostile fashion with J.R.D. Whenever J.R.D. set up appointments with him to discuss issues of mutual concern, the appointments were cancelled by Mukharji at the last minute without any explanation or apology. This wayward behaviour continued till J.R.D. took up the matter with the minister, who settled the differences between the two.

Then one day, ironically, it was Mukharji who was in need of J.R.D.'s help. Mukharji was over-burdened with work and decided he needed a helping hand. He wanted to appoint a General Manager for Indian Airlines, but the ministry refused, as they felt that Mukharji, as full-time Chairman, should be able to lead and manage the airline by himself. Mukharji approached J.R.D. for support, and J.R.D., rather than taking this opportunity to get back for the earlier obnoxious behaviour displayed by Mukharji, instead said he would help him.

J.R.D. went to the minister and stoutly defended Mukharji, saying that Mukharji was absolutely justified in requesting for a General Manager as the airline was too large to be handled by one man alone.

J.R.D. did not hold a grudge. In fact, he even made allowances for Mukharji's earlier peculiar behaviour, saying the man did it not because he was hostile, but rather because he was insecure about his position, as he had been wrongly advised by some that J.R.D. would try to dominate him if he allowed J.R.D. to get too close.

A TRUE AND TOUCHING STORY ABOUT FORGIVENESS

Steven McDonald was a young white police officer with a lot to look forward to in life, when in 1986 he was shot by a black teenager in New York's Central Park. The incident left him paralysed from the neck down. But stunningly, McDonald forgave his assailant. He said, "I forgave because I believe the only thing worse than receiving a bullet in my spine would have been to nurture revenge in my heart." And while the shooter was serving his prison sentence, McDonald corresponded with him, hoping that one day they could work together to demonstrate forgiveness and nonviolence. Although the young man died in a motorcycle accident three days after his release from prison, McDonald still travels across the country to deliver his message of forgiveness.

LEARNINGS
FOR LEADERS

> **The first to apologise is the bravest, the first to forgive is the strongest, and the first to forget is the happiest**
>
> -UNKNOWN

The world is a small place.

And the world of business is even smaller.

Holding grudges and getting back at someone when the opportunity comes your way serves no purpose except massaging the fragile ego.

A wise leader rightly forgoes this perverse, purposeless pleasure. It is far more sensible to convert enemies into friends when the opportunity arises, as in today's complex and highly networked world, the more support a leader can secure for his organisation, from whichever source, the stronger his organisation becomes.

One never knows when an enemy or an opponent who is treated well can turn into a useful friend.

It may be difficult for an individual to forget a wrong, but **it makes sense to at least OUTWARDLY FORGET, if you do not have the capacity to INWARDLY FORGIVE.**

Getting along with people, while maintaining your own dignity and self-respect, is after all the crux of the art and science of leadership.

A SHORT AND SWEET SUFI STORY TO PONDER OVER

A Sufi saint was once asked the true meaning of forgiveness.

He replied: **"It is the sweet fragrance that flowers offer when they are mercilessly crushed."**

REACH OUT TO RESOLVE CONFLICT

How exactly does one convert even the bitterest of enemies into friends? Through sincerity and a genuine desire to resolve conflict – a great former president of the U.S.A. shows us the way.

William McKinley was the president of the United States from 1897 to 1901. Throughout his election campaign, a reporter from a newspaper opposed to his campaign followed him around, trying hard to show McKinley in poor light at every meeting he addressed, often resorting to unfair reporting and twisting McKinley's words to misrepresent the truth. McKinley had every right to feel upset with this reporter, but he did not retaliate, did not hold a grudge; and in fact he rather admired the young reporter's persistence.

Finally, the campaign reached a stage where the weather turned bitterly cold, and McKinley noted with pity that the young reporter, still persistently following him, was shivering with cold as he obviously didn't have the money to buy himself some warm clothing. On one such day, when McKinley was riding in his enclosed horse-drawn carriage, he saw the reporter seated shivering outside on the driver's seat, alongside the driver. McKinley had the carriage stopped, gave the young reporter his own warm overcoat, and invited the reporter to sit inside the carriage with him.

The puzzled reporter told McKinley that he had been tearing apart his election campaign ever since it had begun, and added that he did not intend to stop doing his job.

'Yes, yes, I know very well who you are, but now just put on this coat and get inside the carriage where it is warm,' said McKinley, with genuine concern.

In the balance part of the campaign, the reporter still doggedly opposed McKinley's campaign, but he never wrote anything unfair, biased, or untrue about McKinley ever again.

POINTS TO PONDER AND PRACTICE

- Ask yourself – What practical purpose does holding a grudge serve?

- Conflicts, misunderstandings and disputes constantly arise in business. The higher up you progress in the corporate hierarchy, the more people you will meet and interact with, and the more the personal and professional differences which would probably arise as a result

- You as a leader cannot afford to be too sensitive. Rather, display maturity and a large heart and take the first step to resolving misunderstandings, rather than allowing them to fester like sores, destroying your own creative thought and productive output

359

SPAN OF CONTROL IS A VERY REAL AND PHYSICAL LIMITATION WHICH LEADERS NEED TO APPRECIATE

" *No man by himself is a Superman. But the right men coming together under a super leader can create a super organisation* "

-CYRUS M. GONDA

WHAT **J.R.D.** BELIEVED IN AND **PRACTICED**

" *Always remember, the soul of man may have the potential to reach the stars, but in human form, man has a physical boundary to his body, along with which come physical limitations. The leader who appreciates and acts based on this indisputable fact is the leader who will do justice to all that he thoughtfully takes up, and more importantly, all that he thoughtfully leaves for others to handle* "

-CYRUS M. GONDA

Every human being, however brilliant, qualified and experienced, has physical limitations.

It is the superior being who realises these limitations, and does not try to bite off more than he can chew. Rather, he prioritises and takes on only that much which he or she is physically capable of doing, and doing well.

It makes no sense to take on umpteen responsibilities, and then either totally neglect them or perform them half-heartedly due to paucity of time.

Today, many of our politicians, who are holding official portfolios that should occupy their full energies, also take on president-ships of various sports bodies and cultural bodies, doing little justice to any of their multiple roles.

J.R.D. realised this basic fact early on, and promptly acted upon it.

In 1938, on the untimely death of his predecessor, Sir Nowroji Saklatwala, J.R.D. was appointed Chairman of the Tata group, (the largest business and industrial conglomerate in India). He suddenly found his hands full with a business empire that dealt in products and services as varied as insurance, cement, oil, textiles, soaps, aviation, steel, electric power, hotels, and a range of other products. (Yes, insurance as well. New India Assurance was at that time a Tata company which was later snatched away by the Government and nationalised.)

J.R.D., thrust into this responsibility at a young age, was not sure of the road ahead (no human being can be), but about one thing he was crystal clear. He would not take up the operational responsibilities of all these diverse companies and rush from Board meeting to Board meeting, with little time to perform the true strategic and creative work of the leader.

He took the **bold decision** to forego and give up the chairmanship of certain group companies, unlike his worthy predecessor, Sir Nowroji, who had held the chairmanship of all companies in the Tata group.

It requires courage to give up positions of prestige and power which are yours for the asking, but which you know you would not be able to do full justice to. The organisation which the individual leads will benefit greatly from such an unselfish decision.

J.R.D. identified able and capable men within these Tata group companies, and commenced handing over positions of power to them. For example, Sir Homi Mody was appointed Chairman of Tata Hydro-Electric. Then J.R.D. found an able individual to run Tata Textiles, and appointed him Chairperson there, and so on.

J.R.D. was very clear with regard to his priorities. The companies where he would personally retain chairmanship were those which he knew best and had a passion for. It made sense to concentrate his energies and creative potential on these firms, and leave the functioning of other companies in the hands of trusted and capable individuals who would do full justice to their roles.

J.R.D. retained Chairmanship of Tata Sons, the parent company, and also of Tata Steel, a company which he knew well, as he had apprenticed there. He also retained Chairmanship of Tata Air Lines, a company he had personally founded and was passionate about.

In this way, J.R.D. literally revolutionised management thought in India, by delegating positions of power which he could have retained for himself, to others whom he knew would do more justice to these roles. **This is the hallmark of a true leader, who puts the organisation and its interests before himself.**

" Twenty-five years ago I didn't know the meaning of the word **BALANCE**.

Now I know.

It means learning to say **NO** to yet another meeting, association dinner, sales pitch, or "It would be nice if you could attend....."

I know now that balance means saying **YES** to leaving the office early to watch your son's Little League (baseball) game, and without your cellular phone. It means arriving late to the office because you wanted to drive your daughter to class; or not coming in at all so you can do something that can't be done on the weekend, and is important to you. What a difference twenty-five years makes. "

– BRAD BALL (President – Davis, Ball & Colombatto)

LEARNINGS
FOR LEADERS

> ❝ *Voluntarily giving up a position of power which has been gifted to you on a platter requires courage of a different kind. It requires the courage to sacrifice, to give up a personal benefit for the greater good. It needs the inner-strength to implicitly believe that it is far more important to concentrate and focus on and do a good job in a few chosen areas, rather than spread your energies and attention thinly across a vast stretch of ground, and add no real value anywhere as a consequence* ❞
>
> -CYRUS M. GONDA

The theory of '**Span of Control**' is a very practical concept in the managerial and leadership spheres. Unfortunately, it is little understood and is often ignored by many managers and leaders in the mad rush to 'achieve' and to 'prove one's self.'

WE ARE BORN, WE GROW, WE LIVE, WE DIE.

IN SHORT, WE ARE HUMAN.

AND WE ARE BY NATURE RESTRICTED BY PHYSICAL LIMITATIONS WHICH APPLY TO ALL HUMAN BEINGS.

THIS IS WHAT ALL OF US, INCLUDING LEADERS, NEED TO REALISE.

Apart from any other consideration, there are **physical constraints** and human boundaries **beyond which** if we attempt to focus our attention and take matters under our control, the quality of our output will suffer and fatigue will result. So it is imperative that as a leader, you develop a good dependable team that shares your philosophy of sensible delegation.

The members of this team can and should have differences of opinion on tactical and operational issues, but need to be aligned on the firm platform of a common organisational ideology, else they will be pulling at cross purposes.

'Span of Control,' in brief, espouses that there is a limitation to the number of subordinates that a superior can effectively lead or manage. **The key word here is 'effectively.'** In practice, an over-ambitious leader could take on much more than he is capable of handling, and even ensure that twenty-five, thirty, or even more subordinates report to him.

But would he be handling them **effectively**?

Would he be able to give all of them sufficient time and attention?

Would he have the time to understand the implications and repercussions of all the resource-allocation dilemmas and other top-level decisions that his multiple subordinates handle? Would he have sufficient energy to guide each one of them when they need it the most?

The actual number of subordinates, according to the theory of 'Span of Control,' that a leader or manager can effectively handle, lies **between five to fifteen**; not more than fifteen.

This is not some arbitrary figure, but has been scientifically identified through on-field and hands-on research. The number ranges from five to fifteen based on:

- The complexity of the work involved
- The experience and dependability of the subordinates concerned
- The experience and the ability of the leader in charge

'Span of Control' being a practical reality is why the managerial concepts of **hierarchy, chain of command**, and **departmentation** were formulated and put into practice.

Bear in mind, that in your aim to be over-ambitious and rise up the corporate leader faster, you do not go overboard and take on more responsibilities than you can effectively handle.

Share the burden, share the reward. That is what a sound leader believes in and practices.

ADOPTING AN APPROPRIATE 'SPAN OF CONTROL' PAYS RICH DIVIDENDS

Charles Duhigg in *Smarter Faster Better*, writes about how in the late 1990s, two economists and a sociologist from MIT decided to study how exactly the most productive people develop strong mental models to take quick and accurate business decisions when most needed.

To conduct this research, they convinced a mid-sized recruiting firm to provide them access to their profit-and-loss data, employees' appointment calendars, and the 1,25,000 email messages the firm's executives had sent over the previous ten months.

The first thing that the researchers noticed as they began sifting through all that data, was that **the firm's most productive workers (its 'superstars'), shared a number of traits.** The trait these 'superstars' had in common was that **THEY TENDED TO WORK ON ONLY FIVE PROJECTS AT ONCE** – a healthy load, but not extraordinary. **There were other employees who handled ten or twelve projects at a time, but these employees had a lower profit rate than the 'superstars' who handled only five projects at a time, and who were more selective about how they invested their time.**

The researchers initially figured that the 'superstars' were pickier because they were seeking out assignments that were similar to previous work they had done. This is because conventional wisdom suggests that productivity rises when people do the same kind of tasks over and over again. Repetition makes us faster and more efficient because we don't have to learn fresh skills with each new assignment. But as the researchers studied these 'superstars,' they found the opposite. The 'superstars' weren't choosing tasks and assignments that leveraged existing skills, but in fact were signing up for projects that required them to seek out new colleagues and which demanded new abilities.

The key to their high productivity lay in the fact they did not exceed working on more than five assignments at a given time.

POINTS TO PONDER AND PRACTICE

- As a leader, you will have many offers and opportunities to take up new responsibilities, in addition to your existing ones. You may be offered chairmanship of various committees and associations, secretaryship of social organisations and clubs, and so on, all of which add power and prestige to your resume

- But before you take on any of these positions offered, pause and reflect whether you will have the time to do justice to these new roles, and will your existing responsibilities suffer as a result. If you feel the need to take on a new role and your hands are already full, you need to give up an existing one. Give up existing roles and responsibilities gradually and gracefully, not leaving your existing stakeholders in the lurch simply because a more attractive opportunity to demonstrate and display your leadership skills has presented itself. These things are noticed and observed, and your future reputation as a leader depends upon how professionally you handle such decisions

- Also ensure that you do not have too many subordinates reporting to you. Keep in mind the concept of 'Span of Control' to attain and maintain leadership effectiveness

A TRUE LEADER SHOWS GENEROSITY BY GIVING MORE IMPORTANCE TO OTHERS THAN TO HIMSELF

" In the midst of all this darkness I sacrifice my ego. There ain't no room for selfish, we do it all for the people "

-ALICIA KEYS

(*LINES FROM THE SONG - 'IT'S ON AGAIN'*)

WHAT **J.R.D.** BELIEVED IN AND **PRACTICED**

" Yes, do give of your wealth. But also give of your time, your expertise, your knowledge; give of yourself "

-CYRUS M. GONDA

Generosity does not equate with the parameters of money and wealth alone. That J.R.D. was never one to hoard his wealth is a well-known fact.

But what is even more important is that he was generous in giving of his own self, **by suppressing his supreme designation as Chairman of the Tata group and letting others in his companies have their say, often at his expense**. He was generous enough to keep his personal philosophies aside and accept people as they were, never discrediting them if they held personal views which were contrary to his own.

When a man can have multiple senior people working under him at any point in time, each of them burdened with their own egos and idiosyncrasies, and yet manage to get along with each one of them, and more importantly get the best from each one of them for the good of the organisation and its many stakeholders, it shows a generous and healthy outlook towards life in general.

As J.R.D. once mentioned, "If I have any merit, it is getting on with individuals according to their ways and characteristics. In fifty years, I have dealt with a hundred top directors and I got on with all of them. **At times it involves suppressing yourself. It is painful but necessary.....**To be a leader you have to lead human beings with affection."

J.R.D. also said: "....**Philanthropy does not mean the donating of money alone. The trouble one takes over someone in need often demands more of oneself than the giving of funds**."

Such was J.R.D. – generous not only with his money, but with his time, and also the sacrifice of his personal ego, which is an act that requires immense courage.

> **" If I have any merit, it is getting along with individuals, according to their ways and characteristics. At times it involves suppressing yourself. It is painful, but necessary "**
>
> -J.R.D. TATA

370

LEARNINGS
FOR LEADERS

> **❝ I've learned that people will forget what you said, people will forget what you did, but people will never forget how you made them feel ❞**

-MAYA ANGELOU

A lovely little lesson on the contradictions between miserliness and generosity, authored by Dieter Franke, says all one needs to know on the subject of giving of one's self, as J.R.D. demonstrated for over half a century. Franke writes:

'Author Stefan Zweig, in his book *Twenty-four Hours in the Life of a Woman*, places his heroine behind a group of gamblers at a gaming table at a casino. **She is not watching the expressions on their faces; she is concentrating on their hands**. Each has a different form and colour, some hands are naked, others glittering with jewellery, some as hairy as any animal's, some moist, some twisted like an eel, but all vibrating with impatience to win.....These hands tell many stories from how they wait, how they grasp things. One notices the claws of the selfish, stingy person, the loose hand of the generous person, the tight fist of the exasperated. **The way a hand treats money tells stories: does it grasp, wrinkle the money together, snap at it, let it lie in the hand?**'

Similarly, following Dieter Franke's advice, if you want to truly understand a leader, observe his actions over a period of time:

- Is he generous with those who report to him?

- Does he respect their ideas?

- Does he appreciate them as individuals with their own merit and standing?

- Does he feel he can rule over them because he is paying for their services?

- Does he often give in to them when it can do no harm to the organisation even when they are wrong, not because he feels they are right, but because he realises the value of a generous act?

These are things a person intending to tread all the way up the path of leadership needs to ponder upon, and find within himself the COURAGE and the largeness of heart to do, if his leadership is to be of value to the organisation he represents.

POINTS TO PONDER AND PRACTICE

- Do not attempt at every stage to push your own agenda forward, even though you may be in a position to do so

- **Let others have their say, let them also feel that their views matter. Then, at crucial junctures, when you need to take a quick decision without consulting others, they will not mind, as you have respected their opinion at other times**

- Remember the words of **Mary Kay Ash**, who said:
  "No matter how busy you are, you MUST take time to make the other person feel important"

FOR **EXCEPTIONAL** LEADERS, **ETHICS** ALWAYS LIES **AT A** HIGHER LEVEL THAN MERE LEGALITY

" *Integrity has no need of rules* "

-ALBERT CAMUS

WHAT **J.R.D.** BELIEVED IN AND **PRACTICED**

" *The greatest homage we can pay to truth is to use it* "

-RALPH WALDO EMERSON

In the early days when J.R.D. had commenced the Tata Air Lines or the Tata Aviation Department, his close friend and partner, Nevill Vintcent, who was a key figure in the Tata Aviation Department coming into being, had been promised a third share of the profits. This had not caused a problem until 1938, when a sudden change in certain government policies resulted in vastly increased business for the airline and saw the profits shoot up over ten times than what they had previously been.

This is when solicitor J.D. Choksi suggested that a third of the share of profits for Vintcent would be a very substantial amount, and recommended that the airline work out a new arrangement with him, reducing his share of profits. J.R.D.'s colleagues agreed with the solicitor. So J.R.D., very unwillingly, approached Vintcent with this suggestion. Vintcent was adamant that an agreement was an agreement, so J.R.D. approached another solicitor, Dinshaw Daji, for advice. Daji was a very honourable man. J.R.D. put the entire situation in front of Daji, telling Daji, "**I want to do the right thing.**"

Daji responded that although in view of the changed circumstances, Vintcent was not legally entitled to the original third share agreed upon, morally he was.

Thus J.R.D. went to Vintcent and told him he would continue to receive his promised third share of profits.

In fact, J.R.D. later revealed that he felt guilty about having let such a situation arise in the first place where he had initially not been fair to Vintcent. **He reiterated that the Tatas respected the moral position above the legalities of an issue, and that is where their strength lay.**

Another instance of J.R.D. choosing ethics over legality comes from the 1970s, when the trucks manufactured by Tatas were high in demand and were short in supply. Unscrupulous individuals outside the company were purchasing and then re-selling these trucks at a premium of Rs. 40,000. **Yet the Tatas refused to increase the prices of their trucks though it was obvious that customers were willing to pay a higher price for them.** As Sumant Moolgaonkar, who headed TELCO, and who had a similar philosophy as that of J.R.D., said, **"Profits should come from productivity and not by raising prices in a favourable market. Our greatest asset is customer affection."**

TATA Truck

J.R.D. supported Sumant Moolgaonkar whole-heartedly and backed him all the way in this ethical decision.

It needs great inner strength of character and courage of conviction to take such decisions, stand by them, and more importantly, implicitly believe that they are the right ones. But J.R.D. had developed reserves of strength and courage which were almost super-human.

There are many other instances of J.R.D. having taken decisions in an ethical manner, losing substantial sums of money in the bargain, but gaining incalculable goodwill and repute for himself as well as for the Tata brand which he represented.

> *Ambition is essential for advancement. But for ambition to remain healthy, it cannot be kept naked. It must be clothed with a cloak of integrity. Because when ambition runs around with no 'clothes' on, it transforms into greed*
>
> -CYRUS M. GONDA

Ambition is a good thing. It helps you reach places. J.R.D. too had high ambition. When he took over as Chairman, the Tata Group consisted of 14 companies; when he retired, the number had risen to an astounding 95. Group revenue had soared under his leadership from 17 crore rupees to over Rs. 10,000 crores. TCS, Titan, Tata Tea, Tata Chemicals and Air India (among many others) which are household names today, were his personal brainchilds. J.R.D. certainly demonstrated ambition. **And amazingly, he achieved all this in a pre-liberalisation/pre-privatisation era and economy.**

But J.R.D.'s ambition was always capped and clothed with ethics and integrity. As an example, the Tatas were the business house in the country which had the maximum experience in the airline industry. When India's economy opened up to privatisation in 1991, the Tatas should logically have been the first new entrants into the aviation sector. They had the experience, the funds, and the credibility. But they did not enter the arena, for one very good reason. Permissions and licenses had to be obtained from the authorities, and we are aware of how licenses at that scale are awarded. As J.R.D. had once said: "**....If we had done some of the things that some other (business) groups have done, we would be twice as big as we are today. But we didn't, and I would not have it any other way.**"

And it is this ambition – but coupled and clothed with a fine cloak of sterling integrity (which prevents it from falling prey to naked greed like has happened in the case of so many other global gigantic business houses which have fallen by the wayside) – which is the main ingredient in the recipe of the sustained success of the Tata Group for well over a century and a half.

........*continued*

375

........*continued*

One of the favourite poems of my late father, which he was very fond of reciting, was *The Brook* by Alfred Lord Tennyson. And the last lines in the poem (the poem being narrated by a stream, or brook, as it moves on through the countryside), which are the most stirring, apply aptly to the Tata Group precisely because of the firm bedrock of ethical functioning on which the Group rests:

And out again I curve and flow

To join the brimming river,

For men may come and men may go

But I go on for ever.

" *When I do good, I feel good, and when I do bad, I feel bad. That is my religion* "

-ABRAHAM LINCOLN

A research-based study, titled *The Most Important Leadership Competencies, According To Leaders Around The World*, was published by HBR on 15th March, 2016. Authored by Dr. Sunnie Giles, President of the Quantum Leadership Group, it was based on a study conducted on 195 leaders from 15 countries, spread over 30 global organisations. Participants were asked to choose what they felt were the 15 most important leadership competencies from a list of 74 provided to them.

Based on this study, the **NUMBER ONE LEADERSHIP QUALITY/COMPETENCY/CHARACTERISTIC** was found to be **HAVING HIGH ETHICAL AND MORAL STANDARDS. A stupendous 67 percent of participants in the study selected this competency.**

Yet, ironically, the Master of Management Studies (MMS/MBA) two-year full-time post-graduate degree course, conducted by Mumbai University, which for many years had in its syllabus the subject of 'Business Ethics and Corporate Governance' (the only ethics-related subject in the entire course syllabus, spread over two years), **ELIMINATED** that subject from the syllabus from the academic year 2015-2016. (This being the same period during which this path-breaking study on Global Leadership was conducted.)

LEARNINGS
FOR LEADERS

Our lives improve only when we take chances – and the first and most difficult risk we can take is to be honest with ourselves

-WALTER ANDERSON

On Christmas day, 2002, I was aimlessly wandering the quiet by-lanes in the quiet suburb of Vile Parle (West), Mumbai. Passing the Vidyanidhi School, I saw a board outside which invited people for a free talk on the subject of Ethics by Dr. Atul Nadkarni of Pennsylvania State University to be conducted that morning. (I remember the date clearly because I still have the detailed notes I took down during the session.) Having nothing better to do, I walked in and entered the room where the talk was scheduled to be held. It was just commencing and there were only around five or six of us present, but the session was amazing. The professor began the workshop by playing a video. The story in the video unfolded as follows.

A court scene was in progress, and the man on trial was an architect. Apparently the case against him was that a building for which he had developed the design plan had collapsed soon after construction, resulting in loss of human lives. The architect said in his own defence that his design plan was without flaw, and that his responsibility ended once he provided a stable design. He added that the builder had used poor quality material for construction which resulted in the collapse. Then the architect was asked how he knew the builder had used poor quality material. The architect replied that he used to visit the building site from time to time while the construction was in progress. While visiting the site, he noticed with his trained eye that the material being used was of a poor quality. But, as it was not officially his responsibility to be part of the construction team, he did not interfere. The judge decided that **LEGALLY** the architect was not in the wrong, as he had done his part of the job well. **His design was without flaw, and in the eyes of the law, that is all that mattered.**

378

The architect was let free and the case would now proceed against the builder for having used poor quality raw material.

There the video ended, and the professor facilitating this session on ethics asked us to discuss and deliberate upon what we had just seen. Although legally the architect was in the right, and the court could not convict him, did we feel he was morally in the right? All present agreed he was not.

This – is the difference between legality and ethics.

WHILE THE LAW HAS ITS OWN LIMITATIONS, ETHICS DOES NOT.

Many corporate houses today function very like that architect.

By hiding behind legalities and technicalities.

With '**conditions apply**' being ubiquitous in fine print.

While this may save them from penalty in the eyes of the law, it does little good to their corporate reputation in the eyes of their customer base.

Just as an example, let us consider a brand which is manufacturing and selling televisions and providing a three-year warranty for the same. The brand may spend crores of rupees on advertising and communicating this fact to customers. But if a customer who has purchased a television approaches the company **one single day** after the warranty period has expired, saying his television set has malfunctioned, he would in most cases be told that since the warranty period is over, there is now nothing the company can do about it. **Legally the company is in the right.** It is not 'liable' to do anything for the customer. **But ethically and morally? That's a different story and a different question all together.**

Ask yourself: 'Does it benefit the television company in the above example to take a legal stand or a moral stand?'

A child would tell you that if you spend crores of rupees on advertising to build a brand, but refuse to invest a few thousand to retain an existing customer who has a genuine grievance, the only term applicable in this case would be:
'PENNY WISE AND POUND FOOLISH.'

Ethical functioning builds personal as well as brand repute and earns tremendous goodwill. And for an ethical organisation, goodwill figures for a substantial component on the asset side of its balance sheet. Today, the **speculator** pressure (I refuse to call such short-sighted people as 'investors') on corporate leaders to focus on legalities rather than on ethics is intense. **But this is exactly where the strong leader with a vision in mind and valour in his heart puts his foot down gently but courageously and firmly, understanding the long-term negative repercussions that a deviation from ethical functioning can have for the organisation which he leads and represents.**

J.R.D. understood this well, and courageously steered the Tata group on the high ethical path for well over fifty long years.

POINTS TO PONDER AND PRACTICE

- If you want to be an outstanding leader, you first need to understand and appreciate the clear distinction between legality and ethics

- Develop the will-power and innate discipline to base your decisions on ethical grounds rather than on mere legal ones, if there is a discrepancy between the two

- Inculcate in your followers the same discipline and insist that this is the path you wish them to take. Let your actions speak to them as loud as your words do

- Often, when individuals in a position of leadership are faced with a challenging situation, the easy way out is to take recourse in legalities and technicalities. But the person who takes the courageous ethical stance is the one who will rise to great heights in his leadership journey. **As an example, Shri Lal Bahadur Shastri, when he was the Railway Minister of India, resigned on moral grounds after a horrific train disaster, accepting personal responsibility for the same. But this did not halt his career. Rather, he went on to become one of the most loved of the Prime Ministers the country has ever had till date**

AUTHENTIC LEADERS ENCOURAGE INNOVATION THROUGHOUT THE ORGANISATION BY GIVING CREDIT WHERE IT IS DUE

> **" A good leader is one who takes a little more than his share of the blame and a little less than his share of the credit "**
>
> -JOHN C. MAXWELL

WHAT **J.R.D.** BELIEVED IN AND **PRACTICED**

> **" It's amazing what you can accomplish if you do not care who gets the credit "**
>
> -HARRY S. TRUMAN

It is well known that J.R.D. Tata partnered with Nevill Vintcent, a former British Air Force Officer, to commence his initial aviation venture.

But the story behind this partnership is an interesting one.

In the early 1930s, Vintcent toured the Indian landscape with his old World War I plane, stopping at various cities and towns, earning his living by giving joyrides in the air to adventurous folk, for whom an aeroplane at that time was an extreme novelty.

Once during the course of his travels through India, he met J.R.D., and suggested to J.R.D. that they partner up for a venture which Vintcent had been planning for some time. He suggested that they set up a company to start an airmail service – picking up airmail from Karachi (which was then part of undivided India), and delivering it to Bombay.

J.R.D., who had also been thinking of setting up some kind of commercial venture involving aviation, was excited with the idea and responded positively. The company was set up, with J.R.D. providing ideas for more routes, and it is this company which later grew to become the gigantic Air India under J.R.D.'s visionary stewardship.

But though it was J.R.D. who carried forward Vintcent's proposal spectacularly, he was generous in putting on record and paying tribute (in J.R.D.'s book *Keynote*), to Vintcent's resourcefulness and ingenuity as being the originator of the idea for their joint aviation venture.

Such generosity requires great courage, as it is human tendency to annexe credit for glory and good work, irrespective of who really deserves it.

J.R.D. thus displayed great moral courage by ensuring that Nevill Vintcent received full credit for the original idea which ultimately led to the formation of Air India, India's national carrier.

LEARNINGS
FOR LEADERS

> *" Giving credit where credit is due is a very rewarding habit to form. Its rewards are inestimable "*
>
> -LORETTA YOUNG

Annexation of false credit for ideas which have been initiated or work which has been done by somebody else is a very common leadership failing; all the more common because it is so very tempting.

But such 'misbehaviour' on part of the leader often comes at great cost to the department or to the organisation.

Once employees are aware that their superior is in the habit of plagiarising and carrying forward their good ideas as his own, personally taking the credit for these ideas when he should rightfully be passing on the credit to the subordinate responsible, the flow of creative ideas emanating from the subordinates dries up rapidly, and the 'well of innovation' goes dry.

Without a constant and continuous flow of ideas emanating from all sources, an organisation cannot hope to sustain in this highly competitive era, where innovation is at a premium, and small start-ups are outpacing established giants simply on the basis of a better business idea.

In almost any organisation, across industries, the most practical and profitable ideas emanate from the grass-root level, as it is individuals at this level who are involved with implementation of existing processes and interaction with customers. **And it is in these vital areas that most innovations are needed – to reduce costs, to speed-up processes, to improve quality, to minimise errors, defects and wastages, and to enhance customer delight.** No wonder then, that **3M** (the developer of Post-it), and renowned as the most consistently innovative organisation in the world, has developed an innovative way to circumvent this problem. **3M** has created an **INTERNAL PATENT OFFICE** within the organisation, where any employee who comes up with an innovative idea or concept, can register it with the internal patent office of 3M, and this gets permanently credited to that employee's name. This prevents the possibility of an over-ambitious boss or unethical superior falsely taking credit for the same in future, and ensures the organisation is blessed with a steady stream of innovative ideas it can take to the market-place, without the originator having to worry about whether he will receive his due share of credit or not.

There is the example of an airline of considerable size, operating over 200 flights a day, which initiated a cost-cutting and profit-enhancing exercise. Fortunately, the leadership of this organisation was an enlightened one, and did not restrict this idea-generation exercise only to those from senor levels of hierarchy, but invited people from all rungs across the organisation to participate in the brainstorming process. At first, the standard and typical suggestions were offered. Someone suggested that they increase fares. Another suggested that they **decrease** fares, to attract more passengers and thus increase revenue. This went on till it came the turn of an employee whose job it was to dispose off the consumed trays of food after the flight had landed. He hesitatingly stated, "I don't know anything about pricing and fare-construction. All I know is that when I empty the consumed trays of food into the garbage disposal, I find that passengers have not eaten the olives we provide as part of the meal and the salad. (Although olives are very expensive and are regarded as a delicacy, it is an acquired taste, and those who are not used to it would find the taste slightly offbeat.) Why are we wasting olives by keeping them as part of the meal when most passengers obviously don't much care for them and they're going straight into the garbage disposal?"

The management found merit in the suggestion and stopped adding olives in the dishes on the airline menu. The quality of the meal did not suffer, as most passengers apparently did not even like the taste of olives. The savings for the airline from this simple suggestion? Four to five olives per food tray. Approximately 250 food trays per flight. Around 200 flights a day. The savings from eliminating olives in the meals amounted to over $500,000 over the next few years. The employee who had offered the suggestion was given a handsome sum of money as his contribution towards this cost-saving.

Often, we believe that what we have achieved is primarily due to our own efforts alone. But behind every success, there are many silent, helping hands. The following story, which appeared in the periodical, *United Presbyterian*, vividly reminds of this.

One autumn, a farmer brought in a beautiful bushel of corn he had grown, and showing it to his wife, proudly said, "A man (referring to himself) deserves some credit for raising corn like that."

The corn, hearing this, thought: "God gave this man the soil to start with, and gave health to him and life to the seed, and while the farmer may have attended to us from time to time, God never ceased His care. God taught my tiny roots to push downwards and get nourishment and life from the soil. He guided my sprouts upward to breathe in the air. He gave the sunshine and dew and rain and sent the wind to help me pollinise every growing kernel of corn. In due time, every kernel filled with nutritious and tasty richness. Then He changed my colour to gold to show me how much He loved me and cared for me."

A famous teacher of agriculture has figured out that man does only about five per cent of the work on an ear of corn to make it grow, and God does ninety-five per cent. So it is with wheat, or oats, or potatoes, or any other product of the soil.

The same holds true in the corporate world and in other aspects of life as well. Not only God, to whom the largest share of credit in any achievement must always go, but also many other unsung colleagues, team-mates, subordinates, and other stakeholders need to be acknowledged and appreciated for their valuable contribution, without which the final deliverable would lose much of its value. Good leaders ensure that they never miss out on this task.

The following is extracted from *Six Simple Rules: How To Manage Complexity Without Getting Complicated*, authored by Yves Morieux and Peter Tollman (HBS), and explains exactly the kind of organisational slowing down which occurs when individuals and teams responsible for the innovation do not get their due.

'A manufacturer of robotics had a problem. The company was always late in launching innovations, often being the last among its competitors to integrate new technologies into its products. What's more, its costs were out of line with industry norms. Management explained the problem as one of psychology: "Our company is not innovative enough because our research and development engineers are not creative enough." The solution (the management decided) was to require the engineers to attend creativity workshops. The initiative only made things worse.

When we (the authors of *Six Simple Rules*) analyzed the work context, **we realized the real goal of the hardware and software units was to be recognized as the creator of a new innovation.** After all, the responsible unit would often have a larger budget and more autonomy as a result. When hardware and software cooperated, however, it was difficult for the head of R & D to know which unit was really responsible for the subsequent innovation. Each unit's behavior was therefore to work in isolation, as long as it took to guarantee that any innovation could be traced back unequivocally to its origin. "We are often the real creator of the new thing, but management doesn't know this, if the hardware and software teams bring their elements together too early in the process.'

If the individuals/teams had resort to a simple 'internal patent office' to register their ideas against their name as soon as they thought of them, this unfortunate scenario could easily have been avoided.

386

POINTS TO PONDER AND PRACTICE

- Do not hesitate to give credit wherever it is due. Doing so does not devalue you as a leader, but in fact enhances your personal leadership brand

- Once you develop the reputation of being sufficiently trustworthy to direct the credit for any ideas given to the correct individual, this trust you gain will expand to all other areas of your leadership aura as well. And once your people trust you, you and your organisation can achieve wonders

- Just like 3M has implemented, your organisation can also consider and commence the setting-up of an internal patent office. In this era of innovation ruling the marketplace, it is something which no organisation can afford to be devoid of

- Once you have set up your internal patent office, publicise it throughout your organisation. Announce that a percentage of the additional profits accrued or a portion of the sum saved from any idea offered will be awarded to the initiator

- Do not operate under the mistaken belief that profitable and productive ideas can only come from individuals in the managerial levels of the hierarchy. Keep your eyes and ears open for ideas which can emanate from any source

- Do not criticise any idea which is offered, even if it sounds weird or impossible to implement, as this may demotivate the person from giving other excellent ideas in the future

- Marina Abramovic rightly observed: **'Your ego can become an obstacle in your work. If you start believing in your greatness, it is the death of your creativity.'** If you insist on crediting the innovative ideas of others to your own account, you will soon lose the urge to be creative yourself. By opting for the easy way to be thought of as creative, you stop working at being really creative, and the creative touch will then elude you forever

NEVER TERMINATE STAFF (UNLESS THEY REALLY DESERVE IT)

> *Great leaders sacrifice the numbers to save the people, because when push comes to shove, numbers won't save you, people will*
>
> -SIMON SINEK

WHAT J.R.D. BELIEVED IN AND PRACTICED

> *Employees who believe that management is concerned about them, as a whole person – not just as an employee – are more productive, more satisfied, more fulfilled. Satisfied employees mean more customers, which leads to profitability*
>
> -ANNE M. MULCAHY

J.R.D. was once asked whether he had ever sacked or terminated anybody during his long stint as head of the Tata group. He replied that he had indeed moved and rotated people to jobs where he felt their talents could be more suitably utilised. He added that at the most he did have to get rid of one or two people, and that too, the decision was taken in consultation with his colleagues. And these one or two people were terminated for genuine reasons, not merely as a cost-cutting measure.

He never even considered retrenching employees in large numbers simply because the economic cycle had taken a short-term downturn as is the accepted norm in many other large organisations.

They were **HIS** people, and he would take care of them, just as they had taken care of his organisation.

CARL SANDBURG

Read the poem *The Muckers* by **Carl Sandburg**. It tells of the time during the Great Depression of 1929 in the U.S.A., where jobs were lost over-night, and men had no money left to feed their families.

The poem depicts a crew of workmen engaged in the dirty and dangerous work of digging a deep ditch to lay a pipeline.

Above them, a group of unemployed men who are unable to find work, stand watching the men at work below.

The men at work below, tired and dirty, are wiping the sweat from their brow and saying, "**What an awful filthy job to be doing.**"

While each of the unemployed men looking on from above, are enviously saying, "**I wish I had that job.**"

LEARNINGS
FOR LEADERS

Employee loyalty begins with employer loyalty.
Your employees should know that if they do the job
they were hired to do with a reasonable amount of
competence and efficiency, you will support them

-HARVEY MACKAY

This is a crucial lesson to learn. The utmost priority for an average worker today as far as his requirements from his organisation and leader are concerned is a sense of **job security**. This is the least he can hope to expect, especially if the worker works hard and intelligently, is an asset to the organisation, and the organisation is a profitable one. This would also seem to be a 'no-brainer' from the organisational point of view, as it stands to reason that a right-thinking organisation would not like to lose an employee who is an asset.

Unfortunately, this is not the way the world works today. Despite the employee being productive and loyal, he has every chance of being sacked without notice, even though he may be on the permanent payroll. The reason for this is simple. It does not benefit the organisation to do so, but it certainly seems to benefit certain short-sighted individuals at top echelons of decision-making in certain organisations. The following illustration will clarify what I mean.

Speaking the other day with a former MBA student of mine, who is now employed with middle-management of a multinational finance organisation with global headquarters in the United Kingdom, was an eye opener. He explained how he headed a team of about ten knowledge workers, all of whom were dedicated and productive people. The organisation too was a profitable one. **Yet, every year around appraisal time, the fear of job loss would strike them all and work at that time would almost come to a stand-still.** The reason for this sorry state of affairs? A directive from Asia-Pacific headquarters in Hong Kong each year to reduce the manpower in his department (and all other departments and teams across the

391

organisation), by fifteen to twenty percent. The Asia-Pacific headquarters in turn gets its instructions for doing so from the global headquarters in the United Kingdom. This has become an annual affair, and my former student, and many other sane and sensible team-leaders like him, struggle and fight hard to not lose their performing team members to such inexplicable and literally insane policies.

The reason why such orders are given is so that the top management can display and demonstrate to key shareholders and investors that they are able to extract the same amount of profits as they did the previous year by using lesser staff. This results in a super-bonus for the top management, and the cycle perpetuates year after year. There are many instances where the recommended strength of a department is ten people, and after people leave/retire/are retrenched, the same department with the same (or even increased) workload, is now functioning with three employees doing the work of ten. **Needless to say, quality of output suffers drastically, impacting customer satisfaction.**

I recently terminated an approximately forty-year-old savings account of mine with a foreign bank, as they had astronomically raised the amount to be kept in the account as a minimum balance. When I informed the person at the branch that I wished to close my account, there was not the slightest iota of concern shown as to why I wished to terminate an account of such long standing. Instead, I was simply handed an 'account-closing form' to fill up. In the form was a question which read: **'Please state your reasons for closing the account.'** Since there was only a single-line space in the form after this question to fill my response, and I wanted to respond in detail and use this as an opportunity to provide what I felt would be valuable feedback, I asked the bank officer assisting me as to what I should fill in the limited space provided. To my surprise, he told me to simply **leave that space blank**. Amazed, I asked him, "**I am closing a forty-year-old account with your bank and you are not interested in the reason I am terminating it?**" His response, though said in a polite tone, floored me. "**Sir, there were once six people doing the work which I alone am doing today. The other five have either retired, resigned, or been retrenched. I really have no time to follow up on such issues. Just fill up the basic details and I will ensure your account is closed and you receive your cheque for the settlement amount.**"

Needless retrenchment has become an unfortunate corporate reality today, and it does the organisation no good for the following reasons:

- Many organisations which resort to such measures are currently profitable, and do not need to slash staff

- The fear of such annual retrenchment makes work stall for at least a couple of months around appraisal time, as everyone is on tenterhooks and cannot concentrate on their work if they are not sure of keeping their jobs

- Such policies prevent the best talent from joining the organisation

- Employees who are good at their work, seeing that their services could be terminated any time, without reason, would look for the first opportunity to quit the organisation

- It also tends to give the organisation a bad name; as being an organisation which cannot show loyalty towards staff who have performed for the organisation

- Errors and mistakes in work are bound to increase, as more work is assigned to less people. As a result, **the customer suffers**, complaints and grievances pile up. The brand loses its reputation and collapses over a period of time

Many such 'leaders' argue that with current levels of competition and shrinking profits, slashing staff is the only alternative. This need not be the case.

SOUTHWEST AIRLINES

A classic positive example in this regard is that of Southwest Airlines, a domestic carrier based in the United States. After the tragic World Trade Centre attacks in the year 2001, the number of passengers using flying as a mode of transport fell sharply in the U.S.A. for at least a year. Of course, this did affect revenues and profitability of all airlines concerned. **But while other airlines used the opportunity to retrench staff, Southwest made a policy decision not to let a single employee go.** Southwest too, could have used the drop in business to justify staff-cuts, but the thought never even entered the minds of Southwest's leaders.

Southwest's **Mission Statement** says: **'Above all, Employees will be provided the same concern, respect, and caring attitude within the organisation that they are expected to share externally with every Southwest customer.'**

What is amazing is, in the last thirty-odd years, Southwest is the ONLY airline in the United States to have NEVER retrenched employees, AND it is also the ONLY airline to have consistently shown a profit year after year in all these thirty-odd years. All other airlines who have often retrenched staff have often shown a loss in their balance sheets at the end of many financial years.

HERB KELLEHER
CEO - SOUTHWEST

The leadership of Southwest (just like J.R.D.) are to be commended for their courage in formulating and implementing such path-breaking policies which ensure job security to deserving employees.

It is also the way to Southwest's profitability, as it is these same loyal staff which keep customers coming back.

This story is from an old issue of the magazine *Gospel Herald*, and beautifully encapsulates the Southwest philosophy outlined previously.

'There were three children in the home, one of whom was much younger than the others. A terrific storm came up and the two older children were greatly frightened and cried very hard. The little fellow paid no attention to the storm and finally said to them, "Oh, stop your howling. Don't you suppose God knows His business?" **The small boy realised that God can take care of you just as well in a storm as when the sun shines.**'

I recently attended a seminar where the speaker, a senior Vice-President of Human Resources with a leading organisation, pompously proclaimed on stage: "**We may not be able to guarantee employment to our staff. But we ensure they become employable.**" He went on to explain that this meant we train them so well, and they become so good at their jobs as a result of our training, that even if we ask them to leave, they can easily get a job elsewhere.

When he asked the audience if they had any questions, someone put forward: "**If they are so good at their jobs and are such assets that any organisation would be proud to have, why does YOUR organisation (which is a profitable one), terminate their services in the first place?**" There was no answer.

Of course, in order to ensure that your employees are assets and worthy of guaranteed employment; time and effort needs to be invested in selecting the right people, thoroughly training them, instilling in them the value systems of the founders of the organisation, motivating them to perform at their peak with a set of intelligently devised monetary and non-monetary motivators. If this is given importance by the leader, then almost every single employee will be an asset who will add value to the top-line and bottom-line of the organisation.

Negative decisions on part of top management with regard to mass retrenchment for no substantial cause is nothing short of playing with people's lives and the lives of their families. These employees may have recently got married or obtained a housing loan on the strength of their permanent job. And now, for absolutely no fault of theirs, their jobs are lost and their lives could be destroyed. Simply because the organisation feels it should '**let go of people periodically in the garb of restructuring.**'

How and why can any employee perform even close to his best, knowing that even if he **does** give his best, the unemployment axe could fall on his neck at any time? **Fear without rhyme or reason is never a motivator that true leaders use to get the best from good people.** In fact, one of the *14 Principles of Quality Management* developed by Dr. Deming (who we have been acquainted with in earlier learnings in this book), states '**Drive out fear from the organisation.**'

The following passage from a book by Michael LeBouef can throw different light on this current mania for staff cutting:

"**When I first came to the United States, I thought how convenient it was for American employers to be able to lay off people whenever business slumped,**" said **Sadami Wada**, vice-president of *Sony Corporation of America*. But Wada soon changed his mind. "**Now I understand why some American companies fail to gain the loyalty and dedication of their employees. Employees cannot care for an employer who is prepared to take their livelihood away at the first sign of trouble.**"

LeBouef continues – '**How loyal would you feel towards your parents had they thrown you out during hard times? Providing job security is not just a pipe dream – it's good business. Layoffs are very expensive and prevent companies from attracting and keeping good people who demand job stability.**'

In Japan, if technology is introduced which makes a particular job redundant, the person does not lose his job as a result. Rather, it is appreciated that he is a loyal, trained and valuable resource and an asset for the organisation, and he is retrained to perform some other job within the organisation. **Of course, this requires more effort on the part of the leader and the human resources department than merely 'letting people go,' but this is what true leaders believe – that their employees are their greatest assets, not merely on paper, but in reality, and the leadership will do all they can to retain them.**

> *It is always easier to dismiss a man than it is to train him. No great leader ever built a reputation on firing people. Many have built a reputation on developing them*
>
> —UNKNOWN

It is sad that among the priorities that many organisations expect from the Indian Government is an easy hire-and-fire employment policy, which permits organisations to recruit employees when times are good, and dump them when the economic cycle shows the first sign of downturn. As a speaker at a seminar on the Chinese business model, where the audience consisted of senior executives and entrepreneurs, I was surprised that almost all the audience members felt that the only thing necessary for Indian companies to compete with their Chinese counterparts was an easy hire-and-fire policy. **There was no mention of the Chinese ethic of hard-work, creativity, talent scouting, ideation, hunger for organic growth, their focus on quality and new product development, and no wastage on excessive advertising nor squandering humongous amounts on senseless celebrity endorsement.** All that most of these executives and entrepreneurs wanted was an easy hire-and-fire policy. A clear case of focusing on the negative rather than on the positive.

Many organisations and their managements today moan the lack of talent, but do not take concrete steps to retain the talent they already have on board. Retention often gets lower priority than attraction.

Please ensure that you as a leader focus on the positive rather than the negative. This is one of the qualities that made J.R.D. (and also Ratan Tata after him) a much loved and respected leader.

The newly elected mayor of a small town called on the chief of police to discuss matters related to security and the strength of the police force. "Well, Mr. Mayor," said the chief, "there's me, and I have three officers and eleven constables so that's a total of fifteen of us on the police force."

The mayor, ever ready to spot an opportunity to save a buck, said, "Fifteen of you? Surely in a small town like this, there is not enough crime to keep you all busy?"

The police chief, who had years of efficient experience behind him, smiled knowingly and replied, "That's certainly correct. Currently there's not enough crime in this town to keep us all busy. **But if we didn't have fifteen of us patrolling the streets, there would be.**"

POINTS TO PONDER AND PRACTICE

- You may not currently be at a level where you decide human resource and staffing policies for the entire organisation. If you are, then you would do well to reflect on the Southwest example and realise that your role as a leader is to steer the organisation to long-term success

- But even if you are currently a department head, a regional head, or heading a team, you should and must do all that is humanly possible to support and retain the people who perform and who are loyal and dedicated to the organisation. This would also ensure commitment from your team when you need it the most

- Practice the words of the wise man who once said:

'Real leaders don't ELIMINATE, they ILLUMINATE'

THE LEARNING FROM THE RUSSIAN DOLLS

> **If each of us hires people who are smaller than we are, we shall become a company of dwarfs. But if each of us hires people who are bigger than we are, we shall become a company of giants**
>
> -DAVID OGILVY

WHAT **J.R.D.** BELIEVED IN AND **PRACTICED**

> **If your actions inspire others to dream more, learn more, do more and become more, you are a leader**
>
> -JOHN QUINCY ADAMS

This quality of a leader ensures that the organisation he has lovingly crafted passes on into good or even better hands than those of the leader himself.

This learning differs from the earlier one on 'succession planning,' which describes a visionary quality of a leader. But the 'Learning from the Russian Dolls' falls under the heading of **VALOUR**.

A little patience, please. The 'Learnings for Leaders' which follow will explain what exactly the 'Russian Dolls' are. But first, let us see what the related quality is that J.R.D. displayed and practiced.

Let us read the words of Dr. Freddy Mehta, an economist qualified from the *London School of Economics*, who joined the Tata Group in 1956 and rose to a very senior level in the Tata hierarchy. This is what Dr. Mehta had to say about J.R.D. :

"In business or industry, the moment the number two man gets too much attention in the press or public and he gets glory, the number one tries to pull him down. J.R.D.'s greatest credit is he never assumed an adversarial role to anybody coming up the hierarchy in the Tata group. He would disagree on policy matters. He would even criticise the personality of someone, but he would never assume an adversarial position."

Now, let us see what the '**Russian Dolls**' are all about and what their connection could be with the art and science of leadership and man-management.

A SET OF 'RUSSIAN DOLLS'

LEARNINGS
FOR LEADERS

" Alone we can do so little, together we can do so much "

-HELEN KELLER

A generation and more ago, we had many leaders in the global corporate arena that we could look up to as true pioneers and leaders.

Henry Ford of **Ford Motors**. **Thomas Watson** of **IBM**. **Akio Morita** of **Sony**. Even **Steve Jobs** of **Apple**, who unfortunately passed away at a relatively young age. And many more.

Leaders in the corporate world today have not really proved to be such shining examples in such large numbers for various reasons.

One reason for this is that the current set of leaders appear to have become insecure about their own positions and designations, and many of them channelise their energies into non-productive areas such as in playing office politics and in-fighting to retain their positions within their own organisations.

Energy which should have been used to carry the organisation forward and ahead of the external competition, is often drained away in the unhealthy focus on internal competition from colleagues and subordinates, who are unfortunately viewed as THREATS rather than as ALLIES.

David Ogilvy, a global giant from the previous generation of advertising professionals, had already sensed this fear of internal competition arising among his subordinates, and developed an effective way of dealing with it. He often sent a set of '**Russian Dolls**' to the various country heads and senior executives of his advertising firm as a reminder to them to not succumb to this self-destructive and irrational fear.

The 'Russian Dolls' are a set of wooden dolls, traditionally a children's toy from Russia, with each doll looking similar to, but smaller than the other, and each placed inside the hollow shell of the outer one. So, there is a large wooden doll, which can be opened up, within which lies another doll, inside which is yet another, and so on.

Ogilvy often sent a set of these dolls to his senior people, and inside the last and the smallest doll in the set, he left a small note. The note, read by the executive when he opened the set of dolls and reached the last doll, read to the effect that, **if we, when we recruit staff, hire people who are as capable or even more capable than ourselves, we shall grow to be a company of giants. But, if like the 'Russian Dolls,' we persist in seeking out and recruiting in our team, persons who are less able and competent and 'smaller' than ourselves, merely to secure our own position in the hierarchy for a short while, we shall become a company of pygmies.**

What a very effective way David Ogilvy thought of to put across an important message which J.R.D. in his wisdom, actively practiced throughout his corporate career.

Though there is no recorded instance of J.R.D. sending across such a set of 'Russian Dolls' to his executives, he implicitly believed in and followed the philosophy of selecting the best people for the good of the organisation. He allowed his executives to flourish and establish their own productive and profitable domains, of course, within the ambit and scope of the well-defined culture of the Tata group.

Truly great leaders are never insecure, nor do they worry about their subordinates superseding them. They will always select the best people and promote them. Only such mature leadership thought can place juniors in the limelight and prepare them to be the super-stars of tomorrow. Such leadership has always believed in 'empowerment,' which has become a buzzword of late. This simple word, which has humongous implications, literally means 'giving your power away to others who are deserving of it, leaving you free for yet more higher levels of responsibility.'

Most family-run organisations often find it difficult to let their senior executives and other employees get the glory they deserve.

Even the famed Walt Disney, the genius cartoonist and entrepreneur, and a great leader in many other aspects, did not permit his junior/subordinate cartoonists to get personal fame. Many brilliant Disney cartoonists worked in relative anonymity. The stories and comic-books these cartoonists animated carried only Walt Disney's name. **Readers of these brilliantly illustrated comic-books would often wonder who drew the bulk of the sketches they viewed in these comics, as the great artists never got their due share of glory.**

Theodore Roosevelt had said: '**The best executive is the one who has enough sense to pick good men to do what he wants done, and self-restraint enough to keep from meddling with them while they do it.**'

It is J.R.D.'s moral courage and magnanimity, apart from the obvious merit of the individuals he placed faith in, that allowed these individuals to flourish and achieve great heights within the Tata group. Only an evolved leader can be as large-hearted as J.R.D. was, and such leaders reap their rightful reward by attracting the best talent to work with them, stay with them, and give their heart and soul for the leader and for the organisation.

POINTS TO PONDER AND PRACTICE

- As a leader, when you have the opportunity to recruit people, go for the most, rather than the lesser capable from those available. It is the most capable who will be a great help to you and the organisation. Of course, while judging on capability, you also need to keep in mind certain character traits which these individuals tend to display, which could hinder or hamper organisational productivity

- Simultaneously, sharpen your personal skills and work on your strengths, making yourself invaluable to the organisation, so that you need not fear the smaller 'Russian Doll' gobbling up your position some day. **Leaders who are confident about their own abilities would always seek the best for their organisation. You as a leader, should do the same**

- Always act keeping in mind the words of Alan L. McGinnis, who said:
  'The ultimate leaders develop followers who will surpass them'

- Keep in mind what the iconic leader Lee Iacocca, who led the stupendous turnaround of *Chrysler*, said:
  "I hire people brighter than me and I get out of their way"

LEE IACOCCA

WALK THE TALK

> ## *An ounce of practice is worth more than tons of preaching*
>
> -MAHATMA GANDHI

WHAT **J.R.D.** BELIEVED IN AND **PRACTICED**

> ## *Never separate the life you live from the words you speak*
>
> -PAUL WELLSTONE

'Walking-the-Talk' has long been advocated as a strong leadership trait.

For J.R.D., with his transparent and honest personality, this trait came naturally, and there was rarely, if ever, a discrepancy between what he spoke and what he did.

If, for example, he expected others to be disciplined and obey rules, he would himself be the first to show the way.

As an example, the following is indeed eye-opening.

B. S. Das, a senior Air India functionary recalls an incident when he was with J.R.D. Tata on-board a flight. At that time, J.R.D. was the Chairman of Air India.

Das mentions that he had called his car up to the tarmac near to where the aircraft landed, and requested J.R.D. to sit in the car. Das did this so J.R.D. could be spared the inconvenience of walking all the way till the terminal with the other passengers.

But J.R.D., rather than accept the offer, told Das: "Who gave you the authority to bring your car near the plane? When you don't give this privilege to others (paying passengers), how can you expect me to take undue advantage? Apart from which, this is a violation of security regulations."

Das says that J.R.D. then walked away to the terminal, picked up his own baggage, and boarded his car in the parking lot, along with other 'non-VIP' passengers.

There are multiple other examples of occasions where J.R.D. ensured that he became a beloved leader by courageously 'walking-the-talk.'

" *A leader leads by example, not by force* "

SUN TZU

LEARNINGS
FOR LEADERS

> *I have a perfect horror of words that are not backed up by deeds*
>
> -THEODORE ROOSEVELT

Walking-the-Talk is indicative of leading by example.

Perhaps, if a leader practices this one single quality alone, and practices it well, nothing else would be required of him. It encapsulates almost every leadership trait within it.

It is good if a leader has inculcated this habit from an early age. But it is never too late to start.

It requires **courage** and **strength of character** to Walk-the-Talk.

As is said, talk is cheap. But talk, followed by relevant action, as J.R.D. constantly displayed, requires the leader to courageously pay a price.

Pay a price in terms of giving up a privilege to demonstrate equality and oneness with subordinates; pay a price in terms of not taking short-cuts, but taking the straight and long way, as advocated through words and speech.

If, for example, the leader has always espoused the importance of punctuality and timeliness in every speech he makes, but himself frequently turns up late for meetings, he will cut a sorry figure, viewed as being incapable of walking-the-talk.

A leader's words are always listened to intently, noted and remembered for future reference, and his actions are observed with great scrutiny to see whether the leader is capable of walking-the-talk. If he is not, he is considered a hollow shell, a good orator, and little else. But if the leader should back up his inspiring words with personal action which is commensurate with the words he has spoken, that leader is the one who is held in high-esteem by all concerned.

407

A most inspiring story of courageously standing up to walk-the-talk, comes from that ancient and mysterious land – China. **GLADYS AYLWARD** was a poor young British woman, who went to China as a Christian missionary. She was extremely passionate about her cause, and in 1932, she spent her life-savings to buy a steamer ticket to China to preach her religion. She learned the Chinese language after reaching China, so she could preach her religion to the Chinese people. Once there, she had a hard time convincing the local people of the benefits of converting to Christianity, and worked at an inn, where she and another missionary gave food and shelter to the poor Chinese people, and told them wonderful stories from the Bible about God and His wonderful creations.

One day, an opportunity to establish her reputation came her way, when a man came breathlessly rushing to the door of the inn, saying a riot had broken out in the local prison. A prisoner, a giant of a man, had lost his temper, and had attacked a couple of other prisoners with a chopper. The messenger had come from the prison to fetch Gladys, as she had always professed about the power of Jesus Christ, and asked her to rush over to the prison to calm down the angry man.

Gladys rushed to the prison, where the pale-faced governor of the prison met her at the entrance. He shouted to Gladys, "The prisoners are killing each other. You must go in and stop the fighting." Gladys replied, bewildered, **"But I'm only the missionary woman. Why don't you send the soldiers to stop it**?" The governor said, **"The soldiers are frightened. They won't go in. You are the only one who can. They can't kill you. You preach to everybody that you have the living God inside you. If you are telling the truth, that your God protects you from harm, then you can stop the riot**."

Gladys stared at him and thought to herself, "It is true that I've been preaching that my Christian God protects me. If I fail now, my mission in China is as good as over. No one will have faith in my preaching anymore. **I will have failed to walk-the-talk**." Steeling herself, knowing that inside the prison walls – murderers, thugs, bandits – were rioting and killing each other, she took a deep breath and said to the governor, "All right. Open the door. I'll go in to them."

The huge, iron-barred gate was opened, and Gladys was pushed inside the prison courtyard. The gate slammed shut behind her. Inside, a minor riot was raging. At the centre of the action was one tall, hefty convict, who was swinging a blood-stained chopper. She looked around and saw a couple of men who had been hacked down with

408

the chopper lying on the ground. Then the convict with the chopper singled out one of the other prisoners and chased him. The victim ran towards Gladys and took shelter behind her. The crazed convict, still swinging the chopper madly, now stood in front of Gladys with a savage look on his face.

Gladys, though sick with fear, went up to him with her hand outstretched and said furiously, "**Give me that chopper. Give it to me AT ONCE.**"The man stepped forward, his crazed eyes glaring at Gladys. Suddenly, meekly, he handed over the chopper. Then Gladys turned towards the other convicts who were watching the scene unfold. She shouted at them, "All of you. Come over here. Form into a line." Obediently, the convicts formed a line and stood before her. She gazed at them. Her fear suddenly left her. It was replaced by a deep pity for these wretched men, who were condemned to spend the better part of their lives behind the prison walls. Like an angry mother, she began scolding them. "You should be ashamed of yourselves. All this noise and mess. Now, if you clean up this courtyard and promise to behave in the future, I will ask the governor to deal lightly with you."

All of a sudden, Gladys realised that the governor and his assistants were standing behind her. Having seen and heard everything through a hole in the prison wall, they had felt it was now safe to enter. Gladys told the prisoners that she would be leaving now, but would be back and would do all she could to help them.

One of the prisoners then said to her, "**Thank you, *Ai-weh-de*.**" Gladys did not understand what the word *Ai-weh-de* meant. Later that evening, she asked a friend, who explained to her that *Ai-weh-de* in the local language meant **The Virtuous One**.

GLADYS AYLWARD

The name stuck. In all the many remaining years she spent in China, wherever she went to preach her religion, Gladys was affectionately known as *Ai-weh-de*. **Her mission in China was a success, all because she brought forward the courage to walk-the-talk of her preachings and to courageously stand up firm when the need arose.**

(The complete story of Gladys Aylward can be viewed in the classic 1958 movie - *The Inn of the Sixth Happiness*)

POINTS TO PONDER AND PRACTICE

- The first step to 'walking-the-talk' is for you as a leader to mix and mingle with your team and clearly and constantly communicate the organisation's values and expected standards of behaviour to them

- What is required next is for you as a leader and your key people and senior managers to be visibly seen practicing these values and standards at every opportunity, even if it means personal hardship and sacrifice to do so. **In fact the more the hardship and sacrifice involved in you walking-the-talk, the more positively your actions will be viewed by subordinates, as they realise the effort you are taking to apply the stated organisational values and standards to yourself**

- This will encourage and motivate all in your organisation or in your department to follow suit, and the harmonious actions of every individual in the organisation or department to uphold the values and standards set in place by you through word and deed will result in organisational objectives being achieved more effectively, and with superior levels of quality

TAKE CALCULATED RISKS TO IMPLEMENT YOUR PASSION

> *Pearls don't lie on the seashore. If you want one, you must dive for it*
>
> -CHINESE PROVERB

WHAT J.R.D. BELIEVED IN AND PRACTICED

> *If you are not willing to risk the unusual, you will have to settle for the ordinary*
>
> -JIM ROHN

J.R.D.'s first love and passion was aviation, for which he was bravely willing to put his very life at risk. It was this passion which gave him the vision, the drive, and the determination to establish the aviation industry in India and be renowned as one of the aviation pioneers of the world.

Having a passion is the first step. But committing available resources, both tangible and intangible, to that passion to convert it into a material entity requires courage and is equally important. It demonstrates that the passion is genuine and comes from deep within, and does not just consist of a set of empty words spoken to gain publicity.

A true leader commits his personal resources, both financial and otherwise, to ensure that his passion becomes a reality, capable of serving others and making the world a better place.

This is exactly what J.R.D. did with his passion for aviation.

As Sir Frederick Tymms, the Director-General of Civil Aviation (also known as the 'Flying Civil Servant'), admiringly wrote in the *Times of India* in the month of October 1934 about J.R.D. courageously committing his personal resources to ensure Tata Air Service was a success – **'Scarcely anywhere in the world was there an air service operating without support from the Government. It could only be done by throwing on the operator the financial risk.'**

The passion J.R.D. evinced for aviation is evident from the words of Mr. A. S. DeSa, an early employee of Tata Aviation, who fondly recalls that the early days of Air India were far different from the later glamour that Air India carved out for itself. He says, "It was not the riches we were after. We loved aviation and we were a happy family. Mr. Tata was very close to us then. We worked very hard."

Simple words, but they mean the world for the leader when spoken with a glad heart by a happy employee.

Take calculated risks. That is quite different from being rash

-GENERAL GEORGE S. PATTON

LEARNINGS
FOR LEADERS

> *A ship in harbour is safe, but that is not what ships are built for*
>
> -JOHN A. SHEDD

Needless to say, the passion that drives a leader needs to be a positive one. This passion is what ultimately translates into the vision and the strategy of the organisation.

Without passion, there can be no positive organisational differentiator.

Passion is always **full of life**, bursting with healthy vitality, never dull and lifeless.

And where there is life, there are bound to be risks involved.

But the key word is '**CALCULATED.' Management and leadership are always involved with the future, and the future is always uncertain. Where there is uncertainty, there are bound to be risks.**

The best leaders understand that taking calculated risks, based on well collated and analysed data, added to which is their intuitive 'gut-feel' developed through years of experience, and honed, sharpened and fine-tuned by their genuine passion, is the only way forward.

The risks taken by the leader should never be thoughtless and reckless, as not only his own, but also the organisation's, and all the people involved with it have their futures at stake.

Remember the words of **Bill Cosby**:

"In order to succeed, your desire for success should be greater than your fear of failure"

Kathleen K. Reardon, writing in the *Harvard Business Review* mentions calculated risk taking as a skill which a leader needs to develop and demonstrate on occasion. She writes: 'In business, courageous action is really a special kind of calculated risk taking. People who become good leaders have a greater than average willingness to make bold moves, but they strengthen their chances of success – and avoid career suicide – through careful deliberation and preparation. Business courage is not so much a visionary leader's inborn characteristic as a skill acquired through decision-making processes that improve with practice. **In other words, most great business leaders teach themselves to make high-risk decisions**.....Learning to take an intelligent gamble requires an understanding of what I call the "**courage calculation**," a method of making success more likely while avoiding rash, unproductive, or irrational behaviour. **Six discrete processes make up the courage calculation:** setting primary and secondary goals, determining the importance of achieving them, tipping the power balance in your favour, weighing risks against benefits, selecting the proper time for action, and developing contingency plans.'

The website, **examiner.com**, offers an interesting insight on the subject of risk taking:

'What you should do is be willing to make mistakes, hold unconventional and unpopular positions, never be afraid to take on a challenge, always keep focused on your dreams and do whatever it takes to achieve them. By taking such risks, your personal growth, integrity and achievements are enhanced. You need to do something that forces you to stretch from your present state to a state of greater personal growth. This applies both in business as well as in our personal lives. Quantum leaps in learning, solving problems, inventing new products, and discovering new phenomena require risk taking…..Make no mistake about it; great leaders are risk takers. The leader understands that at certain times in the life of the business cycle or non-profit organization, change is necessary and will require some risk taking. **Effective risk taker leaders do not set out to be reckless and change business policies and procedures just for the sake of change.** Rather, the leader recognises a definite need within the company or non-profit and seeks to create a path that will require a different technique of doing things and will involve calculated risk.'

Alex Malley, Chief Executive at CPA Australia, writes on LinkedIn:

'To me it is the responsibility of a leader to challenge norms and established processes. To take calculated risks and push boundaries so the business does not stagnate or lose relevance.....
I am astonished by the number of risk-averse leaders that I meet. It is obvious that they fear failure, and their dominant motivation is survival in the 'top job.' An uncharted course that might result in something beneficial for the business, but may also harm their tenure or reputation if it does not work out, is one they consider not worth taking. The great irony is that these leaders are unwittingly running the biggest risk of all: entrenching a culture of 'play it safe' complacency exposes their businesses to missed opportunities and ultimately to becoming irrelevant.'

Malley ends his article with a very pertinent question: 'Do you take risks? If not, what is holding you back?'

I would personally rephrase Malley's question and ask every reader and leader: 'Do you take CALCULATED risks? If not, what is holding you back?'

Display of valour by taking a calculated risk can be best summed up in the wise words of Miguel de Cervantes, who said:

'True valour lies in the middle between cowardice and rashness.'

The following is extracted from *Head, Heart & Guts* authored by David L. Dotlich, Peter C. Cairo, and Stephen H. Rhinesmith:

'....(Are) leaders willing to take risks on innovation? When people come up with an original, daring idea in response to a situation, the idea is usually rooted in the imagination than in the data. Leaders must decide whether to take a cutting-edge concept that can't be verified through data analysis. This can be intimidating, and if a leader doesn't appreciate creativity or people who look at things differently, **HE WON'T TAKE THE RISK**. More than ever before, however, organizations need leaders with this capacity.'

POINTS TO PONDER AND PRACTICE

- If you are not passionate about your business and the uniqueness it offers to your customers, you may not be sufficiently motivated to take the necessary risks to stay ahead of others around you. The key to taking calculated risks is developing a healthy passion (and not a pathological obsession), with what you and your organisation are doing to make a difference to the lives of your stakeholders, in however small a way, as long as that difference is a positive one. Reasonable, sustainable, and sufficient profits will definitely emerge from such a venture, if executed effectively

A POEM TO PONDER

There was a very cautious man
Who never laughed or played.

He never risked, he never tried,
He never sang or prayed.

And when one day he passed away,
His insurance was denied.

For since he never really lived
They claimed he never died

-POET UNKNOWN

SHARE THE
WEALTH

> ***Money is like manure. It stinks when you pile it; it grows when you spread it***
>
> -J.R.D. TATA

WHAT **J.R.D.**
BELIEVED IN
AND **PRACTICED**

> ***Share if you dare***
> ***– It shows you care***
>
> -CYRUS M. GONDA

J.R.D. possessed the key ingredient essential for an individual to be positioned at the highest level of leadership – he had a gigantic and a generous and a giving heart.

J.R.D. believed in keeping an open palm and not a closed fist.

He mentioned once, **"I've made sure that I don't have much money."**

At the relatively young age of forty, J.R.D. gave away a substantial part of his wealth to the J.R.D. Tata Trust. He did this by donating to the Trust his own shares of Tata Sons and shares of other companies which he had held. Over time, he transferred more and more of his shares to add to the corpus of this Trust. He had been the sole contributor to this

Trust which bears his name. The funds for this Trust did not come from the profits of Tata group companies, but from J.R.D.'s personal wealth.

During the course of his lifetime, this Trust disbursed crores of rupees to needy individuals for various causes. The blessings he must have received from all the beneficiaries must be tremendous.

Does it require a special kind of courage and valour to give away such a substantial portion of your personal wealth to those in need?

Yes, it certainly does.

If it did not, you would have seen almost all wealthy individuals doing the same. Such courage is rare. And because it is rare, it is doubly blessed.

As Alexander the Great lay dying of fever after having conquered over half the world at a tender age, he asked his assembled generals to carry out his last three wishes. These were:

ONE: "I wish my physicians to carry my coffin to my grave, so people can realise that no doctor can really save anyone from the power of death."

TWO: "As my coffin is being carried to my grave, the path to it should be covered with the gold and silver I have collected in my treasury so that people can know that it is a sheer waste of time to merely collect wealth and not use it in a fruitful manner."

THREE: "Let both my hands dangle outside my coffin so that people can see that empty-handed I came to this world, and empty-handed I am leaving it."

So saying, he breathed his last.

Alexander The Great

> **"** *The wealth gathered by Jamsetji Tata (the founder of the Tata group) and his sons in half a century of industrial pioneering formed but a minute fraction of the amount by which they enriched the nation. The whole of that wealth is held in trust for the people (of India) and used exclusively for their benefit. THE CYCLE IS THUS COMPLETE. What came from the people has gone back to the people many times over* **"**

-J.R.D. TATA

JAMSETJI TATA

The first president of India, Dr. Rajendra Prasad, accepted only fifty percent of his salary, saying he did not need more than that to live a comfortable life.

Then towards the end of his second term, he reduced this still further and took only twenty-five percent of his allotted salary. And the salary of the president of India at that time was only Rs. 10,000 per month.

No wonder then, that Peter Casey writes in the *Economic Times*:

'It (the Tata Group) is an enterprise that has thrived on the vision of its founder (Jamsetji Tata), a vision of philanthropy as an engine of capitalism, an ethos of doing well by doing good. Moreover, today, the (stock) market rewards the high ethical standards that inform and guide the entire Tata Group. They (the Tata Group) are universally regarded as a safe pair of hands. This is why the market capitalisation of TCS (Tata Consultancy Services) is greater than Accenture and Cognizant combined.'

419

LEARNINGS
FOR LEADERS

"The miracle is this: the more we share, the more we have"
                                                        -LEONARD NIMOY

Arthur Gordon writes – 'A closed hand cannot receive. The phrase has a Biblical ring, and a Biblical wisdom that applies profoundly to everyday human affairs. The one who will not share oneself with one's neighbours receives little friendship in return. The tight parental grip that holds children too closely, defeats its own purpose in the end. **It's no accident, probably, that in many countries, the symbol of totalitarianism is the one that you can't shake hands with: a closed fist.** To be a sower of seeds, one must open one's hand. One must do this, clearly, before one can reap. And the process doesn't stop there. To possess knowledge or wisdom, one must open one's mind. If one wants to receive love – one must offer it – and to do this one will need an open heart. Look around you and you will see the truth of these five words shining everywhere – **A closed hand cannot receive** – partly because it is shut, and nothing can get in. But mostly because it has nothing to give.'

As a lesson from history, in the U.S.A., the periods of highest prosperity were the 1950s and the 1960s, when unemployment rates were low and blue-collar factory workers enjoyed high rates of wages. The entire economy of U.S.A. prospered as wealth was distributed fairly evenly across the population and purchasing power was spread across many hands. **The moment a few leading businessmen got excessively greedy and started out-sourcing American manufacturing jobs to other nations where they could get work done cheaper, unemployment in U.S.A. soared, average salaries dropped, unequal distribution of wealth increased, and the entire economy went into a slump from which it has never really recovered till today.**

420

Henry Ford

A brilliantly imaginative example of a hypothetical conversation that could have taken place between the courageous and visionary **Henry Ford** and his less evolved big-business counterparts on the subject of 'sharing the wealth' has been conjured up by Ken Favaro, Per-Ola Karlsson and Gary L. Neilson in their article titled *The Lives And Times Of The CEO* which was published in the Summer 2014 issue of the magazine *strategy + business*. The following is an extremely interesting extract from this article wherein the imaginary situation is drawn up, with the timeline as 1914, where these pioneers of American industry have gathered to discuss the pressing commercial issues of the day. This is how it goes:

'.....the room are arguing with slim, pale-eyed, 51-year-old Henry Ford, who stands with his back turned to them as he squints out the window at the setting sun. **"You're paying your assembly-line workers a minimum - a minimum! - of $5 a day!"** raves **John Rockefeller** (of **Standard Oil**), waving his arms. **"That's more than twice what the average assembly-line workers make. And you're sending them home after only eight hours!"**

John Rockefeller

Julius Rosenwald

"You're mad, Henry," mutters **Julius Rosenwald**, the head of **Sears, Roebuck & Company. "You'll drive Ford Motor Company straight out of business with this decision."**

421

Harvey Firestone

"John's right, Henry," says **Firestone Tire and Rubber Company** founder **Harvey Firestone**, as he lights his cigar. **"We cannot begin to fathom how you - you, of all people, who have single-handedly opened new frontiers of this country with your mass production of automobiles - can believe it wise to share half of your $25 million in profits with your workers."**

"Especially when the unemployment rate is 15 percent!" huffs **Gillette's Frank J. Fahey**, with a swallow of his bourbon. **"Droves of people are immigrating to the United States each day. All of us are faced with an ample supply of able-bodied men all willing to take whatever jobs and at whatever pay they can find in our companies."**

Ford has so far listened politely without reply. He slips his hand inside his coat pocket and pulls out his gold pocket watch. Flicking the cover open with his thumb, he notes that they have been dressing him down for nearly an hour. He slides his watch back into place, takes a deep breath, and spins on his heel to face his fellow moguls.

"Answer me honestly, Frank," Ford says, fixing him with a stare. **"How do you expect men to be able to purchase your Gillette razors if they don't have money to afford them? Or you, John - how do you think Standard Oil will make a profit if only a handful of people can afford to drive Model T cars?"**

Ford walks slowly to the roaring fireplace. **"Gentlemen, the way I see it, we all want the same thing. We all want to sell more of our goods, services, and products to the public, so that our companies can make more money. Correct?"**

Everyone nods reluctantly.

"Then logic demands that if we are to achieve this goal, we must first produce more products faster. **But then we must also have many more people who can afford to buy those products."**

Henry Ford's decision to increase his workers' wages while reducing their workday shocked the business community - and for good reason. Back then, the founder/owner of a company was like an absolute monarch, and Ford's decree appeared to pass power to the people. **But his actions proved to be correct. His workers repaid him in productivity and loyalty, and his decision turned him into a national hero.**'

It requires courageous leadership of the type which J.R.D. and Henry Ford displayed to take such bold steps. Both J.R.D., as well as Henry Ford, in the interest of their respective nations, as well as all individuals and business entities, invested heavily in ensuring that people in general were better off. **Unfortunately, there are many 'leaders' in Corporate India today who DO believe in giving extremely generously, but 'giving' only in the form of bribes, to officials in decision-making positions, to get underhand work done. They do NOT pay their employees what they deserve, nor do they treat their suppliers fairly, nor do they ensure that their customers get value for money. Such 'leaders' have an open hand when it comes to giving wrongful bribes. But they display a closed fist when it comes to rightfully giving their due to legitimate stakeholders. This policy of distorted giving can never benefit their organisation in the long term.**

As mentioned before, **J.R.D. once said**, "Had we adopted some of the methods that other industrialists have adopted, including having Members of Parliament on their payroll, we would have been twice as big as we are today. But we would not have wanted it any other way."

Be a leader with an open hand towards the right people for the right reasons. Not only will you be blessed and receive your reward in heaven, your organisation will receive its reward right here on earth.

Sharing is natural. Hoarding is not. This holds true even for the animal kingdom, as the following story demonstrates:

On 11th May, 2014, a photograph was featured in the Gujarati edition of the *mid-day* newspaper – In an animal park in Sydney, Australia, a man offered a kangaroo some food kept in an ice-cream cone as a container. The kangaroo gratefully took it, and when a pigeon popped up nearby, the kangaroo was seen offering to share this treat with the hungry pigeon. Anne Cameron snapped the beautiful photograph of this fine art of sharing between beast and bird. **Now if only man can be added to this bird and animal equation of sharing, most of earth's problems would be solved.**

POINTS TO PONDER AND PRACTICE

- Give justly. And then give a little more. The message is clear. Do not withhold anyone their legitimate due. Whether it be money, time, or praise. Practice this with whomever you come in contact with and whoever has done you or your department or your organisation good

- You may not be in a position to raise a person's salary. But at least don't withhold praise for a good job done. Praise lavishly. Don't withhold your time when these people ask for it. Give it generously. Small little things are opportunities for giving, such as sanctioning overtime without a fuss when it is actually performed or sanctioning a conveyance voucher without making the person feel like a thief when it is you have sent him out for legitimate company-related work

- Such acts on your part, acts of giving and sharing with people who have had a hand in your growth, who deserve to share in your success, will ensure prosperity for you and your organisation for a long time to come

- Remember the words of **Robert Bosch**, who was an inventor, engineer, industrialist and the founder of the giant Bosch conglomerate: '**I don't pay good wages because I have a lot of money; I have a lot of money because I pay good wages**'

Robert Bosch

DETERMINED LEADERS TAKE PHYSICAL DISCOMFORT IN THEIR STRIDE

> *The first virtue in a soldier is endurance of fatigue; courage is only the second virtue*
>
> -NAPOLEON BONAPARTE

WHAT **J.R.D.** BELIEVED IN AND **PRACTICED**

> *No victory without suffering*
>
> -J.R.R. TOLKIEN

The following excellent example of J.R.D. calmly taking physical discomfort in his stride to ensure the 'work got done' is narrated in Murad Fyzee's book *Aircraft And Engine Perfect*.

In the early days of the airmail service, J.R.D. and his other pilot colleagues flew the mail in aircraft which had no radio, nor any navigational or landing aids. So naturally the flights were performed during daylight hours. The flights were scheduled in stages, with the first stage being Karachi–Bombay, the second stage from Bombay–Bellary (which lies in what is now the state of Karnataka) and the third and final stage from Bellary–Madras.

On one occasion, J.R.D. was to fly the second stage of the journey, and his colleague Nevill Vintcent would be waiting for him at Bellary to take over and pilot the flight on its third stage to Madras. Bellary was a small town, and Nevill Vintcent had arranged to stay in the only decent accommodation then available, which was a bungalow not far from the airfield where J.R.D. would be landing. He would be bound to hear J.R.D.'s aircraft on its descent, and would then drive out to the landing field to take over from J.R.D. But the plan did not always go as scheduled. The plan went awry on an April day in 1933, when the weather was very hot and the air turbulence was severe.

As J.R.D. was to himself later recall: "I encountered such heavy turbulence that I put the aircraft's nose up and climbed to 16,000 feet in order to get some relief. But I felt so air sick I decided I had better land. So I did in a suitable field, seemingly miles from anywhere, and waited for the weather to cool down and the convection currents and resulting turbulence to cool down. I rested in the shade in the wing of the Moth (his aircraft) and soon, inevitably, was surrounded by a small crowd of villagers and peasants. As curious as they were they were kind enough to bring me some fruit and a coconut which they broke and offered to me. After a while I took off for Bellary. By now, however, it was late evening which soon turned to dusk and then dark. Fortunately there was a half moon and by its reflection I could pick out some rivers and the railway line which I knew would lead straight to Bellary. I kept a very tight and accurate compass course and soon I had no problem in picking out the faint lights of Bellary. Luckily I spotted the landing field by its white circle and was able to land quite well by the light of the faint moon."

As per the plan, Nevill Vintcent was now due to turn up to relieve J.R.D. so that J.R.D. could get much needed rest, but unfortunately Nevill Vintcent had fallen asleep in the bungalow and had not heard J.R.D.'s aircraft approaching the Bellary airfield. **Thus J.R.D., founder and head of India's only airline and a leading light of Indian industry, had no alternative but to spend the night in the open, under the stars, sheltering under the wing of his airplane. He had to remain with the aircraft as it contained their precious cargo of airmail which he had to keep secure.**

J.R.D. took all this in his stride, and when later asked how he had managed, his reply was, **"Oh, there was always a blanket in the airplane, and one of the smaller mail bags was an adequate enough pillow."**

As long as the work of the organisation gets done and the employees are not exploited in the process and the customers have no complaints, true leaders, like J.R.D., are more than happy to take personal physical discomfort in their stride.

LEARNINGS
FOR LEADERS

"Happy are those who dream dreams and are ready to pay the price to make them come true"

-LEON J. SUENES

None of us really **like** to undergo discomfort, but individuals, and moreso those in leadership positions, would encounter it often on their onward journey.

Kevin Eikenberry, a leading thinker on the subject of leadership, lists five reasons why leaders need to experience discomfort in order to become better leaders. The reasons he states are:

1. **Discomfort allows growth**: All true growth, whether physical, mental or emotional, lies outside the comfort zone. And to move outside your comfort zone in any of these areas, you have to undergo some amount of discomfort.

2. **Discomfort builds confidence**: The more successfully you perform a task, the more confident you become and the better you become at doing it. And growth requires that you acquire new skills, undergoing some discomfort while in the process.

3. **Discomfort provides creativity**: Most creativity is born out of pain areas; out of need and necessity. New products, new services, new concepts and ideas come up when people are faced with a problem, when they face discomfort in the existing situation.

4. **Discomfort overcomes resistance to change**: When we are comfortable, we do not want change. And change is the only constant.

5. **Discomfort facilitates goal achievement**: As Eikenberry says, "Ask yourself, do you want your goals enough to put up with a bit of discomfort, even fear?" Your goals will often require to push yourself through pressure situations, and that involves discomfort.

Imran Khan, the former Pakistan cricket captain, is acknowledged as one of the all-time greatest leaders on the cricket field. Imran led ably by motivating his team, and he had the ability to inspire, and lead not necessarily only as a thinker and a strategist (which he was very capable of doing), but also lead from the front with zeal and passion when the occasion demanded and his team needed.

In the 1982-83 series when Imran was the captain, the Pakistani team led by him played against the Indian team which was led by Sunil Gavaskar.

Both teams appeared equally matched and well balanced, but Imran Khan was in such great form, that he got forty wickets in the series and literally demolished the Indian side single-handed.

What is more important is that in the latter part of the same series, although Imran had injured his ankle and was advised rest, he insisted on bowling, to inspire and to lead, to ache in silence for the good of the team and in pursuit of glorious achievement.

This demonstrates the hallmark of a leader for whom his team or organisation is paramount – to sacrifice personal pain, perform to the best of individual ability when the team or organisation needs it most, thus putting team before self in a glorious display of superlative leadership.

Possibly no example could be more instructive and motivating to cement this learning than that of the American president – **Theodore Roosevelt**. Roosevelt had already completed two terms as president, and was campaigning to secure his party's nomination for a third term, when, on 14th October, 1912, he was shot in his chest by a would-be assassin outside the hotel he had just emerged from.

Rather than asking to be rushed to hospital, he insisted on first delivering his scheduled speech of 90 minutes. "You get me to that speech," he ordered the driver of his car. He reached the venue (the Milwaukee auditorium), mounted the stage, and then began his campaign speech with the words, "**Friends, I shall ask you to be as quiet as possible. I don't know whether you understand that I have just been shot.**"

THEODORE ROOSEVELT

With these words he proceeded to unbutton his vest and reveal his blood-stained shirt. As the audience watched, stunned into silence, Roosevelt reached into his coat packet and pulled out a 50-page speech which had two big bullet holes blasted through each page. Holding the pages aloft for the fascinated audience, Roosevelt continued, "**Fortunately I had my manuscript, so you see I was going to make a long speech, and there is a bullet – there is where the bullet went through – and it probably saved me from it going into my heart. The bullet is in me now, so that I cannot make a very long speech, but I will try my best.**"

Although his breath had shortened and his voice had weakened, only after he completed his full 90-minute speech did he agree to seek medical assistance. The X-rays taken at the hospital revealed that the bullet had lodged against his fourth right rib on an upward path to his heart and had been slowed down by the heavy overcoat he had worn and the 50-page speech in his coat pocket.

As another great American president (probably the greatest of them all), Abraham Lincoln, had once said:

"**I am not concerned that you have fallen. I am concerned that you arise.**"

Officers in the Indian defence forces are expected to be tougher, faster, and stronger than the men they lead in war and in peace.

When it comes to outdoor sports and games (which occupy a substantial portion of time of an officer's average day when not in front-line action), the officers push themselves to lift more, jump longer and higher, and run ahead of their men whom they participate in these activities with.

**FIELD MARSHAL
PHILIP WALHOUSE CHETWODE**

The message being clear – the officers should not expect their men to undergo physical stress and discomfort in battle which the officers cannot or are not willing to undergo themselves.

No wonder the **motto** of the **officers** passing out of the **Indian Military Academy** is:

"THE SAFETY, HONOUR AND WELFARE OF YOUR COUNTRY COME FIRST, ALWAYS AND EVERY TIME. THE HONOUR, WELFARE AND COMFORT OF THE MEN YOU COMMAND COME NEXT. YOUR OWN EASE, COMFORT AND SAFETY COME LAST, ALWAYS AND EVERY TIME."

This is also known as the '**Chetwode motto**' as these words are extracted from the address delivered by **Field Marshal Philip Walhouse Chetwode**, (who was also Commander-in-Chief of the Indian forces in the 1930s) at the Indian Military Academy at Dehradun in 1932. These words are also engraved on the entrance to the central hall of the Academy.

- Very rarely does success come without struggle

- **'Adversity causes some men to break, and other men to break records.'** Unfortunately who first said this is not known, but it is very relevant for aspiring leaders to realise that the path to leadership success has many unpleasant detours along the way, and they cannot afford to be shy of moments of physical discomfort that could arise

- After all, what better way can there be to gain the respect of the men whom you lead than to show them that you are willing to share in the discomforts which they face on a daily basis to 'get the job done'

NO PAIN
NO GAIN

SECTION FOUR - VICTORY

INTRODUCTION TO THE
VICTORY SECTION

> *" It is better to conquer yourself than to win a thousand battles. Then the victory is yours. It cannot be taken from you, not by angels or by demons, heaven or hell "*
>
> -GAUTAMA BUDDHA

Victory.

The ultimate objective of every human endeavour, and of every leader.

Of course, the concept of victory differs from individual to individual, from organisation to organisation, and from leader to leader.

Which is why what is considered as sweet victory by some is considered as bitter defeat by others.

For some, victory is wealth; for others, fame; and yet for others, a beaming smile on the face of the customer.

The fortunate corporate leader is one who manages to achieve all these and more, and achieve them consistently.

Indeed, the effectiveness of a leader's vision, the depth of his values, and the impact of his courage and valour can all be quantified through the victories he achieves.

433

Victory for a leader in multiple forms is essential. After all, if the myriad and multiple efforts and resources channelised into formulating the vision, practicing the values, and displaying valour do not bear fruit over time in the form of positive tangible and intangible results, then the leader needs to do a serious rethink.

There are many aspects to victory, all not as obvious as winning a gold medal in the 100 metres dash at the Olympic Games, nor as obvious as being awarded the Best Actor at the Oscars.

Sometimes, the apparent 'loser' is the real winner.

———————————

Many of you may have seen and admired the performance of **Marlon Brando** in the title role of *The Godfather*.

MARLON BRANDO

MARLON BRANDO
AS THE GODFATHER

But what is not so well known is that on the 5th of March, 1973, Marlon Brando **DECLINED** the *Oscar Academy Award* for Best Actor for that awe-inspiring performance he had played as Don Vito Corleone – the Godfather himself.

The reason? He was protesting Hollywood's negative portrayal of the Red Indians over the years. Although Brando was not a Red Indian, he felt this perennial injustice could not be left unaddressed. In Hollywood, the Red Indians had been primarily used as extras. Even leading roles depicting Red Indians in several generations of Western and cowboy movies were almost always given to white actors.

So on the evening of March the 5th, 1973, when Liv Ullman and Roger Moore (both hosting the Oscar's that year), read out Marlon Brando's name as recipient of the Best Actor award, they were stunned to find not Brando coming up to receive his award, but a brilliantly beautiful Red Indian woman in Apache Red Indian attire, ascending the stairs of the stage. Roger Moore offered the award to the woman (who was **Sacheen Littlefeather**, the then-president of the National Native American Affirmative Image Committee).

Littlefeather waved away the award, set a letter down on the podium, introduced herself, and addressed the amazed audience, saying, **"I'm representing Marlon Brando this evening and he has asked me to tell you....that he very regretfully cannot accept this very generous award. And the reasons for this being are the treatment of American Indians today by the film industry...."**

Extracts from the speech which Brando had thoughtfully conceived and which Littlefeather proceeded to read on stage – 'For 200 years we have said to the Red Indian people who are fighting for their land, their life, their families and their right to be free: "Lay down your arms, my friends, and then we will remain together. Only if you lay down your arms, my friends, can we then talk of peace and come to an agreement which will be good for you." When they laid down their arms, we murdered them. We lied to them.....Perhaps at this moment you are saying to yourself what the hell has all this got to do with the Academy Awards? Why is this woman standing up here, ruining our evening, invading our lives with things that don't concern us, and that we don't care about?....I think the answer to those unspoken questions is that the motion picture community has been as

435

responsible for degrading the Red Indian and making a mockery of his character, describing him as savage, hostile and evil. It's hard enough for children to grow up in this world. When Red Indian children....see their race depicted as they are in films, their minds become injured in ways we can never know.....I (Marlon Brando) would have been here tonight to speak to you directly, but I felt that perhaps I could be of better use if I went to Wounded Knee (Wounded Knee was a place where a team of 200 Red Indian activists were then protesting poor treatment at the hands of the American Government and were under siege by U.S. military forces) to help forestall in whatever way I can the establishment of a peace which would be dishonourable as long as the rivers shall run and the grass shall grow. I hope that those who are listening would not look upon this as a rude intrusion but as an earnest effort to focus attention on an issue that might very well determine whether or not this country has the right to say from this point forward we believe in the inalienable rights of all people to remain free and independent on lands that have supported their life beyond living memory. Thank you for your kindness and your courtesy to Miss Littlefeather. Thank you and good night.'

Thus the immortal Marlon Brando offered the Red Indian community a once-in-a-lifetime opportunity to raise awareness of their just cause in front of 85 million television viewers around the world. Victory indeed under any circumstances, even though it cost him the coveted Oscar Academy Award for a brilliantly gut-wrenching performance as the Godfather.

> " *The moment we begin to fear the opinions of others and hesitate to tell the truth that is in us, and from motives of policy are silent when we should speak, the divine floods of light and life no longer flow into our souls* "
>
> -ELIZABETH CADY STANTON

And then there is the true story of brave-heart **Eric Liddell**, immortalised in the film *Chariots of Fire*, a man who actually **achieved victory** by **GIVING UP** an **Olympic gold medal in the 100 yards dash**, just as Marlon Brando gained his victory by rejecting an Oscar for his principled stand.

This incident occurred in the 1924 Paris Olympics, and Eric Liddell, a Scotsman and the then world-record holder in that event, was almost certain to win it. But when the dates for the preliminary heats for this event were announced, Eric saw that the day on which the preliminary heats were to be held fell on a Sunday.

Eric, a devout Christian, implicitly believed in the Biblical concept of the Sabbath – the belief that Sunday is the day of rest, and no nature of work, including running a race, shall be done on it.

For Eric, the decision was easy – "I will not run," he said. There was no fuss, nor any announcement at a hastily-called press conference to gain mileage and publicity from his act of genuine sacrifice.

Just a quiet, dignified – **"Since it is a Sunday, I will not run. I cannot run. It would be going against what is written in the Bible. The Sabbath is sacred and cannot be violated."**

Eric, despite intense pressure from his countrymen to reverse his decision, did not run the 100 yards dash, his pet event. But however, he did decide on-the-spot to run the 400 yards race, an event he had hardly ever run before, not even in practice. The preliminary heats for the 400 yards event did not fall on a Sunday, so Eric could participate. No one expected him to even reach the finals of that event.

But he DID reach the finals, and went on to win the gold medal for the 400 yards in grand style. It is said that the roar of the crowd when Eric breasted the finish-line, went from Paris clear across the English Channel and was heard over a hundred miles away in London. Of course, this is part of the myth that has now grown around Eric, this saint-like, simple man.

The story of his victory is not over. Eric later renounced athletics and went to China as a Christian missionary. While he was there, World War II broke out, and Eric, along with many others, was taken prisoner by the Japanese and interned in a prisoner-of-war camp. In the camp along with him were many families which included a lot of children. The children, being cooped up, were restless, and fights and quarrels often broke out among them. To the children in Welhsien camp, Eric Liddell was their 'Uncle Eric,' the one they could turn to, to lighten their otherwise dull days.

ERIC LIDDELL

Eric, in order to keep the children occupied, organised games and sports for them. **He even organised these games on Sundays and participated in them himself, to keep the children engaged, active, happy and healthy.**

This man, this God-fearing Christian, willingly gave up an Olympic gold medal as it would have meant going against his principles of running or playing on a Sunday. But this same man not only organised, but also participated in and played children's games on Sunday – the Sabbath – the 'Day of Rest' – to keep a few imprisoned children engaged, occupied, and free from boredom.

Eric may have voluntarily lost out on an Olympic gold, but he had clearly achieved victory in his spiritual race.

The words: **"First of all, absolute surrender to the Will of God. Absolute surrender,"** were often on Eric's lips.

Sadly, Eric died in the prisoner-of-war camp at the young age of 43. When the news of his passing away filtered through to his native country, all of Scotland mourned.

For Eric, the smiles on the faces and the laughter on the lips of these children was a victory greater than winning dozens of Olympic gold medals.

How then **can** we, and who **are** we, to decide, **what** victory really means?

A REMARKABLE LEADER, THROUGH HIS ACTIONS, WINS THE GENUINE LOVE, RESPECT AND LOYALTY OF HIS PEOPLE

> *You give loyalty, you'll get it back. You give love, you'll get it back*
>
> -TOMMY LASORDA

WHAT **J.R.D.** BELIEVED IN AND **PRACTICED**

> *Love and loyalty do not generate by themselves. They do not spring up from barren soil overnight like mushrooms. They cautiously emerge when people have good reason to believe that their leader has their best interests at heart. That he will not sacrifice their future for his short-term personal gain. That he will play his role responsibly and well and will carry the organisation forward in the right direction. That he will gently correct them when they are wrong, and whole-heartedly support and praise them when they are right*
>
> -CYRUS M. GONDA

One way in which the success of a leader can be identified is by the reaction of his people towards him. J.R.D. was genuinely loved by the people he led. You could say he scores a hundred on hundred on this key parameter of leadership.

A senior staff member nostalgically recalls the days when J.R.D. was the Chairman of Air India . He mentions that at parties, J.R.D. enjoyed meeting and interacting with the junior-most as well as the senior staff. The staff too, responded to his paternal style by blending together as one united family. There was no distinction between the manner in which the seniors treated the juniors when J.R.D. was their leader, as he himself treated them all equally. "Now," said that senior staff member after J.R.D. was no longer the Chairman, "that J.R.D. is not Chairman anymore, it is 'we' and 'they.' The close-knit camaraderie that J.R.D. had personally managed to weave among the senior and junior members of his staff was destroyed with his going. **Love for him and loyalty towards him is what bound all the staff at all levels together."**

Even AFTER J.R.D. left Air India, the staff affectionately and loyally referred to him as THEIR Chairman. He had won a place in their hearts, and he could be replaced by no other.

J.R.D. was also featured and honoured in the Portrait Gallery of the *Sunday Times*, London, in 1951. An extract from this article reads:

'As an employer, he is humane and liberal. Some say almost socialistic. Unspoilt by success, easily approachable, sympathetic in manner, he is admired and respected by labour leaders, who have often appealed to him to intervene in disputes between management and unions. Such personal popularity as he enjoys could hardly be paralleled in an organisation, employing, as his does, over 1,20,000 workers.'

The *Sunday Times*, London, is not a newspaper to be taken lightly, nor does it publish any article without verifying the facts. If this is what this august newspaper had to say about J.R.D., it speaks volumes about the love and respect his employees had for him.

And that, by any standards, is sweet victory indeed.

> **" " Lack of loyalty is one of the major causes of failure in every walk of life " "**
>
> -NAPOLEON HILL

LEARNINGS
FOR LEADERS

The **Great Wall of China** is a unique structure.

Built many centuries ago, it is even today the only structure made by man that is said to be visible from the moon with the naked eye.

It was not built, however, as a decorative marvel to be gazed at, but rather as a secure boundary for the Chinese kingdom. Once its construction was complete, the people of the land felt they were safe. No enemy could possibly attack or invade them now. The wall was so solidly and intelligently constructed that it would be impossible for enemies to either climb over or break through this superb piece of protective architecture.

THE GREAT WALL OF CHINA

B ut yet, surprisingly, or perhaps not so surprisingly, the enemies got through easily. How? They did not need to break down the solid wall or batter down one of the equally solid gates. **They simply bribed one of the gatekeepers who was disgruntled with his superiors and who therefore had no sense of attachment or loyalty to his emperor or to his country. This gatekeeper opened the gate he was assigned to guard, and the enemy walked through unchallenged. The battle was lost before it had begun.**

This does not imply that if a leader behaves in a manner which generates love, respect and loyalty towards him by his people, that there would never be a single, disgruntled individual, who could not be bribed to betray the organisation and the leader.

Rather, when the leader's actions are designed to generate respect and loyalty, the bulk and majority of his people will respond in kind, and will form a strong protective barrier, securing the organisation and its interests against nefarious forces such as unscrupulous competitors from outside and solitary disgruntled individuals from within.

The probability of an employee falling prey to a bribe or other inducement to betray the organisation is far reduced when people have reason to be loyal to their leader.

It is a fact that when most people betray their leader or their own organisation, the primary reason for doing so is not likely to be mere money, but more likely a grudge or a sense of resentment towards the organisation or its leadership which these unhappy people wish to work off.

As has often been said:

"People don't leave jobs; people leave bosses"

Do not give your people a reason to be disloyal to either you or towards the organisation. Rather, lead the J.R.D. way – forthright, loving, simple, honest, direct, and victory is yours.

> *You can buy people's time; you can buy their physical presence at a given place; you can even buy a measured number of their skilled muscular motions per hour. But you cannot buy enthusiasm…you cannot buy loyalty…you cannot buy the devotion of hearts, minds, or souls. You must earn these*
>
> –CLARENCE FRANCIS

A soldier of Emperor Napoleon's army was once captured by the enemy. The enemy soldiers brutally tortured him, and also taunted him. "Where is your Napoleon? Show us where he is," they jeered.

The loyal soldier, though much in pain, bared his chest to the enemies and said, **"Thrust your spear into my heart. When the blood flows from there, you will see my dear emperor, for he resides in my heart."**

Such was the loyalty that **NAPOLEON BONAPARTE** inspired among his troops.

Rome's greatest statesman, **MARCUS TULLIUS CICERO**, witnessed the end of the Roman Republic. Before paying with his life for speaking out against the misrule he was witnessing, he spoke to the Roman Senate:

"A nation can survive its fools, and even the ambitious. **But it cannot survive treason from within.** An enemy at the gates is less formidable, for he is known and carries his banner openly. But the traitor moves amongst those within the gate freely, his sly whispers rustling through all the alleys, heard in the very halls of government itself. For the traitor appears not a traitor; he speaks in accents familiar to his victims, and he wears their face and their arguments, he appeals to the baseness that lies deep in the hearts of all men. He rots the soul of a nation, he works secretly and unknown in the night to undermine the pillars of the city, he infects the body politic so that it can no longer resist. A murderer is less to fear."

POINTS TO PONDER AND PRACTICE

- Remember, loyalty is a reciprocated phenomenon and can never be a one-way-street. And for a leader who wishes to revel victorious by securing the loyalty of his subordinates, he first needs to demonstrate loyalty to his people

- As a leader, practice from today onwards the components which result in loyalty, and gradually and then rapidly, a surge of loyalty emanating from your people will form a protective layer which will rise up like a tidal wave to support you whenever you as a leader or the organisation face tough times

" *Loyalty is the one thing a leader cannot do without* "

-A.P. GOUTHEY

EVOLVED LEADERS ENABLE THEIR COMPETITORS (AND THEIR INDUSTRY) TO GROW

> *Effectively, change is almost impossible without industry-wide collaboration, cooperation and consensus*
>
> -SIMON MAINWARING

WHAT **J.R.D.** BELIEVED IN AND **PRACTICED**

> *Competition doesn't kill an organisation. Rather, it is the irrational fear of inevitable competition that forces insecure decision-makers at the helm of an organisation to commit needless mistakes, which then proceed to kill the organisation*
>
> -CYRUS M. GONDA

It is rare today to find a leader who puts his nation beyond his own organisation, especially if the public sector company controlled by the nation is a direct competitor to the leader's own organisation. But this is precisely what J.R.D. did.

Tata Steel was a well established and world renowned producer of high quality steel in Jamshedpur by the 1950s.

This is the time period when the Indian government considered erecting its own factories for steel production. Most corporate leaders would have viewed the government as unwanted competition, and would have tried to use every underhand trick possible to ensure that the proposed government enterprise in the area of steel failed.

But not J.R.D.

He had a genuine desire to see the country progress, even if it meant adding competition to his own existing organisation. **He thus gave full technical and knowledge-based support to the government's foray into steel.** Employees who had gained expertise and experience at Tata Steel were deputed by J.R.D. to provide know-how to the government venture.

In fact, while the government wanted to put up smaller steel plants (which would have been beneficial to the Tatas, as it would have meant less competition), it was J.R.D., who in his wisdom and integrity, argued with Prime Minister Jawaharlal Nehru that the government should not think small when it came to erecting steel plants. **While the government was considering erecting steel plants on a small scale, it was J.R.D. who convinced the concerned authorities to think big and to erect public sector steel plants with a larger capacity. Today, India reaps the benefit of J.R.D.'s honest and selfless advice to his competitor.**

J.R.D. gave full and unconditional support to the government to set up steel plants which would ultimately compete with Tata Steel, sharing with the government his know-how, his expertise, and most importantly his vision of having large scale plants where the Government had been looking at smaller and mid-sized ones.

How does 'adding to the competition' in this manner result in **victory** for the leader and his organisation? Let us read on and see.

LEARNINGS
▌FOR LEADERS

"Evolved leaders realise that the world and all that lies in it is inter-connected with an invisible thread, and that the destiny of each of us is inextricably linked with that of the other. They understand that when all players in an industry succeed (and as Mahatma Gandhi said, there is enough in the world to satisfy everybody's need, but not enough to satisfy a single individual's/ organisation's greed), the industry as a whole itself advances and benefits"

-CYRUS M. GONDA

It is only enlightened and courageous leaders who realise and appreciate that by helping genuine new entrants and players set foot into their industry, the industry as a whole grows, expands, professionalises and gets the benefit of becoming a mature industry and secures the advantages thereof.

This results into a win-win situation for all players concerned, as even the existing organisation which welcomes and supports the newcomers is motivated to improve its own standards and quality on all parameters and curb unnecessary costs and curtail wasteful expenditure, as it is now no longer in a monopoly situation. Thus, with the entry of new players, the existing organisations themselves improve on the parameter of quality and customer satisfaction, as well as lower their costs of production, becoming fitter and healthier.

All stand to benefit – the existing organisions, the new entrants, the customers, and of course the eco-system at large.

This results in a state of **win-win, and win-win is the highest form of victory for all involved.**

447

 As the iconic **Steve Jobs** correctly observed way back in 1997:

"We HAVE to let go of the notion that for Apple to win, Microsoft has to lose....The era of setting this up as a competition between Apple and Microsoft is over as far as I'm concerned."

Unfortunately, many managers in corporate entities today do all they possibly can to destroy their competition and spend valuable limited resources and energy in pulling competitors and newcomers down, rather than invest those same limited resources into pulling their own organisation, and the entire industry up.

A very pertinent experiment in human behaviour was recently conducted upon employees across organisations in a Western country. A number of employees were given two options regarding their own increments in salary. They could choose one of these two options. The two options offered to the employees in the survey were:

1. They would be given a salary increase of 25 percent, in which case their colleagues at work would get a salary increase of 30 percent

2. They would be given a salary increase of only 20 percent, in which case their colleagues at work would be given an even lower salary increase of 15 percent

The choice sounds like a 'no-brainer,' but, believe it or not, a majority of the employees in the survey opted for the SECOND option, in which case THEY THEMSELVES would receive a LOWER salary increment.

Getting a lower increment themselves was fine by them, as long as their colleagues got an even lower increment.

Sounds amazing.

But this is merely representative of typical human behaviour, which unfortunately leads to an outcome of lose-lose rather than win-win, and is not only exhibited by employees when it comes to decisions regarding their increments, but is also demonstrated by 'leaders' when it comes to choices regarding how they view and treat other firms operating within their industry. It is clear that the employees who were part of this experiment in human behaviour, as well as some 'leaders,' view others around them as competitors to be crushed rather than colleagues to be cherished, even if it means being dragged down themselves in the bargain.

In mature industries, such as the pharmaceutical industry for example, many competing organisations get together on a common platform and **collaborate on research they have individually conducted in areas such as safety measures, and share their findings with one another.**This saves time, cost, and effort all around, and benefits all players concerned. Then each player goes ahead and develops their individual products to the best of their ability and competes in the open market.

Leaders who are confident about the inherent strengths and abilities of their own organisation and their people would have the sensibility to operate in this manner.

Such a positive and collaborative approach also demonstrates the faith which the leader displays and exhibits in his own organisation and the people who constitute it. **It boosts the confidence of his people, telling them in no uncertain terms that they have nothing to fear from competition, as their leader himself welcomes it in a healthy spirit.**

Such a perspective is similar to that of a brilliant and hard-working student who knows he need fear no competitor. Such a student would have no hesitation in helping weaker students with their studies, and in the process himself gaining the benefit of a second revision.

Leaders of this calibre and mind-set always win by rising to greater heights along with the organisations they lead, as not only their abilities, but also their sterling character is recognised and appreciated by all stakeholders concerned. Such leaders are **victors** not only for their own organisation, but also in the eyes of the industry they operate in. They have truly understood the essence of win-win.

James Frederick Bender narrates the beautiful story of a simple farmer who grew award-winning corn, year after year. Hearing of this, a curious journalist approached the farmer to hear his success story.

To his surprise, one of the first things the journalist learned was that the farmer did not jealously guard his special corn seed, but shared it with neighbouring farmers.

The journalist queried the farmer, "**How is it that you can afford to share your best and special seed with your neighbouring farmers, when they too are entering the same contest for growing the best corn? Don't you consider them as your competitors?**"

The farmer smiled and replied, "**Why Sir, didn't you know that the wind picks up pollen from the ripening corn and swirls It from field to field? If my neighbouring farmers grow inferior corn, the cross-pollination from their pollen will steadily degrade the quality of my own corn too over the years. THUS, IF I AM TO GROW GOOD CORN, I MUST HELP MY NEIGHBOURING FARMERS TO GROW GOOD CORN IN THEIR FIELDS AS WELL.**"

Remember the words of the tennis great – **ARTHUR ASHE** – who said, "**True heroism....is not the urge to SURPASS all others at whatever cost but the urge to SERVE others at whatever cost.**"

Roger Federer is an outstanding sportsperson. A rare individual  who has become a true legend not only during his lifetime, but even before his retirement.

With his win in the 2018 Australian Open men's singles title, Roger now has won an incredible 20 Grand Slam singles titles. Along with his impressive victories, Roger also has the distinction of being a tennis professional since the last 20 years, which in the highly competitive world of professional tennis is almost an unbelievable feat.

You would expect an individual who has reached the peak that his sport has to offer, to jealously guard his 'trade secrets' so that he could scale even greater heights. But that is not in Roger's DNA.

Federer also won the singles title at the Gerry Weber Open tournament (Germany) in February 2018. He defeated local  German lad **Alexander Zverev**, the 4th seed, in the fnal match of that tournament. Zverev was physically fit, but was mentally unable to rise to the occasion, and the crowd was disappointed.

After the tournament, Federer realised that his opponent was a quality player who had a great future ahead of him, and just needed a few right words to overcome the mental block he found himself in. So Federer gave the 20-year-old Zverev some precious words of advice, knowing full well that as competitors, they are liable to meet on the court in the future.

What Federer did was the equivalent of not only giving your direct competitor expert tips on how to improve, but possibly even beat you in the future. A true leader in every sense of the word.

Whenever you are confronted with an opponent, conquer him with love

-MAHATMA GANDHI

Great industries are never made from single companies. There is room and space for a lot of winners

-JEFF BEZOS (FOUNDER OF AMAZON.COM)

Basketball is a highly competitive game at college level in the U.S.A. And the most successful college basketball coach of all time was **JOHN WOODEN, who coached the team at the University of California, Los Angeles (UCLA).** During his 27 year tenure there, his teams never had a losing season. And in his last 12 years as coach, his teams won 10 national championships, with a record seven of those in succession. When a winner like Wooden spoke on the subject of winning, you could be sure what he said was worth listening to.

Here is what John Wooden had to say on success:

'**To me, success isn't outscoring anyone**, it's the peace of mind that comes from self-satisfaction in knowing you did your best. That's something each individual must determine. You can fool others, but you can't fool yourself…. Many people are surprised to know that in all my years at UCLA (as coach), I never once talked about winning. Instead, I would tell my players before games, "When it's over, I want your head up. And there's only one way your head can be up – that's for you to know, not me, that you gave your best effort. If you do that, then the score doesn't really matter, although I have a feeling that **if you do give your best, the score will be to your liking.**"

I honestly believe that in not stressing winning as such, we won more than we would have if I'd stressed outscoring opponents.'

Once upon a time, in a suburb in a faraway land, there were two cobbler shops. Both were obviously competitors to each other, and both men strived hard to retain their clientele. Yet, one day, there was a huge surge of business at the first shop, which continued throughout the week. This cobbler learned that the reason for the extra crowd in his shop was that the other cobbler was ill and home in bed, his shop closed for the week.

The first cobbler worked hard from Monday to Saturday, with almost no time to rest or even have his mid-day meals. And on Sunday morning, he gathered all the excess money he had made during the week because of the extra business that had come his way, went to the house of the second cobbler, visited him in his sick-bed, and put that excess money gently onto the side-table in the room. "Some cash to tide you over your illness. Get well soon," the first cobbler smiled and cheerily wished his competitor, and then left to attend church with a light and happy heart.

The following is extracted from an article titled *The Amazon Model: If You Can't Beat 'Em, Work With 'Em*, authored by Matt Palmquist, and appearing on the Strategy Plus Business Blog:

'Firms can use their resources more efficiently when they share or leverage them with competitors through a coopetition-based setup. The well-documented relationship between Sony and Samsung enabled the two direct competitors to establish joint technology and manufacturing plants in South Korea that has helped them become market leaders in the LCD TV segment over the past decade. In addition, Sony's advantages in technological knowledge and Samsung's marketing abilities dovetailed in a competitive alliance that has expanded the global LCD TV market and made the two companies dominant in their fields.

Examples abound in other industries as well. Rival automobile manufacturers such as Citroën, Peugeot, and Toyota share technology and resources while simultaneously competing for customers through branding and by producing slightly different car models. Similarly, Swedish breweries work together to return empty beer bottles from wholesalers in order to cut down on transport costs. In the airline industry, the Star Alliance network and Oneworld links between competing carriers help them save on logistics, marketing, and ticketing.'

POINTS TO PONDER AND PRACTICE

- You may not as yet be a CEO, and you may not currently be in a position to assist new players or existing smaller players to strengthen themselves within the industry. But whenever you do get an opportunity to talk about your competitors in the industry; for example, if a customer asks you how your product or service compares to those of your competitors, **resist the temptation to run down your competitors.** Mention that the competitor's products or services are also good, but explain where your product or service scores better as far as the customer's needs are concerned. In order to do this, you will need to make an in-depth study of your products or services as compared to those of your competitors, but this effort will be well worth it

- Your customers will respect you for this confidence in your own products or services, and for your honesty. The value of your own product and service will go up in their esteem. You and your organisation will be seen as winners in your customer's eyes. And these are the eyes which truly matter

SIGNIFICANT AWARDS
FOR MERITORIOUS ACHIEVEMENT – BOTH AT PERSONAL AS WELL AS AT ORGANISATIONAL LEVEL

Greatness is defined by public recognition of one's contribution to society, and therefore, true greatness is a bit more elusive to obtain than mere success

-KEN POIROT

WHAT **J.R.D.** BELIEVED IN AND **PRACTICED**

The truth of the matter is that there's nothing you can't accomplish if: (1) You clearly decide what it is that you're absolutely committed to achieving, (2) You're willing to take massive action, (3) You notice what's working or not, and (4) You continue to change your approach until you achieve what you want, using whatever life gives you along the way

-ANTHONY ROBBINS

Though J.R.D., with his humble and simple nature, never strove to secure awards for the work he did, they came to him in large numbers because of the good he personally did and the causes he implicitly believed in and espoused, and also the organisational resources he committed towards these ends . These were not awards for mere material targets achieved, but were in admiration and recognition for genuine work in multiple spheres, most of which were oriented towards aspects other than simply gaining revenues and profits for his organisation.

457

J.R.D. in his lifetime and throughout his career secured numerous, almost innumerable awards. And these were bestowed by the most credible international organisations and in many cases even by the governments of developed nations.

A list of just a few of the more notable of these awards and honours (not in chronological or in any particular order of importance) include:

- Given the rank of Group Captain of the Indian Air Force in 1948 and elevated to the rank of honorary Air Commodore in 1965 and further promoted in 1974 to the rank of Air Vice Marshal

- The Daniel Guggenheim Award in 1988 (This Award is considered one of the highest international honours awarded to only one person throughout the world every year for a lifetime of work and contribution to aeronautics. In fact, the first winner of this Award when it was initiated in 1929 was the famed Orville Wright, 'For the design and construction, with his brother now deceased, of the first successful engine-propelled airplane')

- The Tony Jannus Award in 1979 (Awarded once a year to one person throughout the world for extraordinary achievements in the field of commercial aviation)

- The Edward Warner Award of the International Civil Aviation Organisation, Canada, in 1986

- The Padma Vibhushan in 1957 on the eve of the silver jubilee of the commencement of his initial airline

- The Bharat Ratna (Government of India's highest civilian honour) in 1992 for his personal contribution to Indian society and selfless service to the nation – one of the rare instances where this award was bestowed during an individual's lifetime

- The United Nations Population Award in 1992 for his pioneering efforts to promote the philosophy of Family Planning in India

- The French Legion of Honour in 1983

- Awarded Honorary Doctorates from the Universities of Allahabad, Benares, Bombay and Roorkee

- He had been a Member of the Atomic Energy Commission since its inception, and was President of the Court of the Indian Institute of Science, Bangalore

An extremely prestigious award secured by the Tata group under J.R.D.'s able stewardship was the **selection of the Tata Steel Township - Jamshedpur, as a United Nations Global Compact City** based on the hygienic conditions of sanitation, the well planned, thoughtfully laid-out and impeccably maintained roads, other various positive comprehensive measures offered by Tata Steel, and the overall quality of life that its fortunate residents enjoyed.

Note: Especially in our current era, when the thrust of the Central Government is towards developing 'smart cities' to accelerate growth and enhance the standard of living of our citizens, it is important to remember that the Tata group has since long conceptualised, implemented, and even won global recognition for the same.

And, on J.R.D.'s passing away in 1993, the Indian Parliament was adjourned in his memory – an honour not usually given to persons who are not members of parliament.

In the 62 years since the Bharat Ratna (India's highest civilian honour) has been initiated, it has been **AWARDED ONLY ONCE TO A BUSINESSMAN** – and that is to Mr. J.R.D. Tata in 1992.

In contrast, in the U.S.A., the Presidential Medal of Freedom (U.S.A.'s highest civilian honour), has over the years been conferred upon multiple business-persons. Some of them being – Warren Buffet, Henry Ford II, Thomas Watson, Jr. (of IBM), Sam Walton, Walter Wriston (of Citibank), David Rockefeller, Estee Lauder, and many others.

Truly, J.R.D. was a remarkably unique and positively outstanding individual in every sense of the word.

LEARNINGS
FOR LEADERS

Gold medals aren't really made of gold – They're made of sweat, determination, and a hard-to-find alloy called guts

-DAN GABLE

Though certain awards can be considered merely of token value, others, when awarded by those organisations which matter, are worth more than their weight in gold. They are representative of the recognition of significant and victorious achievements, and as Dan Gable has said, they are made of sweat, determination, and often of even tears and blood.

Winning significant individual awards is a great feeling, but it always feels even greater when you win awards on behalf of the organisation you represent or lead.

 **Zhang Ning** has been the only player to win consecutive Olympic singles gold medals in badminton. Her various medals secured with great effort and toil give her immense personal satisfaction, but as she puts it, **"Every player who enters the national team is certain to suffer great pressure because every game you play at the international level is on the behalf of China instead of yourself.... you have to train harder and keep challenging and conquering yourself all the time for the sake of our nation...I have told myself years ago that an Olympic medal was good, but securing the gold for China was above all."**

Significant awards definitely add honour and prestige to the recipient individual and organisation, but DO THEY ADD VALUE IN MATERIAL TERMS AS WELL? Darrell Zahorsky, (writing in an article titled *The Strategic Value Of Corporate Awards* on the stevieawards.com site) certainly believes so.

Zahorsky quotes Lynne S. Marcus, owner of an awards and recognition consulting company, who feels **businesses need to plan a CORPORATE AWARDS STRATEGY with corporate initiatives in mind**. Marcus says, "If the company is making a push for ethical behaviour or corporate leadership, then it can look for awards competitions that recognise these traits." Another example provided is that of the Coca-Cola Company, which has embraced the philosophy of having a diverse and supportive workplace culture. The 38 business awards that Coca-Cola has won in this regard add credibility to the company's commitment towards workplace diversity.

Zahorsky adds that the **right awards also help to attract and retain the best talent**. As an example, the renowned consulting firm, Booz; Allen & Hamilton likes to be known as a family-friendly company, and the five consecutive years that it has been placed in the 100 Best Companies for Working Mothers award given by *Working Mother* magazine, gives the firm a vote of confidence in this regard for the best new hires in that category.

And **awards can also help secure a sales advantage**. Here is quoted Paula Dickerson, manager of industry honours and awards program for the software leader SAS. Dickerson believes that awards provide the "....benefits of increased awareness, third-party validation and establishing market leadership....**Used effectively, industry awards are yet another sales tool to aid in the close of business (deals)**."

Significant **awards also greatly enhance an organisation's Public Relations efforts**, bringing the firm positively into the limelight in the eyes of those who matter.

Last, but definitely not the least, Zahorsky refers to a research study conducted by Hendricks and Singhal of the *University of Western Ontario* and *Georgia Institute of Technology*, which revealed that more than **600 firms which were the winners of corporate quality awards achieved 37% more sales growth** and **44% higher stock price return** than their peers who had not been the recipients of such awards.

All the above are sufficient reasons indeed for a leader to strive to win significant awards, especially those awards which are in sync with the organisation's stated objective and choice of strategic offering.

Yet it must be remembered that J.R.D. never undertook the challenges he did keeping awards in mind as his objective. He was far above such things. The awards came to him by default for the nature of his work and the causes he dedicated himself to and the efforts that he undertook and the attention that he paid not only towards strategising and planning, but also towards execution and implementation of the same. **Once you succeed by adopting this approach, that is when your victory will be the sweetest.**

POINTS TO PONDER AND PRACTICE

- Encourage and nominate your people to participate in external industry-related and other relevant competitions at their level, which relate to their roles and profiles. Let your people also feel the pride of victory, but instil in them the value-system that they should win in the 'right way.' Regular participation will enhance their confidence and open their horizons and help them hone their skills which will help them at work as well

- Offer internal non-monetary awards to your employees for various aspects of performance. Substantial research shows that such awards enhance productivity, decrease absenteeism, and motivate employees

- When you select individuals from among your people to honour them with awards, ensure you select those individuals who have 'played in the spirit of the game.' That is the way a healthy work-culture gets inculcated, when people know that not only are results rewarded, but also the means of achieving them

- Develop a mindset towards envisioning forward-thinking concepts and involving yourself with new initiatives similar to that of J.R.D.'s, and significant awards and their related benefits will certainly follow for you as well as for your organisation as a by-product of the good work you undertake

463

UNITE THE GROUP WITH A COMMON IDEOLOGY

" *Where there is unity there is always victory* "

-PUBLILIUS SYRUS

WHAT **J.R.D.** BELIEVED IN AND **PRACTICED**

" *It would not surprise me if certain billion dollar conglomerates (not the Tatas), who have only the profit motive at their core (such conglomerates only have cores, not hearts), even start selling balloons on the beach to babies if they see a chance of adding a single rupee to their vast coffers. The only ideology the group companies in such a conglomerate would share in common is: 'Sabse bada Rupaiya.' In such a scenario, it is often only the organisational name which is the binding factor among the various group companies of the conglomerate. This serves little purpose, as the reason why a business group should ideally choose to get into diverse businesses is to share a common philosophy among the group companies and conduct its operations with a certain common ideology (other than only the profit motive), in mind* "

-CYRUS M. GONDA

Organisations today are no more the simple entities they once were.

They are complex spiders' webs of holding companies and parent companies; which are rapidly and constantly expanding and contracting through mergers and acquisitions, divestments and diversifications – both through organic and inorganic means.

Most organisations today will no longer be operating in only their core area of expertise, but will expand and spread their tentacles to wherever they see a business opportunity.

In such a scenario, often, diverse sets and types of people and diverse business entities get grouped under one head for the sake of mere convenience and economies of scale.

To maintain a common ideology among all the various and varied group entities becomes vitally important, yet is a vastly difficult task. Different group entities could in reality be led by individuals with different ideologies, and getting them to come on a common platform would be the true test of top-level leadership. As Jesse Jackson once wisely remarked: **'Leadership has a harder job to do than just choose sides. It must bring sides together.'**

J.R.D. ensured that even though the number of Tata group companies rose steadily during his tenure at the helm of affairs, a common Tata ethos and value system stayed firm, binding the various Tata group companies together. Tata firms in such far-flung arenas as hospitality, aviation, insurance, chemicals, tea, salt, consultancy services, cellular services, and many more; came together under J.R.D.'s sound stewardship. And what is more, **they came together happily and not grudgingly**. This was possible because J.R.D. never ruled with a dictatorial hand or an iron fist, but was democratic in his approach, and never imposed himself on his executives.

J.R.D. took concrete steps to ensure that the entire Tata group, through its senior executives and various Heads of Department, thought and acted as one when it came to ethical functioning, decision-making based on Tata values, care and concern for people and the environment, long-term thinking, and similar other parameters which make the Tata group what it is known for even today. Whether selling insurance or table-salt, the common Tata ethos of **'TRUST'** stood firmly behind all brands emanating from the Tata stable.

In the early 1950s, J.R.D. initiated the concept of the **Inter-Departmental Conference**. The members, senior executives from across Tata companies, met once a month, and would discuss, debate, deliberate, and attempt to find solutions to problems such as how to jointly cope with government policies, how to face ethical dilemmas in a united manner, and the like. **The issues discussed were not specific to one Tata company alone, but were pertaining to a range of issues with broad applicability across Tata companies; areas of concern for the whole of Tatas, so to speak.**

This is how J.R.D. achieved victory through unity.

An interesting aspect of 'Tata Group Unity' is mentioned in the book on the life of J.R.D. Tata authored by Mr. D.R. Pendse (former Chief Economist of the Tata Group). The book, titled *Beyond The Giant*, reveals, among other things, the daily lunch schedule in the director's lunch-room in the Tata headquarters building, where for a long period during J.R.D.'s tenure, directors of Tata Group companies were expected to share time together over their afternoon meal.

Mr. Pendse writes: 'The primary objective (of these lunch meetings) was that top Tata men should spend some time together in a relaxed mood, so as to help an exchange of views informally over national issues, and through it to **foster an atmosphere of comradeship**.......Patriotism, (sharing of) high expertise, and devotion - all these flowed naturally during the lunch hour. **Most importantly, the lunchtime get-together helped build a sense of cohesion among the top Tata men.**'

LEARNINGS ■■■■■■■
FOR LEADERS

"We are only as strong as we are united; as weak as we are divided"

-J.K. ROWLING

Today is the era of conglomerates – giant corporate entities, with revenues larger than the GDPs of small nations. Many of these entities are into the manufacturing / marketing of almost every product and service under the sun – from chalk to cheese to cellular-services to computer software.

Though the product and service offerings of the various group companies of a conglomerate would obviously differ, having a common thread to link them together would result in synergy and a common objective and ideology, which is so essential to elevate the individual companies into a stratosphere where group values bind the distinct entities together for the common good.

It is in this context that the following matter, extracted and adapted from *In Search Of Leaders*, authored by Hilarie Owen, is instructive: **– As long as organisations break everything into separate parts it is very difficult, if not impossible, for all employees to express their leadership.** Instead 'protectionist' behaviour is visible throughout the length and breadth of the organisation. **At Board meetings, directors fight to protect their 'areas' and carved out territories.** You can plainly see finance arguing with sales, operations with marketing, and so on. **They often do this not for the good of the organisation, but to secure and safeguard their personal interests.** Personal assistants protect their bosses with phone techniques such as "He's so busy right now," when taking the call would have been in the organisation's and also in the customer's interest. Flatter hierarchies with less bureaucracy are definitely an improvement over the earlier tall structures, but in many cases these flatter structures have simply resulted in fewer people doing more work. These structures go against human nature. Stephen Bergman and Janet Surrey found **the primary motive for all humans ...(is) a desire for connection. Matter, which is a basic of life, is by its nature about connections and relationships.**

As author Sally Helgesen observed, **great leaders tended to put themselves at the CENTRES of their organisations rather than at the top, thus emphasising both accessibility and equality.** They constantly laboured to include people in their decision making. This had the effect of undermining the boundaries so characteristic of mainstream organisations, with their strict job descriptions, categorising of people according to rank, and restrictions on the flow of information. Helgesen describes such happy organisations as '**webs of inclusion.**' Such webs or circular structures take leadership away from the attachment of position. They allow and encourage a systemic approach towards work with creativity and fluidity abounding. **Control is replaced with connectedness.** Leadership can be expressed by every human being and learning becomes part of the day-to-day experience. **A web structure moves leaders away from seeing organisations as machines broken down into constituent parts. Instead, the organisation is viewed as and becomes a living entity with energy, which evolves and changes its shape as the different parts interact. Fundamental to this is the concept of relationships – both with people inside and outside the structure, and with the organisation itself.** The web structure takes us to the new era, leaving behind remnants of the Industrial Age with its emphasis on control and absence of the human spirit and creativity.

It is indeed a considerable achievement and victory when a leader can manage to hold together such a diverse group of companies under a common and forward-looking ideology, each company individually led by an individual with his own philosophy, idiosyncrasies, set of beliefs and way of working. This enlightened way of functioning certainly describes J.R.D.'s inclusive and visionary leadership style to a 'T.'

At a time where mandatory norms impacting the entire conglomerate are coming in force, if only one group company 'fouls up,' every company which is part of the group could suffer as a consequence. Thus this learning from J.R.D. now becomes more important than ever. On the 10th September, 2014, the *Times of India* (Mumbai edition) carried the front page story titled – '**Wilful defaulter tag for entire group if one firm defaults**': 'In a move that will put intense pressure on businessmen whose companies default in future, the Reserve Bank of India (RBI) has tightened wilful defaulter norms and said failure of a company to repay could result in other group units and management being termed wilful defaulters.....'

J.R.D. was, as usual, a man far ahead of his time.

POINTS TO PONDER AND PRACTICE

- At whichever level of leadership you currently are, and whatever be the size of the organisation you represent, it would be one of your many responsibilities to ensure that a sense of unity is constantly being forged among the people and departments over which you have a certain degree of influence

- This can be done in many ways – formally, through the creation of work-teams and intelligent policy-framing – and also informally, through constant internal networking and playing the role of mediator among different individuals and departments to prevent and resolve conflict

- It is only when such internal unity is achieved, that organisational victory as a whole can be assured

" If everyone is moving forward together, then success takes care of itself "

-HENRY FORD

470

WHAT'S IN A NAME?
EVERYTHING!

> **The sweetest sound to anyone's ears is the sound of his own name**
>
> -ROBERT C. LEE

WHAT **J.R.D.**
BELIEVED IN
AND **PRACTICED**

> **Remember my name and you add to my feeling of importance**
>
> -DALE CARNEGIE

During the course of writing this book, I was fortunate to secure an interview with Mr. Ronjon Mookerjee, who retired after 32 years of loyal service to Air India as a Deputy Manager – In-Flight Services. A large part of his Air India days overlapped with J.R.D.'s tenure as Air India's chairman.

Mr. Mookerjee fondly recalls that J.R.D. knew all the regular cabin-crew, (including Mr. Mookerjee himself), by first name and lovingly addressed them as such. He particularly remembers an incident when he was attending to Mr. J.R.D. Tata on a flight from New York to London, and J.R.D. was seated in his favourite seat in first-class, (4A, last row, window seat.)

The meal was served, and as was the custom, chocolates needed to be offered. But when the grand box of chocolates was opened by Mr. Mookerjee's assistant, they found the chocolates had melted in

471

their silver wrapping. Mr. Mookerjee decided to obviously not offer them in this melted condition. After the dinner service, he approached J.R.D. and asked him how he had found the service. J.R.D. said, "Ronjon, the service was excellent, but where are the chocolates?" Mr. Mookerjee explained that the chocolates had melted and hence had not been served. J.R.D. smiled and jokingly said, "All right, Ronjon, you can carry the box home for your wife." At departure from London, when the crew changed, Mr. Mookerjee handed the box of chocolates to Mr. Tata, saying maybe he could gift it to Mrs. Tata. J.R.D. retorted; "Ronjon, do you want me to get a firing from my wife, giving her melted chocolates?" Mr. Mookerjee responded, "Sir, I would have the same problem at my place if I were to take them home." J.R.D. laughed and said, "Anyway, I'll take the chocolates." A couple of days later, the catering manager of Air India in New York called up Mr. Mookerjee and said he had received a memo regarding the melted chocolates. J.R.D. had followed up.

Till date, Mr. Mookerjee's eyes moist over as he once again hears in his mind's eye J.R.D. addressing him by first name – 'Ronjon.'

RONJON MOOKERJEE

Among other fond memories of J.R.D., Mr. Mookerjee has this to say about the airline when J.R.D. Tata was the Chairman. "J.R.D. considered Air India to be his baby. And he knew every function of the airline. He used to carry a notebook along with him when he was travelling, and would note down any discrepancies he observed, and would call for explanations from concerned departments. The staff was always on tenterhooks when J.R.D. was on board, as he would often take out his handkerchief and check the air-vents in the aircraft. If they were dirty, the cleaning staff had had it."

A few years ago, while addressing a Rotary Club group on the subject of business ethics, I was fortunate to meet a fine gentleman – **Niki Jariwala**, a Rotarian and a businessman.

During the course of the interaction on business ethics, I had prominently mentioned the name of J.R.D. Tata as being a passionate practitioner of doing business the ethical way.

After the talk, Niki approached me saying that he had always been a fan of J.R.D. and of the Tata group.

NIKI JARIWALA

Then he mentioned that a friend of his, an Air India purser named Ashok Thakur, had told Niki about the time when he (Ashok) had served J.R.D. on an Air India flight. J.R.D. had courteously thanked Ashok and asked him his name. The next time Ashok met J.R.D. was eight years later, yet Ashok remembers that J.R.D. addressed him by name. J.R.D. had remembered. And Ashok was pleasantly astounded.

Another fact that Niki fondly recalls is how J.R.D. used to attend the Ganesh Visarjan festival at Chowpatty Beach in Mumbai and mingle with the crowd assembled there. Niki was a young lad in school then, but he still remembers this simple humility of J.R.D. which made him participate in the festivities of all faiths and communities.

Nowadays, when you travel by Air India (or other airlines), you can see all the cabin-crew have name-tags on their shirts/blouses/sarees, which makes it easy for passengers to address them by name. But this was not always so.

Mr. Mookerjee told me that in the early days, when he was a cabin-crew, they did not have name-tags on their uniforms. In those days, the fleet of Air India consisted of Boeing 707s, which had a cabin-crew strength of two pursers, two assistant pursers and three air-hostesses on board. None of them wore name-tags, only the half-wing badges which indicated they were cabin-crew. In those days, J.R.D. used to ask the cabin-crew serving him their names, so he could remember them and politely address them by name during future interactions.

CABIN-CREW HALF-WING BADGE

Then in 1971 came the 'Jumbo' aircraft (Boeing 747s). This is when the cabin-crew strength increased to one in-flight supervisor, three pursers, four assistant-pursers and nine air-hostesses. Out of all these, only the in-flight supervisor wore a name-tag.

It is only comparatively recently that the practice of all cabin-crew sporting a name-tag on their uniform has commenced.

All this clearly indicates that J.R.D. really took effort and pain to remember the names of all the various crew members who served him on different flights; not an easy task by any standards.

Dr. W. Edwards Deming, the American statistician who taught the Japanese about the power of quality, was fond of saying, "**In the old days before the industrial era, the tailor, the carpenter, the shoemaker, the milkman and the blacksmith knew his customers by name. He knew whether they were satisfied and what he should do to improve his product.**"

Consider that with the power of technology we have access to today, the opportunity to use the customer's name is so much more widespread than the limited technology which the tailor, the carpenter, the shoemaker, had access to all those years ago. But though the technology exists today, it is rarely used appropriately.

Try this simple exercise the next time you have an opportunity to do so. Hand over your 'Loyalty Card' to a cashier at a retail chain of which you are a member when you make a purchase. In all probability, although the cashier will enter fresh points into your card or redeem existing ones, not once will he address you by name, even though he is holding your loyalty card with your name printed on it in his hand. Unfortunately, this speaks volumes of diluted levels of care and concern in areas where it really matters.

One of the hallmarks of great leadership is to remember the names and faces of people and recall them even after a long time. This quality developed by a leader demonstrates his interest in his people.

You remember what you care for.

J.R.D. obviously cared for his employees who served him and his organisation so well, and they loved him in return.

And this is where the element of **victory** comes in.

It used to be said of old, '**Who Dares Wins**.'

But now, more than ever before, it is an era of:

'WHO CARES WINS.'

THE 'GOOD NAME' YOU HAVE EARNED WILL BRING YOU VICTORY IN MANY WAYS

For individuals and for organisations who have invested years into building a strong reputation of trust, the '**name**' they have earned for themselves over a period of time would be more valued by them than gold.

Not only did J.R.D. invest time and effort in remembering the names of countless people who worked with him, he also ensured that his personal name and the name of the Tata group which he so ably led, became names which symbolised credibility and became the epitome of all that is good and noble.

The following story is a great example of just one of the many ways in which the 'name' you have earned for yourself carries tremendous weight in the marketplace.

During a training programme I was conducting on the subject of Negotiation Skills for the managerial staff of *Tata Motors*, a Purchase Manager of *Tata Motors* who was a participant in the programme narrated his personal experience. He said that he had once been negotiating a lease for a godown situated on prime property on behalf of Tata Motors in a certain city in central India. He specifically mentioned that the owner of that property was what is commonly termed as '*khadoos*,' (stern and rigid). The Purchase Manager said he was expecting a tough negotiation. To his pleasant surprise, he not only got the property on lease on terms and conditions very favourable to Tata Motors, he also got it at a good rate; much lower than what he was expecting to get it at. In fact, the '*khadoos*' owner told him: **"If the Tatas are taking my property on lease, I don't mind giving it at a lower rate and on easier terms and conditions. AT LEAST I'LL SLEEP PEACEFULLY. Their 'name' is enough for me to not worry about a thing."**

Continued....

476

Continued....

The same Purchase Manager further mentioned that he attributed a good part of his success in negotiations throughout his career to the fact that he represents an ethical, trustworthy organisation, which has the strongest possible reputation and goodwill in the market. **Remarkably, he added that in the case of the godown, the owner had been offered a higher rate than what the Tatas got the lease at by another large conglomerate, but he still preferred to give it on lease to the Tatas, simply because of the Tata 'name' and what the Tatas stood for.**

In general, the Tata companies are extended maximum credit by their suppliers and vendors, as there is blind-faith in the Tata 'word'. It is not that every large conglomerate is by default extended credit due to its size. There are other gigantic conglomerates where suppliers fear to extend even miniscule credit, as the past record of these conglomerates goes against them. But the Tatas, through their trustworthy dealings with suppliers over the years and the positive word-of-mouth publicity this has generated, have made life easy for their purchase managers. **Truly, having the backing of a strong 'Name' smoothens the path for an organisation's employees to perform productively and profitably.**

If an organisation can win the genuine trust of its vendors and suppliers, it can then truly be termed a brand leader in every sense of the word. Most organisations give high priority to keeping their shareholders happy, many give the same importance to their customers, a few focus on their employees, but only a handful gain the respect of their vendors and suppliers. Are vendors and suppliers that important from an organisation's perspective? Well, even **Michael Porter, in his '5 Force Model,' has named the vendors / suppliers as one of the forces that can make or mar the fortunes of an organisation.**

On the grand pathway towards building a leading organisation, one needs to cross three essential and distinct 'layers':

1. The first layer is that of '**association**'. The corporate eco-system, which includes customers, employees, shareholders, suppliers, *et al*, needs to in the first place acknowledge and associate with the organisation which is attempting to deliver a product or service offering.

Continued....

2. Once the 'association' stage has been crossed and the products and services have been accepted at a base level, the brand needs to '**communicate**' its values to members of the eco-system. When the communication pathways are clearly laid-out, commitment from the eco-system is secured.

3. Once the brand values have been implicitly and explicitly communicated, and the brand is now trusted based on word-of-mouth from those having past association with it, a '**relationship**' between the brand and the members of the eco-system is strengthened and solidified.

It is this network of relationships and the goodwill which they generate, which when effectively maintained, renewed and strengthened through the visible actions of the organisation, will bring about the ultimate brand loyalty factor.

Loyalty is the result of a process, embedded in the core philosophy of the organisational leadership, and should not be considered as a separate entity which needs to be externally built up. Loyalty with customers and employees is often sought-after, but very few brands (*Toyota* being one of these), focus on building loyalty from their supplier's end as well.

As a global example to justify the importance of developing vendor and supplier loyalty, an anecdote pertaining to **Charles Tandy**, the founder of the world-renowned electronics retail brand – **Radio Shack** – is relevant. In the book 'Business Leaders and Success' (published by McGraw Hill), it is mentioned – 'Tandy knew the importance of having good relationships with his suppliers. To keep the relationship strong, he insisted that bills be paid as soon as they arrived. **In fact, according to John McDaniel, a former accounting executive for the company, Tandy was so anxious to build and retain a good relationship with suppliers, that even when money was tight, he refused to hold off making payments. "In the early days, he didn't even want us to hold a bill until two days before it was due, because he thought we might be one day late if we did that," McDaniel said.'**

Truly, **VICTORY** in the organisational context comes in many forms and is reached through many roads. And J.R.D. and the Tata group seem to have all these 'roads' to **victory** well covered.

LEARNINGS
FOR LEADERS

" *Names have power* "

-RICK RIORDAN

One may think that remembering a person's name by itself is not such a big deal. After all, how much good can simply recalling the name of a person do?

So before we get into the nitty-gritties as to why this is considered such an important leadership trait, we must first understand something basic about human psychology. And that is – **THE SWEETEST SOUND TO A PERSON IS THE SOUND OF HIS OWN NAME**.

When a person is addressed by name, especially by someone who matters, the person feels wanted; important.

The person feels **SPECIAL**.

The person feels he **MATTERS**.

And when the person feels that he is **SPECIAL** and that he **MATTERS**, he is **MOTIVATED**.

And when the person is **MOTIVATED**, he can literally **MOVE MOUNTAINS**.

The sharpest and most successful men of commerce and industry have long since realised how powerful a motivator this apparently simple attribute of leadership can be.

Andrew Carnegie

As an example, consider **Andrew Carnegie**, born to a poor family in Scotland in 1835, who rose from humble beginnings to become one of the first self-made billionaires and at one point of time the **richest man in the world** after he migrated to the United States. He made his fortune in steel, starting off by working as a manual labourer laying railway tracks, and then rapidly acquired good business sense and established a steel rolling mill. He profited and expanded, and when he eventually built his first steel plant, he **NAMED THE STEEL PLANT AFTER J. EDGAR THOMSON** (President of the Pennsylvania Railroad), **WHO WAS ONE OF HIS BEST EXISTING CUSTOMERS**. This was a smart move, as it endeared him to this customer and made his subsequent rise even more rapid.

The same Andrew Carnegie, when a young lad growing up in his native Scotland, had the hobby of keeping pet rabbits. Since the rabbits kept multiplying rapidly, it was not easy for the young Carnegie to provide food for all the young rabbits. Even at that age, Carnegie hit upon the idea of motivating his friends to gather food for all the rabbits, and as a reward he offered to name one baby rabbit after each of his friends who helped him in the feeding task. More than enough greens for the rabbits to munch on were always there as a result.

THIS – is the power of using a person's name.

Joseph T. Straub, the famed management expert, wrote – "I once saw a classic Ferrari at an auto auction with an **engraved plate on the engine's valve cover that read – 'This engine was assembled by (the Italian mechanic's name).'** That worker's name and craftsmanship remained a part of the car for the rest of its life."

Imagine the increased care and attention any worker will take if this 'small' addition of his own name is added to every product the company makes and offers. This simple measure could inspire and elevate the worker to the level of a master craftsman. This is a lesson that all organisations can practice in some way or the other to motivate and empower their employees at no additional cost whatsoever.

Many years ago I was one among around fifteen participants nominated by the firm I was then employed with to attend a training workshop. It was to be conducted by an external trainer who had never met any of us participants before. Yet as we walked into the training room on the day of the programme, the trainer was already in, greeting each one of us not only with a warm smile and a firm handshake, **BUT ALSO WITH OUR NAME.** We were amazed as to how he knew all our names. Later, on being asked, he revealed that he had requested for profiles of the programme participants with their photographs from the training officer of our firm a few days prior to the workshop, and had studied each profile and had taken efforts to memorise the name alongside each photograph.

There is a true story of a university professor who conducted a semester-long course on the subject of Human Resources. His final examination question paper for his students consisted of just five short questions. He asked the students to recall the names of the security guard at the college gate, the elevator boy, the canteen-attendant, the library-clerk, and the person handling the photocopying machine.

The students just had to write five names, and they could score full marks in the subject. On the other hand, if they failed to do so, they would fail the subject.

As the professor wisely said to the students, "What is the use of learning the theory of human resources management when a practical opportunity to put into practice the art and science of man management is frittered away? If you cannot recall the names of persons who have been serving you all semester long, what good would you be at managing human beings at your place of work?"

Lauren Schieffer, an authority on respectful communication, writes on her site: 'My husband and I just returned from a four-day motorcycle run with six other people.....because we were all riding rally style, we gathered for each meal together. It was during dinner on the third day that one of our companions asked the question, "**Lauren, I've noticed you go out of your way to call the waiter or waitress by their first name – every time, in every restaurant we've been in**. Do you find that you get better service that way?" "Well, I suppose I might get better service because of it, but that is not the point or purpose at all.".....**As I explained to my friend, it's that whole respectful communication thing.** The sweetest sound to anyone's ears is the sound of their own name. Furthermore, how much more respectful is it to call someone by name – as compared to "hey you," "darling," "waitress," or worse yet (*don't ever do this*) snapping my fingers at them?'

POINTS TO PONDER AND PRACTICE

- Do you, like many other people, find it difficult to remember and recall the names of the persons you meet? The following are a few tips which could better help you remember them for increased impact:

  1. Pay attention when the name is being said

  2. Repeat the name aloud as soon as possible

  3. You could make a comment on the name, for example, ask how it is spelt

  4. If at a seminar or convention, keep glancing at the name-tag the person is wearing. This helps associate the name with the face of the person

  5. Last but not least, if you reside in the United States, there is an 'app' called Namerick, which can help you to remember names. It operates on U.S. census data (Or maybe you could be the one to develop a similar 'app' for use in India)

- But bear in mind that in certain cultures or organisations, it is best not to become too familiar too soon. Avoid using first names of people till you have established a substantial degree of comfort with them

- Find out what the person likes to be called (by his/her pet-name or so on), ask his permission to call him by that name if that is what he/she prefers

DO YOUR PEOPLE TRUST YOU ?

> *" To be trusted is a greater compliment than being loved "*
>
> -GEORGE MACDONALD

WHAT **J.R.D.** BELIEVED IN AND **PRACTICED**

> *" Trust, for a leader, is not secured by making fine-sounding speeches from a platform alone. It is generated when these speeches are followed up with relevant action. This sounds simple enough, and it IS simple. But it requires a sense of transparency and openness, the ability to share and speak the bitter truth when needed, and the ability to be one with your followers and employees, and not distance yourself from them. Practice all this, and trust follows, as sure as day follows night "*
>
> -CYRUS M. GONDA

J.R.D. devoted almost his entire life to Air India. When the airline (still under Tata management), was nationalised and then divided into two; Air India for the international traveller, and Indian Airlines for the domestic segment, J.R.D. was offered Chairmanship of Air India, but under government control.

He performed this role admirably for decades, taking not a single rupee as remuneration for his services, and brought the airline to even higher levels of glory.

The airline staff, including the unionised cadres, trusted him implicitly, and had full faith that whatever decisions J.R.D. took would always be in the interests of the organisation, its employees, its passengers, and its shareholders.

If unionised employees and cadres implicitly trust the Chairman of their organisation, no further victory can be asked for.

In 1978, without cause, for political rather than for professional reasons, J.R.D. was asked to give up his voluntary Chairmanship of Air India by the then Indian Prime Minister, Morarji Desai.

The government did not even have the courtesy to inform J.R.D. about this drastic step in person before the news was revealed to the entire country on All India Radio.

As soon as this news was made public, both the Managing Director of Air India as well as the Deputy Managing Director, submitted their resignations in protest. The Air India Cabin Crew Association and the Officer's Association also protested the removal of their Chairman.

J.R.D. was the only man the employees and the unions of Air India trusted to successfully handle the airline, and they were right. Within a few months of his being forced to leave the airline that he had built and branded with such love and care, the rot set in. Decline in service, profitability and credibility were swift under the new Chairman. The various and assorted chairpersons who succeeded J.R.D. at Air India were almost like men of straw; absolutely unable and thoroughly incapable of holding the organisation together, or of winning the trust of the staff, and the sad result is there today for all to see.

Truly, when a leader has earned the trust of his people over years by proving his devotion to them and to the organisation, the organisation is capable of achieving wonders.

And conversely, when the man in charge does NOT have the trust of his people, no amount of resources being pumped in can help the organisation to achieve any level of success worth talking about.

After J.R.D. left as Chairman, the staff of Air India wrote on the first page of their Air India journal, the *Magic Carpet*:

'You, Mr. Tata, signify everything to us that is dedication, loyalty and single-minded devotion to a cause....constant in your endeavour to have the latest and the most sophisticated equipment for the airline.....you were unswerving in your attention to detail, in your pursuit of excellence....As you yourself said a little over fifteen years ago: "The international airline business is still the love of my life. Because I was present at the birth of Air India, I feel a little like a mother who can't realise her baby has grown up." Yes, Mr. Tata, babies grow up and one day leave the family fold, but **the indelible stamp of your personality, your love and your affection will forever remain**. And so the time has come to say "au revoir" (good-bye). **As we turn the last page of the Tata Saga we will undoubtedly find some consolation in the thought that what we in Air India did under your stewardship was worth doing, that we set our standards high, that we held our heads up erect both in success and in adversity – and that no one can ever compel us to part with our memories of you.'**

It is my personal challenge that even if the airline continues to remain in existence for another thousand years (not that I would be around to see it), **no other Chairman of Air India will ever get such a glowing and genuine tribute from his entire staff – ever again.**

If your employees themselves have declared you a winner, how can you then lose?

487

Another supreme example of the high trust that not only his employees, who knew him well, but also that the **WORLD BANK**, trusted J.R.D. implicitly, comes from a newspaper article. The following is the text which appeared in the **_Jame-Jamshed_** (a Parsi Gujarati cum English weekly newspaper published every Sunday. It is the second-oldest existing newspaper in Asia, having been in existence for well over 180 years.) The following article appeared in the issue of _Jame-Jamshed_ dated July 31, 2011:

'IT HAS BEEN REPORTED THAT IN THE 1960s, WHEN INDIA WAS IN AN EXTERNAL DEBT TRAP AND REQUIRED FUNDING FROM THE WORLD BANK, THE WORLD BANK TOLD JAWARHARLAL NEHRU (THE THEN INDIAN PRIME MINISTER) THAT THE FUNDING WOULD BE SANCTIONED ONLY ON ONE CONDITION. THE CONDITION WAS THAT J.R.D. TATA SHOULD SIGN ON BEHALF OF THE NATION AND NOT JAWARHARLAL NEHRU.'

THE WORLD BANK

The above is stunning information.

J.R.D. had developed an international reputation for trust and credibility. Even the World Bank decided that no other individual from the country carried the trust that J.R.D. in his personal capacity as head of the Tata group, did. Whether the story reported is true or a myth, the very fact that this story exists says a lot. The media in general do have a tendency to exaggerate, but at the bottom of every story lies at least a kernel of truth. That a reputed, well-established, almost two-centuries-old newspaper printed this article, gives food for thought as to **the humongous trust and credibility that J.R.D. rightfully carried on a global scale**.

After all, as has been said:

'Being good is important.
Being trusted is essential.'

An article authored by **Glenn Llopis** and appearing on the *Forbes Leadership* site lists seven reasons why employees do NOT trust their leaders.

These reasons can be summed up as:

1. The leader lacks courage and fails to stand up for what he/she believes in

2. The leader is devious, lacks authenticity, and carries a hidden agenda

3. The leader is self-obsessed and self-centred and lacks any sense of commitment to the career advancement of subordinates

4. The leader does not have a good reputation and a lot of negative stories are floating about with regard to him/her

5. The approach and behaviour of the leader are inconsistent and waver in their intent and direction

6. The leader is not 'hands-on.' He/she over-delegates and refuses to get his/her hands 'dirty'

7. The leader is not generous with praise and does not appear to appreciate the performance efforts of subordinates

This learning on 'trust' has deliberately been kept towards the end of this section for maximum impact. Trust for a leader is such a vital and essential commodity, that without it, a leader is virtually handicapped.

Gain the trust of your people. It is a slow and steady process, but an indispensible one.

LEARNINGS
■ FOR LEADERS

"Everyone loves to be trusted. But trust is not a commodity that can be bought in the marketplace at any price. It has to be earned. Earned through consistently trustworthy actions and behaviour"

-CYRUS M. GONDA

This is a lesson from that wise sage, Confucius. Once, a disciple asked him, "**What are the fundamental essentials of good government?**"

CONFUCIUS

C onfucius replied, "**Sufficient food, sufficient weapons, and the trust and confidence of the people.**"

The disciple then asked, "Suppose for some reason you had to let go one of these three things. **Which of these three is the most dispensable?**"

"**Weapons**," replied Confucius.

The disciple persisted and asked, "**Suppose, even after that, you were forced to choose between the two that were left. Which of the two would you give up?**"

Confucius replied, "**Food**. From olden times, death for all men has been a constant. So people can even do without food. **BUT A PEOPLE THAT NO LONGER TRUSTS ITS LEADERS IS INDEED TO BE PITIED.**"

Thus, even according to the renowned sage Confucius, for a leader, to have his people truly trust him, could be considered his singularly greatest victory and achievement.

The benefits of being trusted are numerous and well known.

All leaders would want to gain the trust of their people, but few truly achieve it. And those that achieve it are the ones who genuinely deserve it.

These leaders – are winners.

Once, Albert Einstein's wife was asked whether she clearly understood the *Theory of Relativity* that her husband had propounded and developed.

She replied, "**No, but I know my husband and I know he can be trusted.**"

ABRAHAM LINCOLN

Trust is a reciprocal commodity, and for the men to be able to trust their leader, the leader must first have faith in his men. The following is an almost heart-rending story of such a bond of trust between the leader and the led.

The American Civil War was a dark period in U.S. history, with many teenage boys being conscripted into their respective armies to fight their foes. One such lad was soldier **William Scott**, of President Abraham Lincoln's Union army, who was court-martialed and sentenced to be shot dead for the military offence of sleeping at his post while on guard-duty.

But Lincoln, ever merciful and trusting, finding that Scott had taken on sentry-duty to substitute for a colleague, and was sorely exhausted, considered all the circumstances and gave William Scott a reprieve, telling Scott, "**I am going to trust you, and send you back to your regiment**. It will cost you very dearly. I have left my work, and have come up here from Washington just for your sake. There is only one man in the world who can pay the price. His name is William Scott. If from this day William Scott does his duty well so that if I were present at his deathbed, he would look at me in the face as he does now, and say, 'I have kept my promise, and have done my duty as a soldier,' then the debt would be paid. Will you make that promise and try to keep it?"

WILLIAM SCOTT

Scott in turn trusted Lincoln's word and made that promise, and kept it till the very end. He fought nobly in many battles before giving up his life to rescue his comrades. Truly, to function at its best, trust has to be a two-fold affair.

'Having someone's trust is like having money in the bank. Just like a bank account, you must make deposits if you expect to make withdrawals.

When you keep your word, it's like making a deposit into your trust fund. The more often you perform the way you promised, the larger your balance is. Whenever you break your word, you have made a withdrawal from your account.

You have a separate trust fund with each person you have a relationship with. If you have been making regular deposits into your account with that individual, when the time comes that you are unable to keep your word (let's face it, nobody's perfect), you will still have a large enough balance of trust to draw from. That person will recognise that your account is still good. You are trustworthy.'

-MATT DIMAIO

POINTS TO PONDER AND PRACTICE

- Ask yourself whether the actions you currently perform as a leader would make you win the trust of your subordinates

- As an exercise, identify another leader you know from any field who is implicitly trusted by his followers. Observe and study what he or she has done to be trusted. Emulate his or her actions, and soon, trust, that vital ingredient in the leadership recipe, will be yours as well

- Remember what a wise person once said:
  'Without Communication, there is no Relationship.
  Without Respect, there is no Love.
  Without Trust, there is no reason to continue.....'

A MESSAGE FOR READERS

God bless you all, and God speed on your **Leadership Journey.** (Remember, leadership is a journey and not a destination.)

May you achieve all the good that you dream of and desire, and may the people you meet and lead along the way remember you fondly and bless you with their whole heart. May they feel fortunate that they played a part in your success on the leadership road.

Most importantly, may they put in practice what they learned from their association with you, and may you look back fondly at the leaders you helped create who would carry on the good work you began to even greater glory.

-CYRUS M GONDA

THE 'DASH' BETWEEN THE DATES

Napoleon's tombstone is huge. Churchill's is simple. The eternal flame burns over the grave of President John Kennedy. Very different lives, very different markers.

NAPOLEON'S TOMBSTONE

ETERNAL FLAME OVER THE GRAVE OF PRESIDENT JOHN KENNEDY

CHURCHILL'S TOMBSTONE

As different as each was from the other, their lives share at least one common mark. The dash between the dates. **On every tombstone, whether simple or ornate, there is only one dash, or hyphen, between the dates.**

The character and quality of our lives vary greatly. Yet, when all is said and done, we become precisely equal. **They put one dash between the birth date and the death date.**

We get one dash through life. That's it! No seconds! No restarts! Everybody finishes!

Some dash through life with great flair and style. Others become a quiet blur. Some run with long strides, leaving only toe marks in the sand. Most leave an erratic trail of footprints with more than a few heel marks. **Many show evidence of being lost. Yet, having lost their direction, they run all the faster.**

The content of our "dash" varies. But in the end, the workmen will chisel only a dash. It reminds us of the stark truth: "Just as man is destined to die once, and after that to face judgment, so Christ was sacrificed once to take away the sins of many people....."

In the end, men reduce all living to the cold mark on the stone. Those of us who "live a life worthy of the Lord," following in the footsteps of Jesus, find the end of earth's dash to be the beginning of heaven's glory.

-JOSEPH B. FUITEN

LEADERSHIP / EXECUTIVE
COACH OFFERING

The most successful leaders throughout history, be they from the business, the political, the military, or the sporting spheres, have had their potential exponentially enhanced by their mentors and coaches.

Today, more than ever, with competition higher than ever before, a leader needs all the help and inputs he or she can get. The world has gotten increasingly complex, and as leaders struggle with their day-to-day dilemmas and decision-making, the luxury of a strong 'sounding-board' has now become a necessity.

A sound coach needs to be:

- A keen listener

- Empathetic

- Astute thinker

- Effective communicator

- Widely experienced and well informed

- Functional psychologist

- Motivator

..............Cyrus is all these things and much more.

Which is why the following are some of the testimonials he has received with regard to his leadership coaching / executive coaching abilities.

It is always a pleasure to interact with Cyrus and learn so many new things in the fields of strategic thinking, business management, leadership and business ethics. Cyrus is a rare blend of extreme cognitive and creative abilities.

He himself asks the most thought provoking and incisive questions, and encourages the individuals he coaches to do the same and thus raise their thinking process to a higher plane.

He has the uncanny ability to grasp the most complex of situations, and can cut through to the crux of any business dilemma. A genius intellect (as proven by his MENSA-qualified status), coupled with his high level of consequential astuteness, make Cyrus my favourite resource to share and discuss personal and professional dilemmas. He is an awfully intense listener, which I consider a vital quality in an effective coach.

Being a former India Army (ex-NDA) officer and an Ivy League alumnus myself, I can vouch through personal experiences that any promising professional would do well to have Cyrus as his Leadership and Business Coach.

Major Manish Naik (Retd.)
Co-founder and CEO – Vimal Dubey Foundation

I have absolute and total faith in the ability, intelligence and confidentiality of Cyrus as my Executive Coach. After each interaction with him, I find my thought processes getting sharper, and my ability to think and decide getting far better and clearer.

Any business decision I plan to take; I never take without first taking his inputs. An excellent listener, a keen grasper of ideas, a very sound thinker, and an extremely strong support system, taking a decision based on Cyrus' advice has never failed me. Having him validate my thinking process gives me confidence to just 'go ahead and do it.' Conversely, I proceed with caution or drop the idea if that is what he recommends. Any business person or corporate executive would be fortunate to have Cyrus as his Executive Coach.

Vikrant Urval
Director – India International Trade Centre (IITC)

My being a part of the 'tech-gen' and having been near-immersed in tech almost all my life, I often feel the need for solid 'old-school' business, communication, and leadership inputs which are so crucial for professional success.

Being coached by Prof. Cyrus, I have gained refreshing perspectives and unique insights in areas where I often had tunnel vision and over-dependence on technology. This was made possible due to Prof. Cyrus' amazing and literally astronomical wealth of awareness on a multitude of subjects and his ability to absorb my concerns and communicate his responses in simple yet brilliant fashion.

I have been the pioneer of many start-ups, and at each stage of my entrepreneurship journey, I have relied heavily upon Prof. Cyrus for stimulating innovative thought-processes, at the same time staying grounded, which I feel has been the foundation of the success I have enjoyed till date.

Shubham Rai
Founder and CEO – NODD APP
(India's foremost networking App)

It gets lonely at the top. Even though I am quite an extroverted individual by nature, finding an individual with the right combination of intellect, empathy and confidentiality to sound-off my work related issues, stay on track, and move ahead in today's challenging environment is a vital part of business success.

Thankfully I have found this combination in Cyrus, and the one-on-one coaching sessions I have had with him have been excellent value-adds in terms of fine-tuning clarity of vision, sparking of radically new business ideas, and improvement of structured thinking. I would be glad to recommend Cyrus as an Executive Coach to any senior executive looking to carry his or her career or business forward.

Sourav Sachin (IIT – Bombay)
CEO of WoNoBo
(India's only 360 degree immersive and navigable Street View)
Former Head of Tech for Landmark Group, Dubai
Builder of Flipkart's Marketplace

Leadership being the key ingredient in the success of any organisation, it is essential that the development of this vital parameter is not left to chance, but addressed in a systematic and structured manner.

A haphazard approach towards any crucial activity always results in the potential results and outcomes from that activity not being fully realised – the same holds true for the activity termed as Leadership Development.

'The 4V Leadership Scorecard ™' is ideally conceived and formulated for just this purpose – to identify leadership potential and to strengthen leadership talent in a structured and systematic manner.

The four crucial elements which determine a leader's success:

- VISION
- VALUES
- VALOUR
- VICTORY

…..are the primary components of this scorecard and consultancy area.

Similar to this book, in which the four primary elements have been further categorised into sub-elements, the consultancy model based on this scorecard first understands the specific vision, strategy and objectives of the organisation for which the consultancy is being conducted, and then formulates specific sub-objectives on all these four components for its leaders to meet the organisational vision, strategy and objectives.

Thus it is not a static 'one-size-fit-all' scorecard, rather the internal components of the four parameters would be designed keeping in mind the organisation's specific requirements.

Once the specific sub-parameters have been devised, then a workshop is conducted for the leaders/potential leaders of the organisation to familiarise them with the scorecard and its functioning. Following which, the current standing of each of the leaders/potential leaders would be plotted on the scorecard, and the road forward to becoming a holistic leader would be individually shared, with individual inputs for each leader/potential leader provided based on their current standing.

This consultancy input has been found to be highly useful for the leadership of established corporate houses, start-ups, political parties, and non-profits alike, to help them identify individuals for key leadership positions, as well as to strengthen the leadership skills of those already occupying such positions to make them more holistic, and therefore more effective leaders.

'THE MAGIC OF LEADERSHIP™' TRAINING WORKSHOP

> ❝ *Any sufficiently advanced technology is indistinguishable from magic* ❞
>
> -ARTHUR C. CLARKE

Magic, at the end of the day, stripped of the mystique and glamour which surrounds it, can simply be defined as the '**art and science of change and transformation**.'

The term 'Magic' can be very appropriately applied to the discipline of true leadership. For after all, isn't this what an effective leader does best – change, transform and exponentially elevate the inanimate as well as the human resources he works alongside with, into an outcome and output which is sustainably profitable?

This 'Magic' can be absorbed and successfully applied by any type, form and size of individual or firm, in a scientific and structured manner, as outlined in this book. It would certainly be customised according to the specific strategy of the organisation and the needs of the participants.

As can be seen in 'Appreciation For Cyrus' Training Programmes' in this book, these inputs have been well received by the senior personnel of leading corporate houses, and have been fine-tuned and refined over the years, culminating in this book and **The 4-V Leadership Model™** it is based on.

I would be more than happy to share these revolutionary insights with the fine people of your organisation, so that their professional, as well as personal lives too, can be touched and transformed by **The Magic of Leadership™**.

HIGHLIGHTS OF 'THE MAGIC OF LEADERSHIP™' TRAINING WORKSHOP

DURATION

One / two-day workshop, depending on organisation's convenience and requirements. The number of examples and activities will differ based on the duration

CONTENTS

The workshop will be customised according to the specific needs of the organisation. Practical understanding of the expectations that today's workforce and stakeholders have from their leaders will be brought out. 'The 4 V Leadership Model ™' will be discussed in detail, along with elements which comprise the 4 Vs. Key qualities of legendary business leaders will be shared in the form of absorbing anecdotes, and the sub-elements of the 4 Vs will be enumerated, thus ensuring the participants will develop a holistic approach towards effective business leadership

METHODOLOGY

Highly interactive and two-way, with sufficient of industry-specific examples, caselets discussed, and energizing leadership activities

WHO SHOULD ATTEND

Emerging leaders with high potential as well as experienced and seasoned leaders can all gain from attending this scintillating workshop

OUTCOMES AND TAKEAWAYS

- Developing a mindset of a high-performance leader

- Leading your people with confidence and grace

- Building on your leadership strengths

- Developing a holistic style of leadership on all the parameters that matter

- Enhancing decision-making prowess in crucial situations

- Leading positive change effectively

- Winning the trust of your stakeholders

- Motivating people to attain exceptional performance

- Mastering the secrets of leadership communication

........and much more.......

———————————

Mr. Gonda has been conducting regular and extensive training for our Management Team in the areas of Leadership, Strategic Communication, and Customer Service Excellence. Our customers expect us to have the highest GOLD standards in Eye Care and after-sales service, and we value the periodic inputs from Mr. Cyrus M. Gonda in this regard. His case-studies, examples, ideas and style of delivery are path-breaking and innovative and have definitely helped to raise the bar in service standards for the Lawrence & Mayo Group. **If any gentleman really understands, is passionate about, and has proven expertise in improving standards of Customer Delight in India, it is Mr. Cyrus M. Gonda.**

-Mr. Vivek Mendonsa - Marketing Director
Lawrence & Mayo (A 140-year young institution, across 40 cities, having over a 100 Premium Optical owned-retail outlets across India)

This is to place on record the excellent work Mr. Cyrus M. Gonda has been undertaking with our top management team and management staff. The series of workshops he has conducted in the areas of **strategy execution, leadership development, customer service experience, quality initiatives, and communication and presentation skills have been very well appreciated by our team,** who always eagerly await Mr. Gonda's forthcoming sessions with them. **A majority of the inputs he has provided have been profitably and productively put to work by our team in their domain areas. We at Burgmann being very concerned about all the areas he has conducted training for, find his inputs exceptionally useful.** I would have absolutely no hesitation in recommending his expertise in these training areas to any corporate house across industries.

-Mr. Umar Balwa - Managing Director
Burgmann India Pvt. Ltd.

511

Mr. Cyrus M. Gonda has conducted a **series of workshops for the state heads, regional heads and cluster heads of HDFC Bank** in the areas of **Strategy Execution, Systems-oriented Thinking, Customer Experience Excellence, and Leadership Communication. Both the content as well as the style of delivery of these workshops were very well received and kept the participants engrossed the entire days. This was achieved without the aid of any PowerPoint slides or audio-visual aids.**

The workshops were practical, and Mr. Gonda made use of extremely relevant examples and exercises. **Many of the senior participants remarked that Mr. Gonda's workshops were some of the most interesting and informative they had ever attended.** I and my management team who participated in these workshops have no hesitation in recommending Mr. Gonda's training workshops in the above areas to any organization wishing to enhance the effectiveness of their employees.

> **-Mr. Rajesh Naik**
> **Senior Vice President and Head - Treasury Operations**
> **HDFC Bank**

The workshops Mr. Gonda conducts for our senior members in the areas of **leadership, communication skills and soft skills, and customer service excellence** have been extremely helpful to the participants, who find them very educative and stimulating. **I have always been urging and encouraging Mr. Gonda to come out with more books in his areas of expertise, as his unique concepts and wealth of anecdotes need to be shared with a wider audience.**

> **-Dr. Neville Mehta**
> **Executive Administrator (India, South Asia, Africa and Middle East)**
> **Lions Club International**

- **BEST-SELLING LEADERSHIP/MANAGEMENT AUTHOR**
- **THOUGHT LEADER**
  (Originator of several trademarked Models and copyrighted intellectual properties in the key areas of Leadership / Strategy / Customer Service Excellence / Communication / Presentation / Corporate Etiquette and Soft Skills)
- **MASTER TRAINER / AUTHORATATIVE SPEAKER**

Cyrus has rich and diverse work experience in operational as well as executive and administrative roles, in European, American as well as Indian-based multinational and Fortune 500 organisations, in the service and also the manufacturing sectors, both in India and overseas.

Now entrenched in the field of leadership and management development, he brings a unique blend of practicality as well as theory-based insights to his training and consultancy assignments.

He has proven intellectual ability, being a qualified life-member of **MENSA**, the international society for individuals with genius-level IQ. He is a rank-holding MBA from NMIMS, Mumbai University.

A communicator par excellence, he scored the highest grade at the highest level of the Business English Communication examination conducted by Cambridge University. He is also a rank-holder in hospitality management.

Over the years, he has focused on gaining in-depth understanding of the following four disciplines, which now form his areas of expertise.

1. **LEADERSHIP DEVELOPMENT**
2. **CUSTOMER EXPERIENCE EXCELLENCE**
3. **COMMUNICATION ENHANCEMENT**
4. **STRATEGY FORMULATION AND EXECUTION**

He has developed trademarked Models and copyrighted intellectual properties in each of the above, making him one of India's foremost thinkers in these domains, which form the crux of management thinking.

He firmly believes the four areas outlined above are inextricably interlinked, and they form the four-pillared foundation of sustained corporate success.

He has also authored and co-authored ten books (this being the eleventh) which have been translated into Hindi, Gujarati and Marathi on popular demand by localised audiences. The books are highly practical, and are in the areas of customer experience excellence, leadership branding, marketing strategy, and selling techniques. Some have even been reviewed favourably in international management journals. These books and the trademarked Models many of them are based on, are regularly used by many leading corporate houses to train their employees in these vital areas.

During the process of authoring his books on leadership, he has gained keen first-hand insights into the strategic thinking process of titans of industry by having interviewed personalities such as Mr. Nadir Godrej, Mr. Ajay Piramal, Mr. Lalit Kumar Kanodia (founder CEO of TCS and founder CEO of Datamatics), Mr. Marten Pieters (CEO of Vodafone India), Mr. Martin Kriegner (CEO of Lafarge India), Mr. Ronnie Screwvala (CEO of UTV), Mr. Souvik Banerjee (Global Chief Technology Architect of SAP), and many other eminent corporate doyens. Cyrus brings the crucial leadership learnings obtained during these valuable interactions to his training programmes and consultancy work.

A practical, spontaneous, entertaining, and energetic speaker, Cyrus' workshops are filled with relevant and interesting examples and anecdotes, of which he has a memorable wealth at his disposal for every occasion. He enjoys and specialises in conducting training workshops and providing consultancy in the following areas, all of which are based on Models developed and co-developed by him:

- **'The Magic of Leadership™'** (Based on 'The 4-V Leadership Model™' he has designed and developed)

- **'The Magic of Communication™'** (Based on the unique Communication Model he has designed and developed)

- **Corporate Etiquette and Soft Skills** (Based on the **'Master of Business Etiquette MBE™'** Model he has designed and developed)

- **Strategy Formulation and Implementation** (Based on a trademarked Model developed by him)

- **Customer Experience Excellence** (Based on the best-selling book 'Where Is My Ketchup?')

- **Super Sales Success** (Based on the 'Be A Super Salesperson' Model and book)

- **High Performance Presentation Skills** (Based on a trademarked Model developed by him)

He has conducted highly-acclaimed and appreciated training work-shops in the above areas across the spectrum of industries for over a hundred reputed corporate houses, just a few of which include:

- Abbott India Ltd.
- Ashok Piramal Group
- BASF
- Bhabha Atomic Research Centre (BARC)
- BNP Paribas
- Breach Candy Hospital
- Central Depository Services Ltd. (CDSL)
- Godrej and Boyce
- HDFC Bank
- Hindustan Unilever (HUL)
- Indian Navy
- Larsen & Toubro
- Lawrence & Mayo
- Mahindra & Mahindra
- Mini Cooper
- Shoppers Stop
- TajSATS (Taj Mahal Hotel and Singapore Airlines Terminal Services joint venture)
- Tata Motors
- Yes Bank

Cyrus is currently the H.O.D. of Strategic Leadership and Strategic Communication - Rizvi Management Institutes, Mumbai, and also the Jt. Managing Director of the boutique management consultancy firm - Brains Trust India.

517

Cyrus can be contacted for

- **Conducting training workshops**
  (Leadership/Communication/Customer Experience Enhancement/Selling Skills)

- **Coaching**
  (Communication/Leadership)

- **Consulting**
  (Customer Experience Enhancement/ Communication/Leadership)

- **Short speaking assignments on various subjects**
  (Talks to enhance vibrancy of meetings/seminars, pre/post dinner talks)

- **Writing-based assignments**
  (Including co-authoring / speech writing / content writing, and the like)

- **Stimulating new ideas and innovative solutions at the workplace**

 cyrus@cyrusgonda.com